Abbas Khider

CONTEMPORARY GERMAN WRITERS AND FILMMAKERS

Edited by

Julian Preece (Swansea University)
Frank Finlay (University of Leeds)

Editorial Board

Professor Stephen Brockmann (Carnegie Mellon University)
Professor Friederike Eigler (Georgetown University)
Dr Michael Minden (University of Cambridge)
Professor Moritz Baßler (Westfälische Wilhelms-Universität Münster)
Professor Sabine Hake (University of Texas at Austin)

Volume 5

PETER LANG
Oxford • Bern • Berlin • Bruxelles • New York • Wien

Abbas Khider

Edited by David N. Coury and Karolin Machtans

PETER LANG

Oxford • Bern • Berlin • Bruxelles • New York • Wien

Bibliographic information published by Die Deutsche Nationalbibliothek.
Die Deutsche Nationalbibliothek lists this publication in the Deutsche National-
bibliografie; detailed bibliographic data is available on the Internet at
http://dnb.d-nb.de.

A catalogue record for this book is available from the British Library.

Library of Congress Cataloging-in-Publication Data

Names: Coury, David N., editor. | Machtans, Karolin, editor.
Title: Abbas Khider / [edited by] David N. Coury and Karolin Machtans.
Description: Oxford ; New York : Peter Lang, [2021] | Series: Contemporary
    German writers and filmmakers, 1664-6916 ; vol 5 | Includes bibliographical
    references and index.
Identifiers: LCCN 2021009349 (print) | LCCN 2021009350 (ebook) |
    ISBN 9781789974904 (paperback) | ISBN 9781789974911 (ebook) | ISBN
    9781789974928 (epub) | ISBN 9781789974935 (mobi)
Subjects: LCSH: Khiḍr, ʻAbbās, 1973---Criticism and interpretation. | Refugees in
    literature. | Emigration and immigration in literature.
Classification: LCC PT2711.H54 Z53 2021 (print) | LCC PT2711.H54 (ebook) |
    DDC 833/.92--dc23
LC record available at https://lccn.loc.gov/2021009349
LC ebook record available at https://lccn.loc.gov/2021009350

Cover image: Abbas Khider © Peter-Andreas Hassiepen / Munich

ISSN 1664-6916
ISBN 978-1-78997-490-4 (print) • ISBN 978-1-78997-491-1 (ePDF)
ISBN 978-1-78997-492-8 (ePub) • ISBN 978-1-78997-493-5 (mobi)

© Peter Lang Group AG 2021

Published by Peter Lang Ltd, International Academic Publishers,
52 St Giles, Oxford, OX1 3LU, United Kingdom
oxford@peterlang.com, www.peterlang.com

David N. Coury and Karolin Machtans have asserted their right under the
Copyright, Designs and Patents Act, 1988, to be identified as Editors of this Work.

This publication has been peer reviewed.

Contents

Acknowledgements

The editors would like to thank Laurel Plapp at Peter Lang for her assistance and patience with this project. The series editors, including Julian Preece, provided important guidance and support for the volume as well. Karolin Machtans is grateful to Connecticut College for its research support and its generous financial support with the publishing costs. She would also like to thank Abbas Khider for taking the time to meet with her for the interview in Berlin. David Coury would like to thank the Frankenthal Family and their endowed professorship at the University of Wisconsin-Green Bay, which made research on this project possible.

Works by Abbas Khider

Der falsche Inder (2008) = FI
The Village Indian, trans. Donal McLaughlin (2013) = VI

Die Orangen des Präsidenten (2011) [The President's Oranges] = OdP

Brief in die Auberginenrepublik (2013) [Letter to the Aubergine Republic] = BiA

Ohrfeige (2016) = OF
A Slap in the Face, trans. Simon Pare (2019) = SiF

Deutsch für alle: Das endgültige Lehrbuch (2019) [German for Everyone: The Ultimate Textbook] = DfA

Palast der Miserablen (2020) [The Palace of the Wretched] = PdM

DAVID N. COURY AND KAROLIN MACHTANS

Abbas Khider: Introduction

Born in Baghdad in 1973 to a poor and illiterate family, Abbas Khider is one of the most celebrated writers with a migrant background in Germany today. As a teenager, he started reading religious books owned by his parents: 'That way, I actually discovered literature, given that the language of religious texts is often metaphorical. It helped me to read and understand poetry. I thus discovered the world anew.'[1] Supported by his sisters and brother-in-law, the Iraqi literary critic Salhe Zamel, Khider discovered the world of literature and felt encouraged to start writing himself: 'For me, reading was a kind of excursion and refuge. I fled to Germany with Kafka, to Russia with Pushkin and to France with Baudelaire. It was this love of reading that made me write texts of my own.'[2] As a high school graduate, Khider distributed flyers protesting against the regime of Saddam Hussein and was imprisoned for two years on charges of political agitation – an experience that left a profound impact on him as a writer: 'Even after you are freed from prison, the experience accompanies you everywhere you go. The struggle and the pain continue. Over time, that struggle takes on other dimensions and affects language, religion and literature too.'[3] In 1996, he fled Iraq and spent several years as an undocumented refugee in Jordan, Libya, Tunisia, Turkey, Greece and Italy before finally being granted asylum in Germany in 2000. In Germany, he studied literature and philosophy in Munich and Potsdam and soon after began his publishing career.

---

1 Abderrahmane Ammar, '"German is My New Language": Interview with Abbas Khider', trans. Pauline Cumbers, Goethe Institute (2014), <https://www.goethe.de/en/kul/lit/20437059.html>, accessed 15 June 2020.

2 Ibid.

3 Ibid.

To date, Khider has published five novels and a 'grammar book' in German. In 2008, he debuted with *Der falsche Inder* [*The Village Indian*, 2013],[4] a series of vignettes narrating the protagonist's flight from Iraq to Germany in eight different stories, framed by a narrative that engages with questions of traumatic memories and the process of accessing and writing one's own life story. In 2011, he published *Die Orangen des Präsidenten* [The President's Oranges], dealing with the cruelty and suffering in Iraqi torture prisons. In 2013, *Brief in die Auberginenrepublik* [Letter to the Aubergine Republic] was published, telling the story of a love letter written in Benghazi, Libya that passes many hands, but never reaches its intended recipient in Baghdad. The story is told in seven chapters by seven different first-person narrators (a narratological trope that is common in Khider's storytelling), providing insights into the narrators' everyday lives in Libya, Egypt, Jordan, Syria and Iraq at the end of the twentieth century.

It was, however, Khider's 2016 novel *Ohrfeige* [*A Slap in the Face*, 2019] that led to his breakthrough. The overwhelmingly positive reception of the novel must be seen in the context of Germany's 'long summer of migration': the arrival of more than one million refugees in Germany in 2015 and 2016, following Germany's 'open border' politics and Chancellor Merkel's optimistic slogan *Wir schaffen das!* (We will manage!). While Merkel did not, in fact, open the borders, as many have since claimed (in reality the Dublin Regulation was suspended, allowing refugees and asylum seekers to move on to Germany despite having entered the EU in another country), the willingness of the German government to help re-settle so many asylum seekers in such a short period of time triggered a crisis of sorts. On the one hand, enthusiastic pro-refugee initiatives were organised by thousands of volunteers (Germany's proverbial *Willkommenskultur*[5]) and were supported

---

4   After initial introduction, each novel will be referenced by the abbreviations in the list of titles.

5   The term 'Willkommenskultur', as Trauner and Turton have shown, predates the 2015 growth in the number of people seeking asylum and is in and of itself a problematic term due to its suggestion of some migrants being welcome and others not. As such it can also serve as a means of exclusion. – Florian Trauner and Jocelyn Turton, '"Welcome Culture": The Emergence and Transformation of a Public Debate on Migration,' in *OZP – Austrian Journal of Political Science* 46/1 (2017), 33–42.

by the tabloid *Bild*'s campaign *Wir helfen*, while on the other hand, growing anxieties and outright hostility towards immigrants and refugees resulted, especially in the former GDR.[6] This spectrum of competing responses to Germany's 'refugee crisis' is the context in which the reception of Khider's novel must be seen. The term 'refugee crisis' itself is obviously problematic – not only because it stigmatises refugees as cultural others threatening the status quo of Germany's national identity and overlooks the failures of the global North to respond to the humanitarian crisis, but also because it reduces forcibly displaced people to the level of a natural catastrophe, thus dehumanising them and denying them agency.[7] Seemingly in response, Khider's novel *Ohrfeige* tells the story of an Iraqi refugee in Germany in the early 2000s who ostensibly slaps his case agent in the face when she informs him that his asylum status has been revoked, ties her up, and forces her to listen to his story. Critics overwhelmingly highlighted the fact that Khider had finally given refugees in Germany a literary voice and celebrated *Ohrfeige* as 'the book of the hour' and 'a portrayal of refugee life'.[8] There can indeed be no doubt that the narrative is more than timely. However, it is important to note that despite being published in February 2016, at the height of the so-called European 'refugee crisis', the story itself takes place at the beginning of the new millennium, thus dealing with a very specific

6   According to Jan-Jonathan Bock and Sharon Macdonald, the former East Germany, with less than 20 per cent of the German population, witnessed 43 per cent of the acts against asylum seekers and of xenophobic violence as well as a growing electoral support for the right-wing, anti-immigration and anti-Muslim Alternative for Germany. – Jan-Jonathan Bock and Sharon Macdonald, 'Introduction: Making, Experiencing and Managing Difference in a Changing Germany', in Jan-Jonathan Bock and Sharon Macdonald, eds., *Refugees Welcome? Difference and Diversity in a Changing Germany* (Berghahn: New York, 2019), 1–38, 7.

7   Bock and Macdonald, 'Introduction', 2–3.

8   See, for example, the following reviews in the *Frankfurter Allgemeine Zeitung* and the *Hamburger Abendblatt*: Julia Encke, 'Vom Warten wird man immer blöder' (2016), <https://www.faz.net/aktuell/feuilleton/buecher/fluechtlingsroman-vom-warten-wird-man-immer-bloeder-14030679.html>, accessed 15 June 2020. – Thomas Andre, 'Der Roman der Stunde: Das Schicksal eines Asylbewerbers' (2016), <https://www.abendblatt.de/hamburg/article207005593/Der-Roman-der-Stunde-Das-Schicksal-eines-Asylbewerbers.html>, accessed 15 June 2020.

moment in Germany's history of migration. During the 1990s, shortly after German reunification, the arrival of asylum seekers from the former Soviet Union and the former Yugoslavia resulted in a public discourse and media rhetoric about 'floods' and 'waves' of refugees, leading Germany's two main parties, the CDU/CSU coalition and the SPD, to amend Article 16 (the so-called *Asylkompromiss* [asylum compromise]) of Germany's Basic Law.[9] The original intent of the Article was to atone for and help in the process of coming to terms with Germany's anti-immigrant and fascist past. Article 16a declares certain countries *sichere Herkunftsländer* [safe countries of origin] and states that asylum seekers who have crossed a *sicherer Drittstaat* [safe third country] on their flight to Germany have to return to that safe country and cannot claim asylum in Germany.[10] Complicating matters, two million *Aussiedler* (people from Eastern European countries who could demonstrate German ancestry and had not been expelled after the Second World War) arrived in Germany during the 1990s. These *Aussiedler* – unlike many guest workers and their descendants who had lived in Germany for years – were considered Germans (not immigrants), based on Germany's then-citizenship law and its emphasis on descent, rather than place of birth. The recent arrival of these diverse groups of immigrants sparked a heated debate – the so-called *Asyldebatte* [asylum debate] – about an assumed *Asylmissbrauch* [asylum abuse] as well as broader questions of German identity, belonging and nationhood.[11] Despite the growing diversity of German society and the new *Ausländergesetz* [foreigners' legislation] from 1990, which granted guaranteed residency and limited voting rights for those living in Germany without a German passport and made the acquisition of German citizenship possible for guest workers and their children, violent attacks against foreigners, asylum reception centres and accommodations

9   For the following overview of Germany's history of migration, see Bock and Macdonald, 'Introduction', 16–22.
10   Bock and Macdonald, 'Introduction', 18.
11   For further discussion, see Hendrik Cremer, 'Die Asyldebatte in Deutschland: 20 Jahre nach dem "Asylkompromiss"' (Berlin: Deutsches Institut für Menschenrechte, 2013), <https://www.institut-fuer-menschenrechte.de/uploads/tx_commerce/essay_Die_Asyldebatte_in_Deutschland_20_Jahre_nach_dem_Asylkompromiss.pdf>, accessed 15 June 2020.

continued throughout the 1990s across Germany (especially the former German Democratic Republic), and conservative politicians held on to their denial of Germany being a country of immigration.[12]

The situation changed with the 1998 elections and the Social-Democrat/Green coalition's rise to power under Chancellor Gerhard Schröder. The Schröder government officially recognised Germany's status as a country of immigration and promoted integration and participation of immigrants. Most importantly, the 2000 citizenship law reform, recognising the principle of *jus soli*, made it possible for children born in Germany to foreign parents to acquire German citizenship at birth in addition to the foreign citizenship of their parents, under the condition that at least one of their parents has been a legal resident of Germany for at least eight years and has a permanent right of residence at the time of the child's birth. However, by their twenty-first birthday, these children were required to choose between their German citizenship and that of their parents (*Optionspflicht*). This development was far from uncontroversial: CDU politicians like Robert Koch in Hesse and Jürgen Rüttgers in North-Rhine Westphalia ran political campaigns against the broadening of the citizenship laws, greater social inclusion of immigrants and a new skilled immigration law, all issues which inevitably complicate the odyssey of Karim Mensy, the protagonist of *Ohrfeige*.

Furthermore, Khider's novel responds to the 9/11 attacks in 2001 and must therefore be seen in the context of a growing Islamophobia and a 'Muslim turn' in Germany and worldwide.[13] It also includes references

---

12   In 2019, *Zeit Online* digitally collected all speeches in the Bundestag in which the term 'Einwanderungsland' was used, and analysed the change in the debate. – Alicia Lindhoff, 'Einwanderungsland? Wir doch nicht', *Zeit Online* (17 September 2019), <https://www.zeit.de/politik/deutschland/2019-09/migrationsdebatte-einwanderungsland-fluechtlingspolitik-bundeswoerter>, accessed 15 June 2020.

13   As Yasemin Yildiz has convincingly argued, after 9/11, Germany's largest minority, formerly referred to as 'Turks', has been recast as 'Muslims'. – See Yasemin Yildiz, 'Turkish Girls, Allah's Daughters, and the Contemporary German Subject: Itinerary of a Figure', in *German Life and Letters* 62/3 (2009), 465–81. – For a discussion of the growing Islamophobia in the West, see Todd H. Green, *The Fear of Islam: An Introduction to Islamophobia in the West*, 2nd edn (Minneapolis: Fortress Press, 2019).

to the 2003 Iraq War, a conflict which the German government opposed, and its devastating effects on the lives of ordinary people in Iraq. Hence, *Ohrfeige* – as well as Khider's other texts and public statements – must be read as interventions at particular moments in Germany's dynamic history of migration, responding to specific debates about cultural, ethnic, linguistic and religious forms of difference and diversity. At the same time, his interventions are timeless, since refugees, especially those who are not granted full protection, still find themselves in a precarious situation in Germany, despite recent developments such as the German citizenship law reform in 2014 or the relatively new 'immigration courses' that provide access to language courses financed by the German government.[14] As witnessed by the success of Thilo Sarrazin's infamous 2010 book *Deutschland schafft sich ab* [Germany Abolishes Itself], Pegida's anti-immigration and anti-Muslim protests, the NSU murders and the rise of the right-wing party *Alternative für Deutschland*, questions of national and cultural belonging, integration and (post)migration continue to remain highly contested.[15]

In 2020, Khider published his novel *Palast der Miserablen* [The Palace of the Wretched], telling the story of Shams Hussein, a young male protagonist who grows up in the aftermath of the Iran-Iraq War and whose family moves from the South of Iraq to the slums on the outskirts of Baghdad, struggling to survive. Shams discovers his love for literature and, together with his friends, forms a group (named 'The Palace of the Wretched') that secretly meets to talk about literature. According to critics in the German *feuilletons*, Khider succeeds with his unique laconic voice

---

14   For the different forms of protection – entitlement to asylum, refugee protection, subsidiary protection and national ban on deportation – see the website of the Federal Office for Migration and Refugees, 'Forms of Protection', <https://www.bamf.de/EN/Themen/AsylFluechtlingsschutz/AblaufAsylverfahrens/Schutzformen/schutzformen-node.html>, accessed 15 June 2020.

15   For an overview of the recent debates in Germany, see Karolin Machtans, 'Navid Kermani: Advocate for an Antipatriotic Patriotism and a Multireligious, Multicultural Europe', in Axel Hildebrandt and Jill Twark, eds., *Envisioning Social Justice in Contemporary German Culture* (Rochester/NY: Camden House, 2015), 290–311. – See also Jan-Jonathan Bock and Sharon Macdonald, 'Introduction'.

in painting a realistic portrait of daily life in Iraq during Saddam Hussein's reign of terror – a life marked by extreme social inequalities, war, despotism and torture. Furthermore, the novel highlights the role of Iraq as a 'playground' of competing world powers and the effects of world politics on the country's inhabitants' private lives, thus pointing to the role of individual stories for an understanding of historical events.[16] For Khider, writing means to 'engage with history, with time and with lies'. His role as a writer provides him with a public forum and enables him, as he has argued, 'to go on the offensive'.[17]

Although a native speaker of Arabic, Khider writes in German, the language that he acquired when he arrived in Germany at the age of 27. The German language, as he has stated in interviews, provides him with the necessary emotional distance to his subject and allows him to approach a traumatic past that would be too painful to write about in Arabic: 'Whenever I tried to write in Arabic, all the suffering was still in the text. It was only when I started writing in German that the suffering

16   <http://www.new-books-in-german.com/palace-wretched>, accessed 15 June 2020. – As Saul Friedländer has argued in the context of the Holocaust, eyewitnesses' voices not only give us insights into the effects of historical events on their lives. Rather, their voices help us understand their *perception* of the historical events and thus the historical reality itself: 'In many works the implicit assumptions regarding the victims' generalised hopelessness and passivity, or their inability to change the course of events leading to their extermination, have turned them into a static and abstract element of the historical background. It is too often forgotten that Nazi attitudes and policies cannot be fully assessed without knowledge of the lives and indeed of the feelings of the Jewish men, women, and children themselves. (…) Indeed, their voices are essential if we are to attain an understanding of this past. For it is their voices that reveal what was known and what *could* be known; theirs were the only voices that conveyed both the clarity of insight and the total blindness of human beings confronted with an entirely new and utterly horrifying reality.' – Saul Friedländer, *Nazi Germany and the Jews*, Vol. I: *The Years of Persecution, 1933–1939* (New York: Harper Collins, 2007), 2.

17   Abderrahmane Ammar, '"German is My New Language": Interview with Abbas Khider'.

turned into literature.'[18] Psycholinguistic research confirms the connection of memories with the language in which they are encoded. As Jacqueline Amati-Mehler and others have argued, the foreign language serves as a ' "safety barrier" against the tumult of primitive emotions that would immediately have been evoked by the words of [the] mother tongue' (xi).[19] Furthermore, by writing in German – and not in Arabic, his first language – Khider highlights the existence of multiple linguistic and cultural attachments, thus deconstructing 'the illusory stability of fixed identities', to use Rosi Braidotti's words.[20] Neither languages nor cultures are clearly demarcated entities, as Khider playfully hints at in his German 'grammar book' *Deutsch für alle: Das endgültige Lehrbuch* [German for Everyone: The Ultimate Textbook, 2019].[21]

For his literary works, Khider has been awarded numerous prizes and grants and was appointed writer-in-residence for the city of Mainz in 2017 and patron of the Körber Stiftung's 'Hamburger Tage des Exils' in 2018. Among the many awards he has received are the Adelbert von Chamisso Promotional Prize (2010), the Hilde Domin Prize for Literature in Exile (2013), the Nelly Sachs Prize (2013) and, for a second time, the Adelbert von Chamisso Prize for his complete works to date (2017). Khider was, in fact, the last recipient of the Chamisso Prize before it was discontinued, as the Robert Bosch Foundation argued that the prize had run its course and reached its goals and that now such works formed a natural part of German literature, suggesting a 'normalisation' of literature by non-native authors. First established in 1985, the award was initially given to writers who had immigrated to Germany and who wrote in German. In the 1980s, such works were still considered 'guest worker literature' [*Gastarbeiterliteratur*]

---

18   Lewis Gropp, 'Writing More Beautifully than God' (2011), <https://en.qantara. de/content/the-german-iraqi-writer-abbas-khider-writing-more-beautifully-than-god>, accessed 15 June 2020.

19   Jacqueline Amati-Mehler, Simona Argentieri and Jorge Canestri, *The Babel of the Unconscious: Mother Tongue and Foreign Tongues in the Psychoanalytic Dimension* (Madison, CT: International Universities Press, 1993).

20   Rosi Braidotti, *Nomadic Subjects: Embodiment and Sexual Difference in Contemporary Feminist Theory* (New York: Columbia University Press, 1994), 15.

21   Abbas Khider, *Deutsch für alle: Das endgültige Lehrbuch* (Munich: Hanser, 2019).

or 'migrant literature' [*Migrantenliteratur*], but soon, because of the marginalisation associated with such terms, it became known as 'Chamisso literature'.[22] This term, while still referencing the prize's origins, seeks to encompass what has also been called trans- or intercultural literature, literary works that straddle multiple cultural traditions and destabilise a hegemonic cultural discourse without being defined by the nationality of the author.

Khider's novels have contributed to an ongoing debate over what constitutes 'German literature' that perhaps first arose in 1991, when Turkish-born writer Emine Sevgi Özdamar was awarded (somewhat controversially at the time) the Ingeborg Bachmann Prize. The question of both personal and literary identity is one that is important for Khider and is central to his works, as he has explained in interviews:

> [I]ch war, als ich jünger war, Iraker. Später, als ich Irak verlassen habe, war ich jahrelang Flüchtling. Ich kam nach Deutschland und dann war ich Ausländer. Ich habe die Aufenthaltserlaubnis und die Staatsangehörigkeit bekommen und dann wurde ich Migrant. Jetzt habe ich verschiedene Bezeichnungen: Deutsch-Irakischer Autor, Deutsch-sprachiger Autor, Deutsch-schreibender Autor, oder Deutscher oder Iraker.[23]

> [W]hen I was younger, I was an Iraqi. Later after I left Iraq, I was for years a refugee. I came to Germany and then I was a foreigner. I received a residence permit and citizenship and then I was a migrant. Now I have different designations: German-Iraqi writer, German-language writer, a writer of German, or German or Iraqi.

As someone who has experienced flight and exile, Khider uses literature as a means of examining himself and trying to understand who he is in relation to his past and his present circumstances. However, while the topics of exile, flight and expulsion are at the centre of his work, his novels

22   'Adelbert von Chamisso Preis of the Robert Bosch Stiftung', <https://www.bosch-stiftung.de/en/project/adelbert-von-chamisso-prize-robert-bosch-stiftung>, accessed 5 July 2020. Chamisso himself was born in France but was forced to flee with his family first to Belgium, then Holland and finally to Germany in the wake of the French Revolution. He went on to become an important scientist and poet, writing in a second language.

23   Katherine Anderson, *Foreign Writing Agency: Abbas Khider & María Cecilia Barbetta Writing Towards Catharsis in German as a Foreign Language After Trauma* (Philadelphia: The Pennsylvania State University, 2017), 252.

should not simply be reduced to a naturalistic depiction of 'the refugee experience'. Rather, Khider's work deserves much more careful attention from scholars not only in German studies but in a broader European framework for what they contribute to an understanding of a multicultural, cosmopolitan Europe. In his novels, Khider explores the gendered nature of power systems, the Kafkaesque dynamics of bureaucracy and the Agambian notion of the refugee as a biopolitical subject over which the government exercises sovereign power. Taken together, Khider's body of work explores what Lyndsey Stonebridge has referred to as the spectre of rightlessness that has prompted debates over place, belonging and the rights of refugees.[24] Skilfully blending the tragic with the comic, however, as well as the grotesque with the ordinary, Khider highlights the role of laughter as a means of resistance.

To date there have been no comprehensive academic studies of Khider's work, although there have been several published articles on his works and his novels are often discussed at academic conferences.[25] This volume offers

24   Lyndsey Stonebridge, *Placeless People: Writings, Rights and Refugees* (Oxford: Oxford University Press, 2018), 2.

25   See, for example, Moritz Schramm, 'Ironischer Realismus: Selbstdifferenz und Wirklichkeitsnähe bei Abbas Khider', in Søren R. Fauth and Rolf Parr, eds., *Neue Realismen in der Gegenwartsliteratur* (Munich: Fink, 2016), 71–84. – Carola Hilmes, 'Jedes Kapitel ein Anfang und zugleich ein Ende', in Monika Wolting, ed., *Identitätskonstruktionen in der deutschen Gegenwartsliteratur* (Göttingen: Vandenhoeck & Ruprecht, 2017), 135–46. – Warda El-Kaddouri, '"Gott, rette mich aus der Leere!" Verlust, Religiosität und Radikalisierung in den Fluchtnarrativen von Abbas Khider und Sherko Fatah', in Thomas Hardtke et al., eds., *Niemandsbuchten und Schutzbefohlene: Flucht-Räume und Flüchtlingsfiguren in der deutschsprachigen Gegenwartsliteratur* (Göttingen: V&R Unipress, 2017), 23–38. – Hanna Maria Hofmann, 'Erzählungen der Flucht aus raumtheoretischer Sicht: Abbas Khiders *Der falsche Inder* und Anna Seghers' *Transit*', in Thomas Hardtke et al., eds., *Niemandsbuchten und Schutzbefohlene*, 97–124. – Katherine Anderson, 'Von der Wanderung zum Wandel: Die Migration des Abbas Khider in die deutsche Sprache als Traumabewältigung durch Erzählen', in Elke Sturm-Trigonakis, Olga Laskaridou, Evi Petropoulou and Katerina Karakassi, eds., *Turns und kein Ende? Aktuelle Tendenzen in Germanistik und Komparatistik* (Frankfurt am Main: Peter Lang, 2017), 95–104. – Moritz Schramm, 'Experimentelle Erkundungen: Überlegungen zum Verhältnis von Anerkennungstheorie und Literaturwissenschaft am Beispiel von Abbas Khiders Roman *Die Orangen des*

the first comprehensive study of Khider's works, explores important thematic aspects of his novels and contextualises how they form part of an important body of literature on immigrant and exile writing. The essays in this volume are an important contribution to a growing body of scholarship that analyses works by authors from the non-dominant culture, moving the discussion away from the author as someone situated 'between two worlds' whose writing accurately depicts the migratory experience.[26] Instead, as the contributors here argue, these literary texts are rich in topics that help us understand the forces of globalisation and both the challenges and opportunities that migration affords. Using these frames of reference, the contributions here focus on themes such as trauma, historical and individual memory, gender, race, ethnicity and multilingualism. In doing so, these essays will be of value not only to those in German studies, but more broadly to scholars and readers engaged in refugee and migration studies, European studies, transnational studies and global studies.

Katherine Anderson's article explores Khider's first two novels through the lens of trauma, arguing that not only the experience of time is disrupted

Präsidenten', in Martin Baisch, ed., *Anerkennung und die Möglichkeiten der Gabe* (Frankfurt am Main: Peter Lang, 2017), 177–95. – Sarah Steidl, 'Der Flüchtling als Grenzgestalter? Zur Dialektik des Grenzverletzers in Abbas Khiders Debütroman *Der falsche Inder*', in Thomas Hardtke et al., eds., *Niemandsbuchten und Schutzbefohlene*, 305–20. – Ulrike Schneider, 'Darstellungsweisen von Fluchtprozessen in der Gegenwartsliteratur am Beispiel von Merle Kröger und Abbas Khider sowie den Reportagen von Wolfgang Bauer und Navid Kermani', *Argonautenschiff: Jahrbuch der Anna-Seghers-Gesellschaft Berlin und Mainz e.V.* 25 (2017), 82–92. – Corina Stan, 'Novels in the Translation Zone: Abbas Khider, *Weltliteratur*, and the Ethics of the Passerby', *Comparative Literature Studies* 55/2 (2018), 285–302. – Hamid Tafazoli, 'Flüchtlingsfiguren im kulturellen Gedächtnis Europas: Konstruktionen einer Grenzfigur in den Romanen *Schlafgänger*, *Ohrfeige* und *Gehen, ging, gegangen*', *Weimarer Beiträge: Zeitschrift für Literaturwissenschaft, Ästhetik und Kulturwissenschaften* 64/2 (2018), 222–43. – Ana R. Calero Valera, 'Diálogo entre memorias: Perpetradores y víctimas en *Brief in die Auberginenrepublik* de Abbas Khider', *Revista de Filología Alemana* 27 (2019), 117–30.

26 Cf. Leslie Adelson, *The Turkish Turn in Contemporary German Literature: Toward a New Critical Grammar of Migration* (New York: Palgrave Macmillan, 2005). See also B. Venkat Mani, *Cosmopolitical Claims: Turkish-German Literatures from Nadolny to Pamuk* (Iowa City: University of Iowa Press, 2007).

in these two novels, but also the protagonist's experience of reality. Basing her analysis on the work of Robert Eaglestone as well as narrative exposition theory, Anderson explores Khider's treatment of time and reality within these texts, highlighting the close relationship between author and trauma in the creation of narrative form and of narrative content and language within the narrative itself.

Reading the images of refugees' bodies in *Ohrfeige* and *Der falsche Inder* as mirrors of current processes of global mobility and migration, Markus Hallensleben argues that the transnational narratives in Khider's works are examples of a post-migration literature and society, where gender, race and ethnicity have become plural and performative. In depicting his protagonists' identities as transgressive, the question of belonging is replaced by notions of transitional cultural spaces and fluid identities within the context of a global transition at large.

One of the more under-researched aspects of Khider's works is the role of religion and the place of Islam in his novels. Warda El-Kaddouri analyses the protagonists' investigation of their relationship to religion and God as a consequence of a deep existential crisis, resulting from their experiences of war, imprisonment and torture under Iraqi dictatorship, and, ultimately, forced migration. Focusing on intertextual references to the Quran and Sufi thought in *Der falsche Inder* and *Ohrfeige*, she shows that Islam is an essential part of the protagonists' identity formation in exile, thus highlighting the religious and spiritual dimensions of Khider's novels.

In her examination of the prison wall epigraphs in *Die Orangen des Präsidenten*, Carolin Müller argues that walls serve as a metaphor of both boundary and passage. Epigraphs in carceral narratives thus highlight the significance and difficulties of writing memory in in-between places. Using Hannah Arendt's concept of the 'space of appearance', Müller argues that the engraved notes are an act of claiming space and giving a voice to the silenced prisoners – in other words: an act of reclaiming agency that is contrasted with the wardens' efforts to erase these stories and the prisoners' bodies, and thus the writers' existence.

Sabine Zimmermann's contribution deals with narratives of waste production in *Die Orangen des Präsidenten* and *Ohrfeige*. Building on the theoretical works of Giorgio Agamben, Zygmunt Bauman and Liisa

H. Malkki, she examines Khider's portrayals of various power systems as production sites that generate not only material waste, but most importantly 'human waste', or the wasted lives of displaced individuals. Referencing recent studies by Jürgen Habermas, Richard Rorty, Alexander Betts, Peter Collier and others, Zimmermann challenges us to read Khider's novels as representations of a society's treatment of its marginalised groups and as a critical reflection of the interconnectedness of power systems with regard to human rights issues and the politics of refuge.

Jara Schmidt interprets Karim Mensy's overpowering of his female case worker in the foreign registration office in *Ohrfeige* – the embodiment of German bureaucracy – as a carnivalesque reversal of hierarchies. Presenting us with a counternarrative from the perspective of the refugee protagonist, Khider challenges us to critically engage with the power structures inherent in Germany's administrative asylum machinery. Schmidt draws on Bakhtin's concept of the carnivalesque and the grotesque to show that Mensy's body both defies societal norms and is the embodiment of the refugee in German society.

The final two contributions explore the use of language and the relationship between language and identity in Khider's novels. First, basing their analysis on Bonny Norton's concept of social identity construction, Beate Baumann and Corinne Puglisi explore the impact of language acquisition on the construction of identity in Khider's autofictions. All of Khider's novels, Baumann and Puglisi maintain, represent reflections of and display parallels to Khider's own biography and reveal the importance of language and the confrontation with a foreign language on concepts of the self. In doing so, these novels also challenge notions of cultural identity as a clearly defined, homogeneous entity.

Karolin Machtans then analyses Khider's 'grammar book' from 2019, *Deutsch für alle*, and questions of linguistic belonging. Drawing on Yasemin Yildiz' study of German postmonolingualism, Machtans argues that Khider's novels challenge notions of identity linked to one's 'mother-tongue' and instead point to new linguistic and cultural affiliations. Furthermore, Khider examines the relationship between multilingual realities and monolingual power structures in Germany and the sociopolitical consequences of Germany's institutionalised monolingualism.

Thus, Khider's humorous 'grammar book' *Deutsch für alle* can be read as a plea for heightened critical language awareness and an appreciation for multilingual realities in Germany.

The contributions in this volume speak to the array of themes, tropes and narratological innovations that Khider employs in his works. He continues to be a prolific writer, is sought after for interviews and commentaries and has become a recognised figure in the contemporary German literary scene. His works engage at once with the challenges that refugees and immigrants face and at the same time contest the limitations and nomenclature of these categories. His literary aesthetic is steeped in a love of the German language and German literature, yet he brings a fresh look at both, offering the insights of an outsider who is at the same time very much part of contemporary German society.

KAROLIN MACHTANS, TRANS. DAVID N. COURY

Interview with Abbas Khider (Berlin, 24 May 2019)

1. *Du wirst in Interviews häufig nach dem autobiographischen Charakter deiner Werke gefragt. Was antwortest du darauf?*
(Lacht) Unterschiedlich. Jedes Mal fällt mir irgendwie etwas anderes ein. [...] Ich weiß, der Ausgangspunkt meiner Arbeit ist meine Biographie auf jeden Fall, das weiß ich. Aber natürlich, die Figuren meiner Romane haben ihre eigenen Charaktere und ihre eigenen Eigenschaften und ihre eigene Geschichte. [...] Die sind eigene, selbstständige Figuren, und die funktionieren auch in einem Text und sollen in ihrer eigenen Welt existieren. Ich muss hier eigentlich nicht die Rolle eines Gottes spielen und alles bestimmen, auch ihre Eigenschaften. [...] Jede Figur in jedem Roman ist ein anderer Mensch, eine andere Person. Eins ist wichtig, wenn man an meine Biographie, meine Geschichte denkt. [...] Es geht häufig um Exil, Fremde, das Leben am Rande einer Gesellschaft, Gefängnis, Diktatur, Biographie, komplizierte Beziehungen zwischen Menschen, Gruppierungen auch – das sind eigentlich meine Themen, und das betrachte ich als mein literarisches Programm. Und wenn ich das schreibe, natürlich, dann hat man den Eindruck, die Themen sind ähnlich [...], aber das sind eigentlich die Themen der Literatur seit Ewigkeiten. [...] Und ich versuche nicht, meine Autobiographie zu schreiben, sondern tatsächlich meine Zeit. Ich bin in einer Zeit, und ich lebe in dieser Zeit, und diese Zeit bestimmt auch, wie ich denke. [...] Ich glaube, Themen wählen ihre Autoren, nicht die Autoren wählen Themen. [...] Die Zeit schreibt vor, wie wir denken. [...] Jede Generation hat irgendwie bestimmte Themen, die diese Generation auch bewegen und eine große Rolle spielen, und meine Themen sind auch die Themen meiner Zeit, und meine Zeit ist natürlich auch meine Biographie, auf allgemeine Art und Weise.

2. *Eine andere häufig gestellte Frage ist die nach deiner eigenen Mehrsprachigkeit und der Rolle der deutschen Sprache für dein Schreiben. Welche Rolle spielt die deutsche Sprache für dein Schreiben?*
Es ist eine Art Beziehung. [...] Zu einer Muttersprache können wir keine Beziehung aufbauen. Warum? Weil es gegeben ist [...], es ist ein Teil von uns, es wird uns gegeben.

English Translation by David N. Coury

1. *You are often asked in interviews about the autobiographical nature of your works. What do you answer?*

   (Laughs). Various things. Something new occurs to me every time. […] I know that the starting point of my work is my biography for sure – I know that. But naturally the figures in my novels have their own character and their own personalities and their own stories. […] They are their own autonomous figures and they function in a text and should exist in their own world. I shouldn't have to play the role of God here and determine everything, like their personalities. […] Every figure in each novel is a different person, a distinct human being. One thing is important, when you think about my biography, my history. It's often about exile, foreignness, life on the margins of society, prison, dictatorship, biography, complicated relations between people and social groupings as well – those are my themes and I view that as my literary program. And when I write about that, naturally, one then has the impression, the themes are similar […] but those have been the themes of literature forever. […] And I'm not trying to write my autobiography, rather about my time. And I'm in a time and live in a time and this time determines how I think. […] I believe that themes choose their authors, not that authors choose their themes. The era dictates how we think. […] Every generation somehow has certain themes that move that generation and that play a large role, and my themes are the themes of my time and my time is naturally also my biography, in a general sense.

2. *Another often asked question is about multilingualism and the role of the German language in your writing. What role does the German language play for your writing?*

   It's a kind of relationship […] We cannot build a relationship with our mother tongue. Why? Because it's given […], it's a part of us, it's given to us.

Eine Sprache, die wir selbst auswählen, müssen wir erobern und
alles neu erkennen – alle Eigenschaften, alle Besonderheiten.
Das ist wirklich der Unterschied. Und dann entwickelt sich eine
Beziehung. Und diese Beziehung ist tatsächlich keine einfache
Beziehung. Es ist ziemlich kompliziert. Es ist genauso wie
Beziehungen zwischen mehrsprachigen Menschen. Es ist nicht
kompliziert, aber es ist anders. Weil Kultur eine große Rolle
[spielt], wie man die Welt anschaut, wie man die Worte verwendet,
Missverständnisse entstehen dadurch. Das macht natürlich Dinge
lebendiger, aber nicht einfacher. Und solche Beziehung entwickelt
sich natürlich und bleibt nie gleich. [...] Und meine Beziehung
zu der deutschen Sprache hat tatsächlich unendliche Phasen. Es
begann zum Beispiel am Anfang, als ich Deutsch gelernt habe,
dann später, als ich irgendwann angefangen habe, das erste Buch
zu schreiben, wo ich immer noch unsicher war mit der deutschen
Sprache, aber trotzdem habe ich versucht, irgendwas mit dieser
Sprache zu erreichen zusammen, und das ist zum Beispiel die
erste Phase [...], nicht die Phase des Kennenlernens, sondern
mehr die Phase des Provozierens – man geht dorthin und nimmt
sich irgendein, mehrere Teile von einer Sprache und versucht,
[sie] für sich zu gewinnen und davon irgendwie neu zu formen.
Und das, natürlich, hat auch viel mit Gewalt zu tun. Man zwingt
die Sprache am Anfang, integrationsfähiger zu sein. [...] Und
dann entwickeln sich mehrere Phasen. Die zweite Phase zum
Beispiel in meinem zweiten Buch, *Die Orangen des Präsidenten*,
da schrieb ich über Gefängniserfahrungen [...]. Ich bin jemand,
der selbst im Knast war. Und ich kenne diese Welt und was es
bedeutet, in einem Gefängnis unter der Erde zu leben. [...] Und
über diese Erfahrung zu schreiben, das ist tatsächlich literarisch
überhaupt nicht einfach. Man kann nicht mal darüber reden,
das dauert manchmal Jahrzehnte, Menschen können nicht
darüber reden. Das kennen wir von der Literatur übrigens, [...]
das ist seltsamerweise immer irgendeine Hauptfigur, die mit
den Großeltern redet, und die Großeltern wollen nie über die
Vergangenheit reden. In meinem Fall, ich bin nicht mit diesen
Großeltern [gewesen], sondern ich bin die Hauptfigur [...],

A language that we ourselves choose, we have to conquer and to discover everything new – all of its characteristics, all of its peculiarities. That's really the difference. And then a relationship develops. And this relationship is no easy relationship. It's rather complicated. It's just like relationships between multilingual people. It's not complicated but it's different. Because culture plays an important role, as to how one views the world, and how one uses words. Misunderstandings arise as a result. That makes things livelier of course, but not simpler. And such a relationship develops naturally and never stays the same. And my relationship to the German language has indeed many unending phases. It started for instance at the beginning, when I first learned German and then later, when I at some point began to write my first book when I was still insecure with the German language but nevertheless I tried to achieve something together with this language. And so that is for instance, the first phase [...], not the phase of acquaintance, rather more the phase of provocation – you go there and take some piece, several pieces of the language and try to win them over and somehow to shape something new from it. And that of course has a lot to do with violence. You force the language at the beginning, to be better able to integrate. [...] Then more phases develop. The second phase, for instance, in my second book, *The President's Oranges*, where I wrote about prison experiences [...]. I am someone who has himself been in prison. And I know this world and what it means to live in a prison below ground. [...] And to write about this experience is, in fact, not easy to do literarily. One cannot even really talk about it; it sometimes takes decades, people cannot talk about it. That we know from the literature, by the way, [...] there is always, strangely enough some kind of a main character, who speaks with his grandparents, and the grandparents never want to talk about the past. In my case, I didn't grow up with these grandparents, rather I am the main character

und ich erzähle von diesen Erfahrungen. Und diese Erfahrungen zu erzählen, tatsächlich, war mir am Anfang unmöglich auf Arabisch. […] Die deutsche Sprache entwickelte tatsächlich eine Art Distanz zu den Ereignissen, so dass ich wirklich – ich konnte wirklich mehrere Türen aufmachen und [in] Bereiche eintreten, [in] die ich früher nie […] gedacht habe, hineinzugehen. […] Und das ist zum Beispiel eine zweite Phase. […] Was ich sagen will: Eine Fremdsprache ist ein Mysterium. Und in diesem Mysterium befinden sich Schmerzen, aber auch Fröhlichkeiten und Schönheiten. Und durch die Eigenschaften dieser Sprache kann man unheimlich gut unterscheiden zwischen Schmerzen und Schönheiten, und man verwandelt sogar Schmerzen in Feinheit, und manchmal Feinheit in traurige, melancholische Momente. Das heißt, man kann tatsächlich alles auf den Kopf stellen. Und das ist, natürlich, die Beziehung mit einer neuen Sprache. Man bekommt neue Erfahrung, und man sieht die Welt mit einem anderen Blick. Und man hat die Möglichkeit, durch die andere Sprache, die Muttersprache, […] neue Bilder und neue Metaphern entstehen zu lassen. […] Jeder von uns versucht natürlich, eine neue Beschreibung, neue Metaphern, neue Bilder zu finden. Und manchmal, wenn mir nicht was einfällt, tatsächlich hilft in diesem Fall die andere Sprache oder die andere Kultur – Ausdrücke und Umgangssprache. […] Wenn man das im Deutschen verwendet, mit ein bisschen kleineren Änderungen, entstehen manchmal seltsame Metaphern, die vermutlich von einem deutschen Autoren […] nicht kommen. Und das zum Beispiel, das ist wie diese Beziehung zu der Sprache, und was diese Mehrsprachigkeit mit einem auch macht, ist tatsächlich ein langer Prozess.

3. *In der aktuellen Migrationsforschung wird die Pluralität kultureller Identitäten und die gleichzeitige Bindung an verschiedene Orte hervorgehoben. Migration ist das Normale geworden, kulturelle Identitäten werden als grenzüberschreitend verstanden. Ist der Begriff 'Heimat' obsolet geworden – oder wie definierst du ihn?*
Darüber […] kann man unendlich diskutieren, aber ich versuche mal. Ich glaube, das ist auch sehr persönlich auf jeden Fall,

and I tell of these experiences. And to narrate these experiences was at the beginning really impossible for me in Arabic. The German language helped develop a kind of distance to the events so that I could really open more doors and enter into areas where I had earlier never thought to go. [...] And that, for instance, is a second phase. [...]

What I want to say is: a foreign language is a mystery. And within this mystery we find pain, but also happiness and beauty. And through the characteristics of the language one can differentiate wonderfully between pain and beauty and one even turns pain into subtlety and sometimes subtlety into sad, melancholy moments. That is to say, one can actually turn everything upside down. And that is of course the relationship with a new language. You get a new experience and you see the world from a different perspective. And you have the possibility, through the other language, your mother tongue, to allow new images and metaphors to arise. Each of us tries naturally to find new descriptions, new metaphors and new images. And sometimes, when nothing occurs to me, the other language or the other culture actually helps, in this case – with expressions and colloquial language. If you use that in German, with some minor changes, strange metaphors sometimes arise that would probably not come from a German writer. And that for example, that is why the relationship to language and what multilingualism does for you, is such a long process.

3. *In current immigration research, there is an emphasis on the plurality of cultural identity and the connection to different places at the same time. Migration has become the norm and cultural identities are understood as transgressive. Has the concept of 'Heimat' then become obsolete – or how would you define it?*

One could discuss this forever, but I'll give it a try. I believe in any case that it's something very personal and

bestimmt über die Biographie einer Person, wie man die Dinge sieht, und wie viel man selbst auch erlebt hat, weltweit. Ob man ein Weltbürger ist, oder man das ganze Leben an einem Ort gehockt [hat] und nur an sich und seinen Garten und seine Mitmenschen denkt […]. In diesem Fall, ich denke an Heimat: Ich glaube, das Wort ist für mich […] so ein sinnentleertes Gefühl. Es ist ein Gefühl, aber sinnentleert. Es ist nicht was Konkretes, [wenn] man hundertprozentig sagt, was ist Heimat. Wir wissen, wie Heimat entstanden [ist], oder wie diese Länder, die wir als Heimat bezeichnen [entstanden sind]. Wenn ich sehe, zum Beispiel, was bedeutet Heimat, Deutschland. Oder, wenn ich sehe, wie sich die deutsche [Land-]Karte in dem letzten zwanzigsten Jahrhundert geändert hat, durch die Kriege und so. […] Und die Frage ist: Die Menschen, die in diesen Gebieten an den Grenzen [leben], die jetzt nicht mehr zu Deutschland gehören, […] viele von ihnen gehören jetzt zu anderen [Ländern]. Die Frage ist: Ist diese Beziehung, Heimat, immer noch die gleiche wie damals, als sie zu Deutschland gehörten, oder ist es eine andere? Ist Heimat ein politischer Begriff oder ein Gefühl? Wahrscheinlich unterscheiden wir nicht so richtig zwischen Zuhause und Heimat. Ist es Zuhause, meinen wir vermutlich Heimat, Zuhause sein, Geborgenheit, miteinander zusammen sein […]. Ist das Heimat? […] Wenn wir einen richtigen Begriff für das Wort finden, dann kann ich sagen, das ist ein sinnvolles Gefühl, aber vorher, bis jetzt, ist es tatsächlich ein sinnentleertes Gefühl, weil alles sich ändert, und es ist nicht geographisch [auch] verbunden, weil Geographie ändert sich sowieso. Es ist auch verbunden mit der politischen Situation und auch mit der geographischen Situation eines Landes. Im Nachhinein, wenn ich daran denke, es ist, wie gesagt, […] persönlich, wie man die Dinge sieht. Ich glaube, die Welt hat sich total geändert, und jeder aber, jeder Mensch braucht ein Zuhause. […] Es ist ein Gefühl, das sich auch durch andere Menschen entwickelt, das heißt, Anerkennung, miteinander leben, […] innerlich eine Ruhe mit anderen Menschen zu finden. Dann entwickelt sich das Gefühl, zu Hause zu sein.

determined by the biography of the person, and how one sees things and how much one has experienced globally. Whether one is a citizen of the world or has sat one's whole life in one place thinking about one's garden and fellow citizens. In this case, thinking about Heimat: I think the word for me is a feeling devoid of meaning. It's a feeling but one without meaning. It's not something concrete so that one could say one hundred percent what Heimat is. We know how Heimat arises or how these countries that we call 'Heimat' have arisen. If I look, for instance, what does Germany as Heimat mean? Or if I look at how the map of Germany has changed in the twentieth century through wars and such […] and then the question is: the people who live on the borders of these places that no longer belong to Germany many of them now belong to other countries. The questions is: is this relationship, Heimat, still the same as previously when they belonged to Germany or is it something else? Is Heimat a political concept or a feeling? We probably don't differentiate correctly between being 'at home' and 'Heimat'. Is it 'at home' that we mean by Heimat, being at home, a sense of security, being with others – is that Heimat? If we could find the correct meaning for the word, then I could say that it is a meaningful feeling, but for now, it's really a feeling devoid of meaning, because everything changes and it is not tied to geography because geography changes anyways. It's also tied to the political and geographical situation of a country. In retrospect, if I think about it, it is, as I say, personal, how one sees things. I think the world has changed dramatically and everyone needs a home. […] It is a feeling that also develops through other people, that is, through recognition, living together, finding inner peace with others. Then the feeling of being at home arises.

KM: *Bist du hier zu Hause, in Berlin?*
Ja.

4. *Wie würdest du die Rolle von Lachen/Humor für dein Werk
   beschreiben – und für dein Leben?*
   (Lacht) Oh je, oh je, oh je ... Ich würde nur einfach sagen: Lachen
   verbindet! (Lacht)

5. *Wie definierst du die Aufgabe des Schriftstellers und die Aufgabe
   von Literatur?*
   Ich komme aus einer anderen Welt, und ich kenne eine andere
   Welt, mit Unsicherheit, Traurigkeit, Krieg, Tod, keine Perspektive
   von irgendwas [...]. Da sieht man die Dinge ganz anders. [...] Ich
   lebte im Irak, in Bagdad, in der Zeit von Saddam Hussein. Diktatur.
   Es gab viele Autoren im Land, die für den Präsidenten geschrieben
   haben. [...] Andere haben geschwiegen und haben irgendetwas
   Anderes geschrieben. [...] Warum spielen sie mit? Warum –
   Literaten, Denker – spielen sie mit in der Diktatur? Geht es nur
   um Geld? Um Überzeugung? Oder Anderes? Diese Frage, dieses
   Thema von Intellektuellen hat mich jahrelang beschäftigt. [...] Was
   ist die Aufgabe der Intellektuellen? [...] Das Thema wiederholt
   sich immer in der Geschichte. [...] Sind die Autoren ein Teil einer
   Gesellschaft und einer Welt – oder nicht? Diese Frage muss jeder
   Autor für sich selbst beantworten. Ich meine, es ist die Aufgabe der
   Autoren, nicht nur gute Bücher zu schreiben, die sich verkaufen,
   sondern auch, etwas zu schreiben für die nächste Generation.
   Dass man eine Kultur aufbaut – keine Kultur der Gewalt, sondern
   eine Kultur des Menschen oder des Menschseins. Weil, wenn ich
   Diktatoren unterstütze oder Unternehmer oder Banditen oder
   [religiöse] Extreme, baue ich eine Gewaltkultur. Und durch diese
   Gewaltkultur werden später viele Menschen auch sterben. [...]
   Wir machen die Grundlage dieser Gewaltkultur durch unsere
   Unterstützung. Und ich glaube, die Aufgabe der Autoren [...] ist
   zuerst, nicht ein Teil einer Gewaltkultur zu werden [...]. Und wenn
   ihr nicht in dieser Rolle [...] als Produzierende von dieser Kultur
   des Menschseins sein wollt, könnt ihr etwas Anderes machen, aber
   niemals Gewaltkultur unterstützen.

KM: *Are you at home in Berlin?*
Yes.

4. *How would you describe the role of laughter or humour for your work – and for your life?*
(Laughs) Oh my, oh my, oh my ... I would only say that laughter unites! (laughs)

5. *How would you define the task of the writer and the task of literature?*
I come from a different world and I know of another world with uncertainty, sadness, war, death, no prospect of anything […]. There you see things completely differently. […] I lived in Iraq, in Baghdad during the time of Saddam Hussein and of a dictatorship. There were many writers in the country who wrote for the president. Others were quiet and wrote something completely different. […] Why do they play along? Why do they – writers, thinkers – play along in a dictatorship? Is it about money? Out of conviction? Or something else? This question, this topic about intellectuals preoccupied me for many years. […] What is the role of intellectuals? The question repeats itself throughout history. Are writers a part of society and of a world or not? This is a question that every author must answer for him- or herself. I believe it is the role of the author not only to write good books which sell but also to write something for the next generation. One must build a culture – not a culture of violence, rather a culture of humanity and of being human. Because if I support dictators or entrepreneurs or bandits or religious extremists, I'm building a culture of violence. And as a result of this culture of violence, many people will later die. We build the foundation of the culture of violence through our support. And I believe the role of writers is, first and foremost, not to become a part of this culture of violence. And if you all in your role as creators don't want a part of this culture of being human, then you can do something else, but never support the culture of violence.

[...] Das ist die einzige Rolle – das, was ich mir von Autoren wünsche. Sie können über alles schreiben, sie können alles sagen. Aber niemals wieder, niemals wieder eine neue Gewaltkultur hervorbringen. Weil, das gab es immer [...] in der Geschichte, und das Ende ist tatsächlich nicht etwas Besonderes. Das Ende heißt Blut und Zerstörung. Und in der Gegenwart entsteht auch eine Gewaltkultur, das sehen wir in dem Denken von vielen Menschen, politisch und auch literarisch [...]. Und ich hoffe nicht, dass ich oder irgendjemand anders irgendwann kommt und sagt, Dichtung wäre barbarisch in dieser Zeit. Das wünsche ich mir nicht.

Die Aufgabe der Literatur: Ich glaube, die Literatur hat nur eine Aufgabe. [lange Pause] Unter jeder Ruine befindet sich irgendet was Wertvolles, womöglich ein Schatz oder ein Gegenstand, die mit Erinnerungen oder Geschichten verbunden [...] [sind]. Und ich glaube, die Kunst und die Literatur [...] können diese Schönheit auch in den Ruinen zeigen. Das, was verborgen ist. [...] Aus dem Nichts kann die Literatur eine Hoffnung hervorbringen. [...] Für mich ist Literatur tatsächlich eine Art Hoffnung, neue Erkenntnisse, neue Welten. Es ist manchmal auch mahnend, die Literatur, dass Dinge sich nicht wiederholen. Die Literatur ist auch eine Bereicherung für bestimmte Aussagen des Lebens, ob Liebe, ob Fußball oder Krieg.

6. *Welchen Einfluss hat die deutsche Literatur auf dein Schreiben? Gibt es bestimmte Werke und Autoren oder Autorinnen, die dich besonders beeinflusst haben? Kafka zum Beispiel?*
(Lacht) Kafka – der sowieso. (Lacht) Der ist der Gott von allem. (Lacht)

Es ist natürlich schwierig zu sagen, wie beeinflusst, weil, ich habe natürlich eine andere Geschichte. [...] Aber Deutschland, am Anfang, als ich hier ankam, habe ich ein paar Autoren entdeckt, wo ich das Gefühl gehabt habe: Ja, hier lese ich etwas, und ich habe das Gefühl, [...] ich verstehe, was sie schreiben. [...] Es gibt Autoren, die erkennen den universellen Schmerz.

That is the only role that I wish for writers. They can write about anything and they can say anything. But never again produce a culture of violence. Because that has always existed in history and its end is not something special. Its end means blood and destruction. And at present a culture of violence is arising; we can see that in the thinking of many people, politically and literarily. [...] And I hope that neither I or someone else comes one day and says, poetry is barbaric these days. I don't wish for that.

The task of literature? I think literature has only one task (long pause). Under all of the ruins, we can find something valuable, possibly a treasure or objects that are connected to memories or history. And I think that art and literature can show this beauty even among the ruins. That which has been buried. Literature can create hope out of nothing. For me, literature is truly a kind of hope – new perceptions, new worlds. Sometimes literature is also a warning, that things should not repeat themselves. Literature is also an enrichment for certain facts of life, be it love, soccer or war.

6. *What influence has German literature had on your writing? Are there certain works or authors who have especially influenced you? Kafka perhaps?*
Kafka for sure! (laughs) He is the God of everything! (laughs)

It's difficult to say what influences me, because I of course have a different history. But at the beginning, when I first arrived in Germany, I discovered a few writers where I had the feeling: yes, here I'm reading something and I have the feeling I understand what they are writing. There are writers who recognise universal pain.

KM: *Wer war das für dich?*

Viele! In meinem Fall waren das zum Beispiel Hilde Domin, Rose Ausländer, Sarah Kirsch, Thomas Brasch [...]. Ich mag den alten Hans Magnus Enzensberger, ich meine, seine frühen Werke [...]. Da haben die [= die Autoren] eine große Rolle gespielt, und später natürlich auch Romane, besonders Exilliteratur [...] von deutschen Exilanten, wie Anna Seghers und so weiter. [...] Weil, ihre Themen waren mir sehr nahe. Und das hat mich natürlich beeinflusst, wie sie geschrieben haben, worüber sie geschrieben haben. Und dieses Gefühl, man ist nicht allein. Und dieses Gefühl, was man hat – es existiert schon vorher, bevor man geboren ist. [...] Literatur verbindet. Nicht nur Lachen verbindet. (Lacht) [...] Am Anfang haben diese Autoren, diese Dichterinnen insbesondere, [...] eine große Rolle gespielt für mich, und begann ich auch [...], mich selbst in der deutschen Literatur zu finden [...].

7. *Welchen Einfluss hat die arabische Literatur bzw. die Tradition des mündlichen Erzählens aus dem arabischen Raum auf dein Schreiben?*

Das kann ich nicht hundertprozentig beantworten, weil ich aus einer sehr, sehr armen Familie komme, und mein Vater und meine Mutter sind Analphabeten, das heißt, sie haben nie für mich ein Kinderbuch vorgelesen, ich kenne das nicht. Aber als Kinder, wir hörten Geschichten. Diese Geschichten kommen von Opa und Oma [...], aber als Kind – ich erinnere mich nicht daran. Aber [...] ich komme aus einer schiitischen Familie, und die Schiiten sind ganz anders als andere islamische Richtungen. Die Schiiten sind verbunden viel mehr mit [der] Vergangenheit und der traurigen Geschichte ihrer Imame [...], eigentlich eine Sammlung von getöteten und eingesperrten Imamen. [...] Und es gibt so einen Imam, der eine große Rolle spielt in der Geschichte der Schiiten, der heißt Al-Hussein. Und der Al-Hussein, der ist ein Enkel des Propheten Mohammed, der wurde von einem Kalifen getötet in Kerbela im Irak.

KM: *Who were they for you?*

Many! In my case for instance it was Hilde Domin, Rose Ausländer, Sarah Kirsch, Thomas Brasch [...]. I like the early works of Hans Magnus Enzensberger. They played an important role for me and later of course many novels, especially the literature of German exiles, like Anna Seghers, etc. Because their themes were very close to me. And that influenced me, how they wrote and what they wrote about. And this feeling that you aren't alone. This feeling that what you have has existed previously, before you were born. Literature unites. Not only laughter unites. (Laughs) At the beginning, these authors and poets played a large role for me and I began to find myself in German literature.

7. *What influence has Arabic literature, or the oral narrative tradition from the Arabic world, had on your writing?*

I can't completely answer that because I come from a very, very poor family and my father and mother are both illiterate; that is, they never read children's books to me, so that's something I never knew. But as children, we heard stories. Those stories came from grandpa and grandma, when I was a child, but I can't remember them. I come, though, from a Shiite family and the Shia are very different than other Muslims. The Shia are much more strongly connected to their history and the sad history of their imams, actually a collection of killed and jailed imams. And there was one imam who played a major role in the history of the Shia, and his name was Al-Husayn. Al-Husayn was the grandson of the prophet Mohammed and was killed by a caliph in Karbala in Iraq.

Und […] bis heute trauern die Schiiten immer ein Mal jährlich um ihn. Und in dieser Zeit kam immer ein Mann in ein Zuhause bei uns damals und dichtet die Geschichte von Al-Hussein. Zehn Tage lang. Zehn Tage war der Krieg, bis Hussein gestorben ist, und dichtet jeden Tag den Verlauf des Krieges, bis er zu Ende ist, bis zum Tod. Und dies dauert immer eine halbe Stunde bis vierzig Minuten. […]

KM: *Und die Person kam in euer Haus?*

Jaja. Die kommen, und da sitzen alle Männer und Frauen und hören zu.

KM: *In einer Nachbarschaft?* Ja.

Und fast alle Schiiten machen das. Und das ist […] wichtig, die Geschichte wird traurig, und die Leute weinen da. Das zum Beispiel, diese Geschichte der Schiiten, das sind eigentlich immer Geschichten von Revolution. Die kämpften gegen Kalifen oder Könige, die Diktatoren waren, und wurden ermordet und eingesperrt. Und diese Geschichten von den Schiiten spielten in der schiitischen Kultur, die ich auch mitgenommen habe, mündliche Überlieferungen, eine unheimliche Rolle. Und das, glaube ich, hat etwas Besonderes, weil, es macht das alles [zu] eine[r] inoffizielle[n] Geschichte, das heißt, in Schulbüchern, in der Schule, da war der Kalif, der Al-Hussein getötet hat, heilig. […] Das lernte ich in der Schule. Zu Hause lernte ich, der war ein Diktator, und der Hussein ist ein Revolutionär. Das heißt, es ist wie zwei Systeme im Kopf, zwei Geschichten […]. […] Diese geheimnisvolle Art, wie man mit der Geschichte umgeht, […], das, glaube ich, hat eine große Rolle gespielt, wie ich mit der Geschichte umgehe.

8. *In deinem Grußwort zu den Hamburger Tagen des Exils hast du Folgendes geschrieben: 'Ankunft. Doch das Eintreffen findet nie statt. Das Zusammengehörigkeitsgefühl ist ein Exilant.' – Bist du persönlich jemals 'angekommen' in Deutschland? Ich frage besonders auch in Hinblick auf die aktuelle politische Lage in Deutschland, den Erfolg der AfD, Rechtsextremismus, Angriffe auf Flüchtlinge.*

Ich glaube, die [Rechtsextremen] haben mir die Möglichkeit gegeben, richtig seelisch anzukommen.

Today the Shia mourn his loss once a year. And during this time a man always came to our house and for ten days told the story of Al-Husayn. The war lasted ten days until Husayn died and every day he told the course of the story up to the end, to his death. And this lasted 30 or 40 minutes [...].

KM: *And this person came to your house?*

Yeah, yeah, they come and all of the men and women sit and listen.

KM: *In one neighbourhood?*

Yes. Almost all Shiites do that. And it's very important. The story is sad and people cry. These stories of the Shiites, they are always stories of revolution. They fought against the Caliphs or kings who were dictators and were murdered or incarcerated. And these Shiite stories, passed on orally, played an important role in the Shia culture that I carried with me. And that, I think, is something unique and it became a kind of unofficial story. In schoolbooks and at school, the caliph who murdered Al-Husayn was always holy. That's what I learned in school. At home I learned that he was a dictator and that Al-Husayn was a revolutionary. It's like there were two systems in my head – two histories. And this mysterious way in which one deals with history, I believe, played an important role in how I deal with history.

8. *In your opening remarks at the Hamburg Exile Days you wrote the following: 'Arrival. But the arrival never occurs. The sense of belonging is an exile.' Did you personally ever 'arrive' in Germany? I ask especially with regard to the current political situation in Germany, the success of the AfD, right-wing extremism, attacks on refugees, etc.*

I think that the right-wing extremists gave me the possibility to really arrive psychologically.

Es ist endlich mal auch dieses Gefühl, dass mich das Land braucht –
mich. Es ist vielleicht naiv [...], das zu sagen, aber man hat plötzlich
eine Aufgabe, dass man irgendwie – man muss was tun. Um den
Menschen, sich selbst, seiner Umgebung und den Menschen um
sich herum zu helfen, irgendwas zu machen, damit Dinge sich
nicht wiederholen. [...] Ich wünsche denjenigen, die sich nach
autoritären Führungen sehnen, eine zweiwöchige Ausbildung in
anderen Ländern wie Saudi-Arabien. Dann bin ich gespannt, ob
sie immer noch diese Sehnsucht haben. Ich kenne Diktaturen [...],
ich weiß, was es bedeutet, dahin zu gehen und in diese Richtung zu
marschieren. Danach würden wir echt viel bereuen. Und jetzt habe
ich die Möglichkeit. Ich lebe in einer demokratischen Gesellschaft.
Ich habe auch eine Leserschaft, und ich kann auch etwas sagen. Ich
habe eine Möglichkeit, Menschen zu erreichen. Auch wenn ich
das Gefühl habe, es gibt viele, die dagegen kämpfen, dass ich diese
Möglichkeit habe, und versuchen, das zu verhindern. Aber dieses
Gefühl: Ja, du bist da, und du kannst jetzt was machen. Mindestens
deine Meinung sagen. [...] Für die Zukunft – dass man sagt, man
ist irgendwie sauber geblieben. Und in dieser Zeit, tatsächlich, bin
ich richtig seelisch gut angekommen, irgendwie. (Lacht)

9. *Ganz aktuell: Am Wochenende ist Europawahl. Verstehst du dich als*
   Europäer – und wenn ja: auf welche Weise?
   (Lacht) Ich verstehe mich wirklich als Europäer. Ich finde,
   europäische Werte sind universal. Wir bezeichnen sie als
   europäische Werte, aber sie sind Werte der Menschen.

10. *Und zum Schluss: Hast du ein Lieblingsbuch – und was liest du*
    gerade?
    (Lacht) Seit gestern habe ich wieder angefangen, das Buch *Dialektik*
    der Aufklärung von Adorno zu lesen. Und mein Lieblingsbuch der
    letzten Jahre [ist] *Das Ministerium der Schmerzen*, die Autorin
    heißt Dubravka Ugrešić. Hier geht es um die Exilanten vom
    Jugoslawien-Krieg, in Europa, in Deutschland, aber auch in den
    Niederlanden, und ihre Probleme mit der Geschichte, mit dem
    Krieg, mit dem Ankommen da, und das Buch fand ich sehr gut.

There is finally this feeling that this country needs me. Perhaps it's naïve to say so, but you suddenly have a task, that somehow you have to do something. In order to help people, help one's self, help one's environment, the people around you, to do something so that things don't repeat themselves. I wish that those people who have some desire for authoritarian leadership could take a two-week educational trip to other countries like Saudi Arabia. Then I'd be curious if they still have this desire. I know dictatorships; I know what it means to go there and march in that direction. Afterwards we would sincerely regret a lot. And now I have this opportunity; I live in a democratic society. I have an audience and I can say something. I have the possibility to reach people. Even if I have the feeling that there are those who fight against me having this possibility and are trying to prevent it. But there's this feeling: yes, you are there, and you can do something now – at least express your opinion. So that you can at least say in the future that you stayed clean. So, at this time, I can really say that I have arrived psychologically somehow (laughs).

9. *Do you see yourself as a European? If so, in what way?*
   (Laughs) I do truly see myself as a European. I think that European values are universal. We call them European values, but they are in fact human values.

10. *And finally – do you have a favourite book? What are you currently reading?*
    (Laughs) Yesterday I started re-reading Adorno's *Dialectic of the Enlightenment*. My favourite book from the past couple of years is Dubravka Ugrešić's *The Ministry of Pain*. It's about exiles during the war in Yugoslavia, in Europe, in Germany and in the Netherlands, and their problems with history, with the war and with arriving there. It's a book that I really liked.

KATHERINE ANDERSON

Productive Ruptures: Trauma as Both a Disruptive and Generative Force in Abbas Khider's *Der falsche Inder* and *Die Orangen des Präsidenten*[1]

Abbas Khider could not have written his first two novels in his native Arabic; rather, he prefers to write in German, a language in which he can be more precise, less emotional and in which he can establish distance between himself and his content.[2] He is now the author of six published novels in German that elaborate on his experiences as a prisoner, refugee and asylum seeker. Khider's fourth book, *Ohrfeige* (2016) [*A Slap in the Face*, 2019], is a timely narrative that sheds light on the plight of asylum seekers in Germany. *Ohrfeige* was released on the heels of what has been commonly referred to as the 'refugee crisis', a massive population shift that brought more than one million fleeing war and persecution in search of asylum to and across Europe's borders. Khider's book was popularly received by many seeking to better understand the experience of the marginalised migrant and the asylum seeker in Germany. Perhaps not independent of this attention, the Robert Bosch

---

1   All translations are my own, unless otherwise noted.

2   See the interview with Michael Kohlstadt of the *Westdeutsche Allgemein Zeitung*: 'Und besonders meine beiden ersten Romane hätte ich nicht auf Arabisch schreiben können. Da war so viel Traurigkeit in den Geschichten, so viel Betroffenheit. […] Auf Deutsch konnte ich Distanz zu den Geschehnissen aufbauen' [I couldn't have written particularly my first novels in Arabic. There was so much sadness in the stories, so much *Betroffenheit* [consternation/dismay] […]. In German, I could distance myself from the events]. – Michael Kohlstadt, 'Abbas Khider Interview: "Abbas Khider und die Liebe zur Sprache der Deutschen"', *Westdeutsche Allgemein Zeitung* (11 December 2013), <http://www.derwesten.de/kultur/abbas-khider-und-die-liebe-zur-sprache-der-deutschenid8762981.html>, accessed 1 October 2019.

foundation awarded Khider its final Adelbert von Chamisso Prize for literature in 2017.[3] While Khider has played a vital role in bringing awareness and sensitivity to the plight of refugees, this primary critical focus on his role as a voice of the marginalised has caused his skill as an author, particularly his contributions to narrative form, to be over-looked. Each of Khider's novels takes on a form uniquely distinct from the others, although the role of a first-person narrator remains con-sistent throughout the novels. Whereas *Der falsche Inder* (2008) [*The Village Indian*, 2013] comprises the same journey in eight thematic vari-ations, *Die Orangen des Präsidenten* (2011) [The President's Oranges] weaves two lines of narrative into an eventual reconciliation. *Brief in die Auberginenrepublik* (2013) [Letter to the Aubergine Republic] as-sembles disparate narratives around the common purpose of delivering a letter, while *Ohrfeige* is a fictional address to a bureaucrat. His fifth text, *Deutsch für Alle* (2019) [German for Everyone], is a collection of satirical essays with his recommendations for making the German language more user-friendly. Because of their shared focus on a disrup-tive traumatic past event and the importance placed on the question of identity within the narratives, this essay concerns itself predomin-antly with the first two novels, *Der falsche Inder* and *Die Orangen des Präsidenten*. Khider constructs both novels as the intentional narratives of his protagonists, detailing their traumatic experiences of flight into exile and of incarceration, respectively. There is a unity generated by the

3   The Robert Bosch Foundation awarded seventy-seven authors the Chamisso Prize between 1985 and 2017. It was created largely through the efforts of Germanist Harald Weinrich to call attention to a body of German-language literature growing outside the traditional canon. See his 1983 essay in *Merkur*. – Harald Weinrich, 'Um eine deutsche Literatur von außen bittend', *Merkur*, 37/422 (1983), 911–20. – The foundation's chief executive, Uta-Micaela Dürig, retired the prize in 2017, ar-guing the prize's goals of promoting cultural diversity had been met. In 2019, the Chamisso Prize was resurrected as the Chamisso Preis Hellerau, linking it to the intentional community created in Hellerau, Germany during the early twentieth century. In its new formulation, the prize recognises German-language literature that crosses linguistic and cultural boundaries. See the website of the Chamisso-Preis/Hellerau: <https://www.chamissopreishellerau.de>, accessed 5 August 2019.

content and form of these two texts around the narrators' experiences of trauma, in that traumatic experience rests at the heart of the narrative and serves as both disruptive and generative force of the narrative form. Contrasting the differing narrative structures, which nonetheless preserve a unity of content and form within the confines of either novel, brings to fore Khider's skill at synthesising experience with form in the creative process of meaning making. Although New Critical theorists might argue against the use of emotional, biographical or heavily psychological approaches to textual analysis, examining the implications of traumatic experience as evidenced within Khider's novels serves two purposes. Not only does this lens provide a context for assessing Khider's work with narrative form, it also provides insight through isolated example into the implications of traumatic experience on creative human expression.

At the heart of Adorno's observation 'nach Auschwitz ein Gedicht zu schreiben, ist barbarisch' [to write a poem after Auschwitz is barbaric] is his recognition of the impact trauma and particularly societal trauma like the Holocaust has on the transmission of both society and culture. One might extend this observation to the impact of trauma on the literary output of twenty-first-century authors like Khider, whose incarceration and torture at the hands of the Iraqi government led to his flight and eventual asylum in Germany. Although observations like Adorno's called attention to the greater societal implications of trauma, the direct impact of trauma on creative human expression has been observed throughout the humanities, including, but not limited to, historical narratives, film and literature, the very crucibles upon which the established constructs governing society and culture are stripped down and reformulated.[4] In his chapter 'Knowledge, "Afterwardness" and the Future of Trauma Theory', Robert Eaglestone proposes harnessing the developing field of trauma theory as a lens for examining not just literature, but the humanities in a post-Holocaust world

---

4   See Freud's *Jenseits des Lustprinzips* and Cathy Caruth's *Unclaimed Experience*.

broad scale.[5] Doing so would allow scholars to better understand trauma's effect on the experience and representation of time, as well as the existential questions that govern the (re)formulation of the ethical structures upon which society is based.[6]

Predating Eaglestone's treatise and responding to trauma studies pioneers like Cathy Caruth, leading critic of trauma theory Wulf Kansteiner has argued that broadly applying a trauma lens across the humanities is problematic. Although he critiques the quality of the research done and the use of trauma as a platform for pushing loosely related scholarly agendas, his main contention is with the ubiquitisation of trauma to a shared human experience, as this conflation detracts from the magnitude of events like the Holocaust.[7] He proposes as an alternative the closer study of violence and power dynamics to better understand their effect on social and cultural transmission.[8] Along this vein, Corina Stan argues in her article identifying Khider's texts as *Weltliteratur* that violence is a key factor in Khider's novels, disrupting understanding of identity and provoking subsequent validation of identity.[9] While focusing on violence does call attention to the complex social interaction between victims, perpetrators and bystanders, such a focus assumes all violence and displays of power as necessarily traumatic, which is not necessarily the case. Trauma predicates simultaneously an irreconcilable loss of agency and a combined existential threat, and subsequently refuses unmediated integration into narrative memory. Further, this focus on the structures of violence ignores the important physiological ramifications of trauma on both body and mind in favour of social dynamics.

Reading trauma narratives for their factual contributions to history is also problematic due to the inherent fallibility of memory. Khider's

---

5   Robert Eaglestone, 'Knowledge, "Afterwardness" and the Future of Trauma Theory', in Gert Buelens, Sam Durrant and Robert Eaglestone, eds., *The Future of Trauma Theory* (London: Routledge, 2013), 11–21, 20.

6   Eaglestone, 'Knowledge, "Afterwardness" and the Future of Trauma Theory', 12.

7   Wulf Kansteiner, 'Genealogy of a Category Mistake: A Critical Intellectual History of the Cultural Trauma Metaphor', *Rethinking History*, 8/2 (2004), 193–221, 194.

8   Ibid., 195.

9   Corina Stan, 'Novels in the Translation Zone: Abbas Khider, *Weltliteratur*, and the Ethics of the Passerby', *Comparative Literature Studies*, 55/2 (2018), 285–302, 286.

narrator questions the historical authenticity of his own narrative in *Der falsche Inder*, 'Ob das, was ich schreibe, das wahre Leben ist? Ich kann es nicht sagen' [If what I'm writing is real life? I can't say] (FI, 25). His first novels draw heavily upon his personal experience as a prisoner, a refugee and as an asylum seeker in Germany. However, the particulars of these novels – the constellation of the protagonists' families, the details of their births, even the cities in which they were raised – differ enough so as to suggest that Khider's narrators are different people.[10] Instead of focusing on the factual authenticity of texts written after trauma, Eaglestone highlights the importance of these texts for their insight into the human experience of trauma, something that adds a human component to history.[11] In this vein, Khider's characters are like shadows cast on Plato's cave walls: they project aspects of Khider's personal experience, but they should be read as projections of the truth rather than the truth itself.

Reading trauma narratives not for their factual contribution to historical accounts, but for an understanding of the both disruptive and generative relationship between trauma, author and text proves a useful tool for examining the individual human experience of trauma. Eaglestone identifies trauma as both an 'originary' and a disruptive force, although I would reorder these to emphasise the causal relationship.[12] Trauma is 'originary', or generative, because it is disruptive, not unlike the oppositional forces of death and life as posited by Sigmund Freud and repurposed by Jacques Derrida in his *Archive Fever*. Recent gains in neuroscience have now proven what nineteenth-century psychotherapists like Freud and Pierre Janet surmised: traumatic experience disrupts the way the brain experiences time and reality as well as its understanding of self. From scans of the brain during triggered flashbacks, psychologist Bessel van der Kolk observed that trauma defies integration into the part of the brain responsible for narrative memory, because the remembered experience of trauma locks

10   The protagonist of *Der falsche Inder* is called Rasul Hamid; in *Die Orangen des Präsidenten*, he is Mahdi Muhsin. Is it merely coincidence that Mahdi is an anagram of Hamid? Perhaps not when one takes into account the importance Khider places in his novels on naming and heritage.

11   Eaglestone, 'Knowledge, "Afterwardness" and the Future of Trauma Theory', 16.

12   Ibid., 12.

the individual into the immediacy of the initial traumatic experience. The inability to convert immediate experience to past memory subsequently disrupts the continued formulation of identity after trauma, creating a tension from which the creative impulse of narrative creation and identity-work springs.[13] Understanding the importance of actively integrating traumatic experience into the narrative memory of his patients, Janet developed a narrative therapy to bring his patients to a feeling of catharsis in the nineteenth century. Psychologists Frank Neuner et al. are currently using a similar narrative therapy to help rehabilitate refugees in Europe in the twenty-first century, but one that prioritises a symbolic ordering of events before a written draft is created.[14] Generally accepted pioneer of trauma studies Cathy Caruth identifies in literature and literary language a perfect tool for processing trauma, because they allow for the incomprehensibility of the experience.[15] Reading Khider's first two novels as trauma narratives provides the context for seeing the disruptive and generative relationship between trauma, the author and the text at work.

Khider's first published novel, *Der falsche Inder*, tells the story of an unnamed protagonist who boards a train in Berlin bound for Munich and discovers a manuscript written in his own hand and in Arabic, but by a stranger called Rasul Hamid. This unnamed protagonist inhabits a frame narrative that transpires in train stations, trains and cafes in Germany. Hamid's manuscript, the embedded narrative, details Hamid's flight from

---

13   Janet surmised that the memory was divided into two repositories, a hot or emotional memory, and a cold or narrative memory. Traumatic events were locked into the hot memory and defied integration into the cold. Van der Kolk's research confirmed Janet's theory that the memory is indeed divided into emotional and narrative memory, and that trauma defies integration into the narrative memory. See van der Kolk's 'Looking into the Brain: The Neuroscience Revolution' in *The Body Keeps the Score* for a more comprehensive explanation. – Bessel van der Kolk, *The Body Keeps the Score* (London: Penguin Books, 2014).

14   Their patients structure their narratives temporally with the help of stones and flowers. See Frank Neuner et al., 'Narrative Exposition', in Andreas Maercker, ed., *Posttraumatische Belastungsstörungen*, 4th edn (Berlin: Springer Medizin, 2013), 327–47, 336.

15   Cathy Caruth, *Unclaimed Experience: Trauma, Narrative, and History* (Baltimore: Johns Hopkins University Press, 1996), 3.

Iraq to Germany in eight thematic variations. The first chapter, which bears the title of the novel, provides various explanations for the narrator's skin colour, which is unusually dark for southern Iraq. Subsequent chapters build in intensity, circling in closer to the heart of the emotional trauma experienced by the narrator, culminating with the final chapter 'Wiederkehr der Gesichter' [Return of the Faces], in which spectres of the loved ones who have died revisit Hamid to take their leave of him. Hamid describes battling his fear of madness throughout the embedded narrative, a loss of reason that he describes as *die Leere* [the void], and an experience that both the unnamed frame narrator and the embedded narrator share. This is almost undoubtedly in reference to Gottfried Benn's poem 'Nur zwei Dinge' [Two things alone], cited in part in the novel, in which Benn identifies the void and the writing self as juxtaposed basic remainder elements. As in Benn's poem, Hamid turns to writing in a concerted effort to stave off madness, going so far as to say, 'Seitdem gab es in meinem Leben nur noch zwei Möglichkeiten: die Leere zu bekämpfen oder meinem Leben ein Ende zu setzen' [Since then, only two options remained: to fight the void, or to put an end to my life] (FI, 71–2).

Khider's *Die Orangen des Präsidenten* tells the story of Mahdi 'Hamama' Muhsin, an Iraqi who grew up during the Iran-Iraq and Gulf Wars and who was falsely imprisoned on the final day of his exams in secondary school. His narrative begins in a refugee camp on the border between Iraq and Kuwait in 1991. The first pages of the narrative set the scene and provide the motivation for the writing: the narrator is afraid the boredom of the refugee camp will rob him of his sanity, and so he begins telling the story of his life, hoping to thereby discover the origin of his peculiar laugh, *Trauerlachen*, or laughter in times of sorrow. Fifteen chapters, introduced as 'Mahdi Hamama. Der Taubenzüchter. Eine wahre Geschichte' [The Pigeon Keeper. A True Story], follow a second introduction, alternating chapter for chapter between two chronological narrative lines: Mahdi's life before his incarceration and his life in prison. These lines eventually merge with his release from prison and conclude with his arrival in the same refugee camp in which the story begins. From the introductory segment, it is clear that the trauma experienced by Mahdi motivates the narrative and its central focus on identity. Mahdi's *Trauerlachen* manifests as a coping mechanism in the face of his torture at the beginning of his incarceration: 'Das Lachen machte mich unempfindlich gegenüber dem Schmerz, gegenüber der Angst und gegenüber der Verzweiflung' [Laughter made me impervious to the pain, to the fear and to the despair] (OdP, 8). This laughter is an essential part of Mahdi's identity, a unique synthesis of his mother's *Glückstränen* [tears of happiness] and his father's inability to cry, being an 'überaus fröhlicher Mensch' [exceedingly cheerful person] (OdP, 7). It is also related to the only remaining characteristic by which his family is able to identify him after his release from prison, as his incarceration has so drastically altered his physical appearance: 'Es ist wirklich Mahdi. Er hat dasselbe Lächeln' [It really is Mahdi. He has the same smile] (OdP, 113).

Comparing Khider's first novels reveals deviations in the narrative form that align with their respective narrative content. What these first novels have in common is that they both contain the embedded manuscript-narratives of their respective protagonists. *Der falsche Inder* contains the memories of Rasul Hamid, and *Die Orangen des Präsidenten* the true story of Mahdi Hamama, the pigeon keeper. Intriguingly, each manuscript is precluded in its respective novel by a description of the colour green. The unnamed protagonist of *Der falsche Inder* describes the sunny landscape radiating green through the train window; and in the introduction of Mahdi's manuscript, he describes the almost shimmering green of a pigeon's feathers catching the sunlight (FI, 10; OdP, 15). While the colour green has long been associated with Islam, representing paradise in the Quran and serving as the dynastic colour of the Shiites, of which Mahdi is a member, it is also the colour of nature, symbolising growth, harmony, freshness and fertility.[16] Perhaps most importantly, it carries a strong emotional correspondence with safety, an important factor in facilitating the return to traumatic memory.[17] Although the novels are said to be largely autobiographical,

16   See John Hutchings, 'Folklore and Symbolism of Green', *Folklore*, 108 (1997), 55–63. – For a discussion of Al-Khidr, the immortal guide in the Islamic tradition, also known as the green man, and the intersections between ego and the environment, see Irfan A. Omar, 'Khiżr-i Rāh: The Pre-Eminent Guide to Action in Muhammad Iqbal's Thought', *Islamic Studies*, 43/1 (2004), 39–50.

17   Janet was deliberate about establishing a safe environment, free from stressors in his narrative therapy treatment.

they deviate significantly in the specifics of and the manner in which the stories are told. The protagonists of the embedded narratives are at most anagrams of each other, *Hamid* and *Mahdi*. Details about family, occupation, hobbies and even place of origin differ between texts, as well as the narrative content and the form in which it is presented.

Turning to Khider's first novel, *Der falsche Inder*, for an understanding of the unity of content with form, the title of the second chapter 'Schreiben und Verlieren' [Writing and Losing] calls attention to an important creative tension. Khider's chosen form aptly reflects this major narrative theme of creative origin and disruptive loss, yet inversely, providing cathartic resolution to a seemingly never-ending cycle of loss. Hamid loses journals and scraps of paper, knowledge to decipher codes he developed to keep his journals secret in his father's home in the Iraqi dictatorship and entire manuscripts. This disruptive loss is met again and again by the compulsion to tell his story; writing, for the narrator, is connected to his inner state of being, 'Das Schreiben hatte immer etwas mit meinem Innenleben zu tun, das mich unaufhörlich dazu zwang' [Writing always had something to do with my inner state, which constantly compelled me to it] (FI, 24–5). In her article, Stan interprets the repetition of the chapters as indicative of the unreliable memory of the narrator.[18] Each chapter returns to the narrator's place of origin, allowing him to explore a different facet of his journey in the cyclical arch of each subsequent chapter. While the impulse of writing does appear to be predicated by a loss of memory, the cyclical structure of the chapters appears to be one of design. The chapters gradually progress into heavier topics, from identity and the desire to write in Chapters 1 and 2, to his incarceration in Chapters 4 and 5, to the guilt he feels at being a harbinger of misfortune and surviving where others did not, in the final chapters. In fact, this inward progression is outlined in the final lines of the final chapter of the embedded manuscript: 'Ich will meine Geschichte endlich zu Ende schreiben. Von den Gesichtern über die Wunder bis zur Geburt – oder umgekehrt. Der Leitsatz steht als Widmung schon fest: "Für die, die eine Sekunde vor dem Tod noch von zwei Flügeln träumen."' [I want to finally finish writing my story. From the faces to the wonders to

18   Stan, 'Novels in the Translation Zone', 286.

my birth – or the other way around. The guiding principle serving as the dedication is already set: 'For those who still dream of wings a second before death.'] (FI, 151). The compulsion to repeat is constructive, however, in that it moderates the narrator's return to the traumas of his past. The first chapters lay foundations for the narrative return to past traumas with happier anecdotes, foundations that later serve to guide the narrative as it journeys into darker subject matter.

Whereas loss and creative impulse dominate the narrative content of *Der falsche Inder*, discovery and preservation dominate the narrative form. Reversing the theme of loss, a found manuscript rests at the heart of the novel between two halves of a frame narrative. Time markers corresponding with the respective opening and closing of a manuscript link these halves. In the first half of the frame, the unnamed protagonist journeys alone, the manuscript lands in his lap at 2.16 p.m. and he opens it at 2.45 p.m. In the second half of the frame story, the protagonist has arrived, is in a loving relationship and feels compelled to write his story. He places an empty envelope on the table before himself at 2.16 p.m. and finally puts his completed manuscript into it and seals it at 2.45 p.m. The novel in this way recovers the lost narrative and preserves it in the enveloping halves of the frame story; the theme of loss is reversed, thereby revealing the key to cathartic resolution through structured narrative creation. As the frame narrator exclaims, not just the content is important, but rather the form as well: 'Ich wusste immer genau, was ich schreiben wollte, aber eben nicht wie!' [I always knew exactly what I wanted to write, just not how!] (FI, 154). The discovery of the appropriate structure enables the frame narrator to speak his first words of dialogue: 'Wirklich, was für ein schöner Tag!' [Really, what a beautiful day!] (FI, 155), an optimistic first utterance indicating the underlying importance of this cathartic experience.

Like *Der falsche Inder*, *Die Orangen des Präsidenten* begins with a frame story before transitioning to a manuscript. Unlike *Der falsche Inder*, however, the novel ends with the conclusion of the manuscript. There is no explicit return to the narrator of the frame. This seeming lack of resolution to the frame at the end of *Die Orangen des Präsidenten* is a deviation in keeping with the content of this second novel. Whereas *Der falsche Inder* represents the frame-narrator's efforts to reclaim his

story and thereby find his voice, *Die Orangen des Präsidenten* is a tale
of reconstructing identity after coming to terms with trauma. The challenge set in the frame, of understanding the origin of Mahdi's peculiar
Trauerlachen, is resolved through the act of creating the manuscript.
The embedded manuscript, through the telling, effectively reconciles
the two identities of the frame narrator, who he was before with who
he was after the traumatic rupture. Were the novel to explicitly resolve
the frame story, it would detract from the implicit resolution facili-
tated by the creation of the embedded trauma narrative. The zipper-like
construction of the manuscript is in union with the narrative content
of reconciliation of identity: the narrator vacillates between two narrative lines detailing his life before and after the traumatic rupture
before merging these lines upon his release from prison. The second
narrative line, although chronologically the first, begins in the second
chapter when Mahdi's parents first meet and concludes with the end
of the tenth chapter, just as Mahdi is beginning to formulate plans for
a future profession: 'Ich dachte, ich könne auch Literatur übersetzen
[…] Oder selbst literarische Werke verfassen' [I thought, I could also
translate literature […] Or compose literary works myself] (OdP, 105).
The first narrative line, which follows the second line chronologically,
begins in the first chapter, as a mass of armed men in uniform encircle
Mahdi and his friend Ali. The two have just finished their last exams
and have driven to Ur to celebrate, according to a brief introduction.
This narrative line then chronicles Mahdi's experience in prison until
his release in the eleventh chapter. The conclusion of this prison narrative, signalled by Mahdi's release, coincides with the conclusion of
the pre-prison narrative chronicling Mahdi's formulation of identity
before his incarceration. Beginning the prison narrative with Mahdi's
incarceration and torture indicates this traumatic experience as being
responsible for the rupture in narrative time represented by the parallel narratives. The conclusion of the pre-prison narrative with Mahdi
choosing a profession, an event meaningful for identity formulation,
confirms this and indicates the important role this narrative plays in re-
establishing identity post-trauma. Whereas each chapter in *Der falsche
Inder* resolves thematically before beginning another thematic cycle

with each subsequent chapter, *Die Orangen des Präsidenten* resolves metaphorically at the end of the narrative with the act of spitting: 'Wir spuckten auf den Boden und setzten unseren Weg fort' [We spat on the ground and continued on our way] (OdP, 158). Mahdi's act of spitting immediately represents his and his companion's contempt for the war and all parties involved, but it also carries the symbolic weight of new beginnings, in this narrative at the very least. After all, Mahdi explains at the beginning of the second chapter, 'Am Anfang war nicht das Wort, sondern die Spucke meiner Mutter im Gesicht meines Vaters. Das war der Anfang meiner Familie' [In the beginning was not the word, but rather the spit of my mother in the face of my father. That was the beginning of my family] (OdP, 30).

The unity of form with content in both *Der falsche Inder* and *Die Orangen des Präsidenten* is a starting point for understanding the concrete implications of trauma on narratives, and by extension, the sociocultural networks to which they contribute. In her article on Khider's *Der falsche Inder*, Carola Hilmes calls attention to the variability of Khider's narrative style, 'die unterschiedlichen Stillagen – Märchen und Bericht' [the differing stylistic registers – fairy-tale and report].[19] Although the novels deviate in form, both *Der falsche Inder* and *Die Orangen des Präsidenten* share this narrative variability. Hilmes recognises that the nature of the narrative content, the protagonist's journey through many countries on his way to exile in *Der falsche Inder*, disrupts the narrative form: 'Kontinuität entsteht erst durch das Schreiben als fortgesetzte Tätigkeit' [continuity is first established through writing as a continuation of agency].[20] Comparing Khider's first novels reveals, however, that it is not just the journey through different countries that contributes to this narrative variability, but also the traumatic ruptures experienced by his protagonists. In both novels, there are shifts in the temporal consciousness of the narrative language through flights into terse descriptive language free of temporal markers,

19   Carola Hilmes, '"Jedes Kapitel ein Anfang und zugleich ein Ende." – Abbas Khiders fiktionalisierte Lebensbeschreibung', in Monika Wolting, ed., *Identitätskonstruktionen in der deutschen Gegenwartsliteratur* (Göttingen: V&R Unipress, 2017), 135–46, 141.
20   Ibid.

what Hilmes refers to as report language, accompanied by shifts in narrative tense entirely. In *Der falsche Inder*, the frame story begins with a description of the unnamed protagonist's surroundings. An announcement blares over the intercom, he sits and takes one long look through the train station at Zoologischer Garten. Suddenly the narrative switches into the terse style of a report:

> Alles leer. Für einen Moment das Gefühl, auf diesem Bahnhof mutterseelenallein zu sein. Die Menschen sind verschwunden, oder genauer, niemals da gewesen. Alles leer. Alles hell und sauber. Keine Züge, keine Reisenden, keine Lautsprecher. Nichts, nur ich und der leere Bahnhof Zoo, das große Nichts um mich herum (FI, 7).

> [Everything empty. For a minute, the feeling of being utterly alone in this train station. The people are gone, or more precisely, had never been there. Everything empty. Everything bright and clean. No trains, no travellers, no loudspeakers. Nothing, just me and the empty Station Zoo, the great nothing all around me.]

But for the helping verbs *to be* and *to have*, which in this quote indicate a completed state rather than action, there are no linguistic markers to anchor this quote in narrative time. The only adverb, *niemals* [never], supports this temporal dissociation, implying that this moment of existential crisis operates outside of time. *Mutterseelenallein*, a word with a linguistic history of displacement, indicates the existential anguish of the narrator at finding himself completely alienated from his surroundings, though the provocation for this dissociative moment is not immediately clear.[21] There are similar shifts in narrative language to the terse style of a report in *Die Orangen des Präsidenten*: 'Mir wurden die Handschellen geöffnet und das Tuch abgenommen. Das grelle Licht der Glühbirne blendete mich. Ich sah einen großen Raum. Ohne Fenster. Weiße Wände' [My handcuffs and the blindfold were removed. The glaring light of the bulb blinded me. I saw a large room. Without windows. White walls] (OdP, 20). In *Der falsche Inder*, this terse language, stripped of all verbs but the primary element of being, of all adverbs but the absolute *niemals*,

---

21   Waltraud Legros traces *mutterseelenallein* to Huguenot refugees in Germany in the seventeenth century. Their cry of loneliness, *moi tout seul*, is argued to have been phonically translated into German in a manner that retained something of its original meaning.

divorces the narrative from time. Perhaps the repetition of *nicht* and *keine* are responsible for the palpable entropy that develops in this part of the narrative, as the reader joins the narrator in the all-consuming void. In contrast, the terse descriptive language in the above-mentioned episode of *Die Orangen des Präsidenten* punctuates the agitation of the narrator, accelerating the narrative. Whereas *Der falsche Inder* demonstrates the dissociative repercussions of suffering from chronic trauma, *Die Orangen des Präsidenten* demonstrates the immediacy of the initial traumatic instance, which divorces itself from narrative time, eloping to the immediacy of the present.

Khider stages the frame narratives in both *Der falsche Inder* and *Die Orangen des Präsidenten* in the narrative present, bringing the reader into the immediate reality of the creative instance. As was explained above, the nature of traumatic memory essentially locks one into the immediacy of the initial traumatic event, as though it were actually happening during the moment of recall. The embedded manuscripts of either novel, however, take almost exclusively the narrative past, an intentional course of action explained by the narrator of the frame in *Die Orangen des Präsidenten*, 'Das Beste wird sein, mir ein Heft und einen Stift zu besorgen und in die Vergangenheit zurückzukehren' [The best thing would be to find a pen and a notebook and return to the past] (OdP, 10). This use of narrative past indicates the embedded narratives as the intentionally rehabilitative efforts of converting traumatic memory to narrative memory. Despite this intention of relegating traumatic memory to the past, the language of the narrative is often interrupted by excurses into either narrator's present reality. In *Der falsche Inder*, the narrator shifts from a description of the past, when he had nothing left, to a continuation into his present reality, every time he feels as if reborn: 'Jedes Mal, wenn ich keine Wege, keine Träume, keine Hoffnung mehr hatte, und jedes Mal, wenn die Leere die Welt um mich herum einschloss. Jedes Mal fühle ich mich danach frei und neugeboren' [Every time I was without a path, dreams or hope, and every time the void of the world closed in around me. Every time, I feel free and reborn afterwards] (FI, 79–80). This shift into the narrative present indicates the persistence of trauma from the past into the narrator's present, although the sentences written in the narrative past immediately preceding it suggest a finality of the described dissociation. And whereas the frame narrator does not immediately recognise himself in the embedded manuscript he finds, this shift in narrative tense serves to reunite the frame narrator with his dissociated former self.

The shifts in narrative tense in *Die Orangen des Präsidenten* also serve to indicate departures from reality, this time through losses of consciousness. For example, after being brought to his cell after his first round of torture, Mahdi ends the section looking out the cell door, 'Gegenüber sah ich nur die gelbe Tür einer anderen Zelle' [Across from me, I saw only the yellow door of another cell] (OdP, 25). Three stars indicate a pause and the narrative begins again, 'Meine Lieblingstauben, der Schwarze Ägypter und die Grüne Taube, fliegen davon, schlagen mit den Flügeln und setzen sich an die Spitze des Schwarms' [My favourite pigeons, the Black Egyptian and the Green Dove, fly away, flap with their wings and position themselves at the head of the swarm] (OdP, 25). After the green pigeon flies away, Mahdi wakes up, 'Ich wachte auf. Schritte näherten sich' [I woke up. Footsteps approached] (OdP, 27). Other than the three stars and the transition to the present tense, there is no clear indication that the narrator is dreaming until the narrator returns to the narrative past and explains that he has woken up. The shift in narrative tense indicates both temporal dissociation as well as a departure from reality. Other excursions from reality are subtler: 'Sami ist wieder da. [...] Sami lässt meine Hand los und verschwindet. Jemand packte meinen Arm und brüllte: "Beweg dich!"' [Sami is back again. [...] Sami releases my hand and disappears. Someone grabbed my arm and yelled: 'Move it!'] (OdP, 28). In this episode, when the spectre of Sami returns to comfort the narrator, the narrative shifts to the present, returning to the narrative past only after Sami disappears, precipitated perhaps by the tactile attack that tears Mahdi back into his immediate reality. These excursions from reality follow Mahdi after his release from prison as well. From the safety of his own room at his uncle's house, Mahdi is visited by the green pigeon before returning to the abyss and the deathly stillness, 'Ich schloss meine Augen und versuchte, wieder einzuschlafen. Später gehe ich auf die Straße. Doch da ist nichts. [...] In der Ferne erblicke ich die grüne Taube. Sie nähert sich. Und verschwindet. Wieder Leere. Dann Totenstille' [I shut my eyes and tried to fall back asleep. Later, I'm walking in the street. But there is nothing there. [...] In the distance, I spy the green pigeon. It approaches. And disappears. The void once more. Then, deathly stillness]

(OdP, 130). The void plays a figurative role in both *Der falsche Inder* and *Die Orangen des Präsidenten* by representing simultaneously the disruptive nature of trauma on the experience of time and reality as well as the productive interference by way of the representation of time and reality within trauma narratives.

Just as trauma has served as the point of origin for the temporal and ontological ruptures within the narratives, its implications reach into the treatment of identity within the texts as well. And as was briefly alluded to above, although trauma serves as the dissociative rupture, the writing it catalyses functions as a cathartic tool in identity reconciliation. In *Der falsche Inder*, the rupture has already occurred, illustrated in the frame-narrator's inability to recognise his own manuscript on the train, though he can recognise his handwriting. Neither is he closer to recognising Hamid after reading his manuscript, as he considers telling his girlfriend Sophie about his experience: 'Aber was soll ich sagen? Dass ich ein Manuskript gefunden habe, in dem meine eigene Geschichte zu finden ist, geschrieben von einem Fremden namens Rasul Hamid?' [But what should I say? That I found a manuscript that contains my own story written by a stranger named Rasul Hamid?] (FI, 153). Although, as was briefly discussed above, the ruptures in the narrative past of the manuscript into the narrative present appear to link the narrator of the embedded manuscript with the narrator of the frame narrative, and although the conspicuous time markers in the frame narrative appear to bind the actions of the frame narrator pre- and post-manuscript, it is not clear whether the rupture in identity rendering the frame narrator incapable of recognising the embedded narrator as himself has been reconciled by the novel's conclusion. The narrator of the frame seals the envelope on his completed manuscript, and this manuscript is indeed backed up on his computer, but there is no guarantee the frame narrator will recognise the envelope should he stumble across this new envelope in the future.

While there was certainly work towards reconciling the dissociated narrative lines chapter for chapter in *Der falsche Inder*, this reconciliatory work figures centrally in *Die Orangen des Präsidenten*. As the discussion of unity and form explained above, the first novel is concerned with finding voice; in contrast, the unity of content and form in *Die Orangen des Präsidenten* identifies the rupture and subsequent reconciliation of identity as the undertaking of this second novel. Upon returning home from prison, Mahdi is almost completely unrecognisable by his family and friends except for his smile. Within the text, this smile serves as the foundation for re-establishing his identity post-trauma. To extend my own metaphor of the two halves of a zipper, Mahdi's smile is the anchor holding both sides together. He explains, 'Alles war ruhig. Und ich spürte zwei Wesen in mir' [Everything was quiet. And I sensed two beings within me] (OdP, 139). One of these beings represents the understanding Mahdi had of himself before his imprisonment, 'Aber ich habe die Gewalt doch immer gehasst' [But I have always hated violence] (OdP, 139), whereas the other fatalistically recognises the loss of self and innocence caused by the imprisonment, 'Du bist kein Engel mehr. Den Engel in dir haben sie längst getötet' [You are no longer an angel. They killed the angel within you long ago] (OdP, 139–40). The voice of Sami enters the text as a temporal and ontological interruption to help Mahdi navigate this rupture in identity. When helping Mahdi to understand what gave pigeon keepers in Iraq a bad reputation and what agency Mahdi can take as a pigeon keeper to decide his own conduct, Sami explains 'Mit einem Messer kann man töten oder Obst schneiden. Jedes Ding in dieser Welt hat zwei Gesichter. Und ein Taubenzüchter eben auch' [With one knife, one can either kill or cut fruit. Everything in the world has two faces. The same is true for a pigeon keeper] (OdP, 99). Sami's advice enters the story in the chapter 'Flügel' [wings], the culmination of the pre-prison narrative. As important as the fixed point of his smile, these words from his mentor reinforce the role of agency in identity. Although Sami was referring to the duality inherent in all things, his advice aptly applies to the rupture in identity Mahdi experiences: agency is the answer. Even after rupture, the ability to decide remains.

From the unity of content and form within Khider's first two novels to the temporal and ontological disruptions within the narratives as well as the ruptures in identity, examining Khider's *Die Orangen des Präsidenten* and *Der falsche Inder* through the lens of trauma serves to return the focus to his work with narrative form. The relationship between an author and traumatic experience is often disruptive and subsequently generative; using an awareness of trauma as a lens for reading a text brings the representation of time and reality in the text into focus and sheds light on the processes of reformulating identity and understanding one's place in the world after trauma has occurred. Eaglestone proposes developing trauma as a lens broadly across the humanities not just to highlight the experience and representation of time and the formulation of existential questions, but rather for greater insight into the impact trauma has on the human experience as manifested in the language and, by extension, on social and cultural transmission. The effectiveness of this lens in texts not associated with traumatic rupture, however, requires further research. Adorno questioned how anyone might conceive of writing poetry after the Holocaust, referring to the collective responsibility of humanity. Within the German context, this question of social responsibility and its implications for the perpetuation of culture is compounded. German author and social theorist Zafer Senoçak, writing from the unique perspective of a German citizen born to immigrant parents, calls attention to the consternation of native Germans in his *Deutschsein* that anyone could choose to live in Germany, let alone learn the language.[22] And yet, perhaps because of its positivist policies of atonement, Germany has become home to a rapidly growing community of authors whose writing crosses linguistic and cultural boundaries, writers like Khider. His own texts, marked by personal and societal traumas of incarceration, flight into exile, war and the plight of the asylum seeker, housed in a language with its own history of trauma, provide a fascinating case study on the interstices of language and trauma.

---

22   Zafer Senoçak, *Deutschsein: Eine Aufklärungsschrift* (Hamburg: Körber Stiftung, 2011), 92.

MARKUS HALLENSLEBEN

Portraying the Refugee as a Transitional Figure of Plurality: The Performance of Gender and Ethnicity in the Postmigrant Narratives of Abbas Khider's *Der falsche Inder* and *Ohrfeige*

Since the surge in the number of asylum seekers into Germany in 2015, the literature on flight and migration has significantly increased. Despite recent insular populism in politics, German-language literature and cultural practices have changed dramatically and have been seen as exemplary in facilitating the transition of Germany towards a postmigrant society.[1] By reading the portrayal of refugees in Abbas Khider's novels *Der falsche Inder* (2008) [*The Village Indian*, 2013][2] and *Ohrfeige* (2016) [*A Slap in the Face*, 2019],[3] I will evaluate the transnational narratives in these works from a new perspective.[4] I suggest that one might take

---

1   Naika Foroutan, 'The Post-Migrant Paradigm', in Jan-Jonathan Bock and Sharon Macdonald, eds., *Refugees welcome? Difference and Diversity in a Changing Germany* (New York: Berghahn, 2019), 142–67; 'Postmigrantische Gesellschaften', in Heinz Ulrich Brinkmann and Martina Sauer, eds., *Einwanderungsgesellschaft Deutschland: Entwicklung und Stand der Integration* (Wiesbaden: Springer Fachmedien, 2016), 227–54, 230–2. <https://doi.org/10.1007/978-3-658-05746-6_9>, accessed 20 August 2018; Mark Terkessidis, *Nach der Flucht: Neue Ideen für die Einwanderungsgesellschaft* (Ditzingen: Reclam, 2017), 18–20; Erol Yildiz, 'Postmigrantische Perspektiven: Aufbruch in eine neue Geschichtlichkeit', in Erol Yildiz and Marc Hill, eds., *Nach der Migration: Postmigrantische Perspektiven jenseits der Parallelgesellschaft* (Bielefeld: transcript, 2015), 19–36, 21.

2   Abbas Khider, *Der falsche Inder* (Hamburg: Edition Nautilus, 2008). All translations follow Khider, *The Village Indian* (London; New York: Seagull Books, 2013).

3   Abbas Khider, *Ohrfeige* (München: Carl Hanser, 2016). All translations follow Khider, *A Slap in the Face* (London: Seagull Books, 2019).

4   See, for instance, Stuart Taberner, *Transnationalism and German-Language Literature in the Twenty-First Century* (Cham: Palgrave Macmillan, 2017), 57–8.

them as instances of a postmigrant condition and society,[5] where identity, gender, race and ethnicity are increasingly viewed as plural[6] and performative.[7] In this sense, Khider's narratives make current societal processes of super-diversity, plurality, mobility and migration visible.

Super-Diversity and Plural Societies: De-Essentialising Cultural Identity

Within the context of the *mobility turn*[8] and a larger global transition of constantly changing societies,[9] the question of belonging is replaced

---

5   While the postmigrant theatre has been established since the opening of the *Ballhaus Naunynstraße* in Berlin in 2008 and the notion of a postmigrant society has been widely discussed, the discourse about German-language postmigrant narratives in literature is still at its beginning. See, for instance, 'Forum: Migration Studies (with contributions by Gizem Arslan, Brooke Kreitinger, Deniz Göktürk, David Gramling, B. Venkat Mani, Olivia Landry, Barbara Mennel, Scott Denham, Robin Ellis, and Roman Utkin)', *The German Quarterly* 90/2 (2017), 212–34, <https://onlinelibrary.wiley.com/doi/full/10.1111/gequ.12033>, accessed 24 September 2017; Anne Ring Petersen and Moritz Schramm, '(Post-)Migration in the Age of Globalisation: New Challenges to Imagination and Representation', *Journal of Aesthetics & Culture* 9/2 (2017), 1–12, <https://doi.org/10.1080/20004214.2017.1356178>, accessed 12 May 2018.

6   Isolde Charim, *Ich und die Anderen: Wie die neue Pluralisierung uns alle verändert* (Wien: Zsolnay, 2018); Paul R. Spickard, ed., *Multiple Identities: Migrants, Ethnicity, and Membership* (Bloomington: Indiana University Press, 2013).

7   Judith Butler, *Undoing Gender* (New York: Routledge, 2004), 42f. and 189–94; Louis F. Mirón and Jonathan Xavier Inda, 'Race as a Kind of Speech Act', in Norman K. Denzin, ed., *Cultural Studies: A Research Volume* (Greenwich: JAI Press, 2000), 85–107.

8   John Urry, 'Moving on the Mobility Turn', in Weert Canzler, Vincent Kaufmann and Sven Kesselring, eds., *Tracing Mobilities: Towards a Cosmopolitan Perspective* (Aldershot; Burlington, VT: Ashgate, 2008), 13–23.

9   See, for instance, Sten Pultz Moslund, Anne Ring Petersen and Moritz Schramm, eds., *The Culture of Migration: Politics, Aesthetics and Histories, International Library of Migration Studies*. Vol. 6 (London: I. B. Tauris, 2015).

by a 'multiplicity of attachments' and deterritorialised identities.[10] Consequently, culture itself has to be seen as something constantly being reiterated, staged and performed, just as gender and ethnic identities are.[11] Within such an understanding, a cultural space is a relational category, whether dynamically performed through social-economic narratives, as in de Certeau's notion of a *practiced place*,[12] or constructed as fluid and 'transitional' through 'its correlation to "habitation"', as Vittoria Borsò points out:

> Die ontologische Priorität des fluiden Raums wird erst durch das Korrelat des 'Aufenthaltes', nämlich der Konsistenz der uns umgebenden Situation (der Praktiken, Kontexte, Mediationen) produktiv und gibt dem Transitorischen Sinn. […] Der Ort wird dabei zum Ereignis einer Beziehung, Öffnung und Veränderung.[13]

> [The ontological priority of fluid space, which becomes productive through its correlation to 'habitation', i.e. the configuration of the environment (practices, contexts, mediations), gives meaning to the transitional as a category. […] Place becomes a relational event, in an open way and through change].

10 'Our sedentarist assumptions about attachment to place lead us to define displacement not as a fact about sociopolitical context but rather as an inner, pathological condition of the displaced […] deterritorialization and identity are intimately linked. […] To plot only "places of birth" and degrees of nativeness is to blind oneself to the multiplicity of attachments that people form to places through living in, remembering, and imagining them.' – Liisa Malkki, 'National Geographic: The Rooting of Peoples and the Territorialization of National Identity among Scholars and Refugees', *Cultural Anthropology* 7/1 (1992), 24–44, 33 and 38, <http://www.jstor.org/stable/656519>, accessed 18 October 2017.

11 For the ethnic discourse within anthropology, the concept of 'De-Essentializing Ethnicity', together with the notion of 'Post-Migration', was first introduced by Gerd Baumann and Thijl Sunier, 'Introduction: De-Essentializing Ethnicity', in Gerd Baumann and Thijl Sunier, eds., *Post-Migration Ethnicity: De-Essentializing Cohesion, Commitments and Comparison* (Amsterdam: Het Spinhuis, 1995), 1–8, especially 4.

12 Cf. Michel de Certeau, *The Practice of Everyday Life* (Berkeley/Los Angeles/London: University of California Press, 1984), 117.

13 Vittoria Borsò, 'Transitorische Räume', in Jörg Dünne and Andreas Mahler, eds., *Handbuch Literatur & Raum* (Berlin/Boston: de Gruyter, 2015), 947–96, 970–71, <http://dx.doi.org/10.1515/9783110301403>, accessed 20 August 2018.

In re-narrating and analysing culture as a *transitional space* and as a *practiced place* of a plural society, literature and literary studies can keep the societal discourses open for change, and possibly provide the key for what Ulrich Beck saw as the missing narrative and 'language through which contemporary super[-]diversity in the world [of global flows of migration] can be described'.[14] In this sense and by taking Khider as a paradigmatic example, I hesitate to define postmigrant literature as a subcategory of migrant literature,[15] but rather see literature as a *transitional space* within a postmigrant condition.[16] Instead of providing another canon based on origins and originality, postmigrant writers demonstrate the mobility and fluidity of cultural borders as well as the super-diversity of cultures, languages, gender and ethnic identities.[17]

As Steven Vertovec has shown through sociographical research for many world cities, including Frankfurt am Main,[18] the qualitative category of the *Other* must be replaced by its concrete pluralities, for which he coined

14   Ulrich Beck, 'Multiculturalism or Cosmopolitanism: How Can We Describe and Understand the Diversity of the World?', *Social Sciences in China* 32/4 (2011), 52–8, <http://dx.doi.org/10.1080/02529203.2011.625169>, accessed 19 January 2018.

15   As suggested by Hansjörg Bay, 'Migrationsliteratur (Gegenwartsliteratur III)', in Dirk Göttsche, Axel Dunker and Gabriele Dürbeck, eds., *Handbuch Postkolonialismus und Literatur* (Stuttgart: Springer, 2017), 323–32, 323, <https://doi.org/10.1007/978-3-476-05386-2_60>, accessed 9 May 2018.

16   Sten Pultz Moslund, Anne Ring Petersen, Hans Christian Post, Moritz Schramm, Mirjam Gebauer, Sabrina Vitting-Seerup and Frauke Wiegand, *Reframing Migration, Diversity and the Arts: The Postmigrant Condition* (New York: Routledge, 2019), <https://www.routledge.com/Migration-Diversity-and-the-Arts-The-Postmigrant-Condition/Schramm-Moslund-Petersen/p/book/9781138584099>, accessed 26 April 2019.

17   See the chapter 'Ohne Zusammenfluß keine Kultur!' [No Confluence, No Culture!] in Ilija Trojanow and Ranjit Hoskote, *Kampfabsage: Kulturen bekämpfen sich nicht, sie fließen zusammen* (Frankfurt am Main: Fischer, 2016), 19–36, especially 22; *Confluences: Forgotten Histories from East and West* (New Delhi: Yoda Press, 2012), 1–18, especially 7.

18   Steven Vertovec, 'Super-Diversity in Frankfurt' (2009), <http://www.mmg.mpg.de/fileadmin/user_upload/powerpoint/Super-diversity_in_Frankfurt/Super-diversity_in_Frankfurt.pdf>, accessed 16 September 2017.

the term 'super-diversity'[19] in order to describe the increasing diversity of
the population beyond ethnicity, especially within immigrant communities
since the 1980s. This concept has had an impact on our understanding of
society as being built by patterns of migration and in our understanding
of culture as being dynamically created by a plurality of belongings that
call for the dissolution of hegemonic principles.[20] It is not only the notion
of the nation as a confined public space drawn by borders that is at question here, but also the notion of identity as being built on sameness and
distinction.[21] Furthermore, as the sociologist Armin Nassehi has disclosed
from a system-critical point of view, the problematic concept of belonging
only works by picturing society as a 'container' into which an individual
integrates and which allows for maintaining the social order through integration.[22] The very concept of cultural identity is indeed 'slippery'[23] and
in itself carries a Eurocentric normative approach, including the definition
of bodily identity (and integrity) in terms of Western languages and cultural traditions.[24]

19   Steven Vertovec, 'Super-Diversity and its Implications', *Ethnic and Racial Studies*
     30/6 (2007), 1024–54, <http://dx.doi.org/10.1080/01419870701599465>, ac-
     cessed 16 September 2017.
20   Cf. Yildiz, 'Postmigrantische Perspektiven', 23.
21   As Peter Wagner and others have emphasised, identity in its literal meaning refers
     to sameness and similarity, and therefore can only lead to a normative approach
     when defining European cultural identity. – Peter Wagner, 'Hat Europa eine
     kulturelle Identität?', in Hans Joas and Klaus Wiegandt, eds., *Die kulturellen Werte
     Europas* (Frankfurt am Main: Fischer, 2010), 494–511, 495; 497.
22   Society here is thought as an integrative space 'im Sinne von Zugehörigkeit' [in
     the sense of belonging], in which social expectations are met in interaction with
     other individuals. – Armin Nassehi, 'Überraschte Identitäten', in Jürgen Straub and
     Joachim Renn, eds., *Transitorische Identität: Der Prozesscharakter des modernen
     Selbst* (Frankfurt am Main/New York: Campus, 2002), 211–37, 219. All translations
     are my own unless otherwise noted.
23   Chiara Bottici and Benoît Challand, *Imagining Europe: Myth, Memory, and
     Identity* (New York: Cambridge University Press, 2013), 115.
24   Markus Hallensleben, 'Introduction: Performative Body Spaces', in Markus
     Hallensleben, ed., *Performative Body Spaces: Corporeal Topographies in Literature,
     Theatre, Dance, and the Visual Arts* (Amsterdam: Rodopi, 2010), 9–27, 12, 17–8.

Khider's literature is political in that he writes against what Chiara Bottici and Benoît Challand pointed out as 'the use of "external Others" in [political] narratives [that] adds specific "dramatic" elements to historical narratives, which play with the emotions and threats and [that] tend, therefore, to turn them into [national] myths'.[25] Khider's postmigrant narratives deconstruct some of these myths and thus challenge the construction of the migrant's body as an alternate cultural space. They show that, within a global mobility at large and in an 'age of diversity',[26] there simply is no *Other*, whether applied to gender, ethnicity, literature or author, and the question of belonging must be replaced by a notion of culture as transitional and of cultural identities as performative.

Furthermore, for postmigrant societies, migration can be seen as central, rather than being marginalised by a 'home-born normality'.[27] Consequently, when reading Khider's narratives as postmigrant, it is crucial to think of culture as a negotiable, relational and super-diverse space, as a *practiced place* of an open and imaginative diversity, which defeats conventional interpretations of migrant identities merely as *other* ethnic identities. Therefore, the portrayal of refugees in the two selected works by Khider discussed here can serve as an example for how plural identities can be aesthetically constructed and how cultural practices of performing belonging have changed within German-language cultures. In eliminating the distinction of bodies as cultural sites of difference,[28] Khider's narrative aesthetics produces a new understanding of cultural belonging as a 'multiplicity of attachments'. It fosters the conceptualisation of societies and sociocultural identities as being plural and super-diverse. Thus, I will interpret these literary characters not only as being transgressive,[29] but also as undermining any binary notions of

---

25   Bottici and Challand, *Imagining Europe*, 116.

26   Steven Vertovec, '"Diversity" and the Social Imaginary', *European Journal of Sociology/Archives Européennes de Sociologie* 53/3 (2012), 287–312, 287, <http://dx.doi.org/10.1017/S000397561200015X>, accessed 16 September 2017.

27   Yildiz, 'Postmigrantische Perspektiven', 22.

28   See also, within a wider German context, Fatima El-Tayeb, *Undeutsch: die Konstruktion des Anderen in der postmigrantischen Gesellschaft* (Bielefeld: transcript, 2016).

29   See, for instance, Hanna M. Hofmann who assumes a cultural in-between stage that is based on *Otherness*: 'Khiders Roman [*Der falsche Inder*] stellt [...] der Verwurzelung ein Modell der Entgrenzung gegenüber. Er ist eine

inter-culturality and in-betweeness,[30] even leading to the abandonment of racial and gendered categories. They will reveal that super-diversity is the sociological basis for portraying the refugee as a transitional figure that bears 'multiple cultural attachments', connections and confluences.

Plural Identities: Gender Performance and Re-narrating Modes of Othering in Khider's *Ohrfeige*

The best example for a transitional figure of plurality is the physical representation of the Iraqi refugee Karim Mensy, the protagonist of Abbas Khider's *Ohrfeige*, who suffers from gynecomastia (OF, 78). The notion of the refugee as a person in transit is translated into a hybrid physical appearance and image of gender, although enlarged breasts in men should not necessarily be considered transgender or intersex. In an ethno-comedic way,[31] Khider plays with the stereotypical image of a male Iraqi refugee and possible terrorist mole after 9/11 who takes 'revenge on all who inflicted pain' on him[32]. The whole book can thus be read as a

---

Grenzüberschreitung zwischen Europa und seinem ("arabischen") Anderen' [Khider's novel puts rootedness in juxtaposition with a model of debordering. It is a transgression between Europe and its ("Arabian") Other]. – Hanna M. Hofmann, 'Erzählungen der Flucht aus raumtheoretischer Sicht: Abbas Khiders *Der falsche Inder* und Anna Seghers' *Transit*', in Thomas Hardtke, Johannes Kleine and Charlton Payne, eds., *Niemandsbuchten und Schutzbefohlene: Flucht-Räume und Flüchtlingsfiguren in der deutschsprachigen Gegenwartsliteratur* (Göttingen: V&R unipress, 2017), 97–124, 117.

30   See also Leslie A. Adelson, 'Against Between: A Manifesto', in Tom Cheesman and Karin E. Yeşilada, eds., *Zafer Şenocak* (Cardiff: University of Wales Press, 2003), 130–43.

31   For an analysis of ethno-comedy in Khider's work see also the chapter by Jara Schmidt within this volume.

32   Qtd. in Ronald Düker, 'Literat Abbas Khider - "Ich stelle der Folter eine sprachliche Form entgegen"', *Cicero* (2013), <https://www.cicero.de/kultur/abbas-khider-auberginenrepublik-ich-stelle-der-folter-eine-sprachliche-form-entgegen/53874>, accessed 25 March 2018. For the motif of revenge in Khider see also Moritz Schramm, 'Experimentelle Erkundungen: Überlegungen zum Verhältnis von

humorous attempt to subvert the stereotypical norms and fears around migration and integration issues.[33]

Since Mensy's gynecomastia does not provide a valid reason for seeking asylum in Germany, he makes use of the experience of his old schoolmate Meki, who had told a joke at the expense of Saddam Hussein that was interpreted as upheaval against the regime and led to his arrest and disappearance (OF, 103). Hence, Mensy's true life story cannot be told. It increasingly becomes the story of others – and this in a double sense – since it is not only someone else's biography that is told in order to seek asylum,[34] but it also becomes a story of othering. This doubling of cultural exclusion, by having to pretend to be someone else and by being excluded from society for reasons of gender and ethnicity, creates a double alienation effect. Moritz Schramm calls this technique an 'aesthetics of difference' by which the expectations for authenticity are undermined. Through this kind of 'ironic realism', the reader becomes defamiliarised with modes of stereotyping gender, ethnicity and nationality.[35] In short, if the concept of the body as a container for gender no longer functions as a proper image, as in Khider's work, how then can society be perceived as an intact body to which one has to integrate into?

While Karim Mensy's physical appearance represents the fluidity of gender identity, his meetings with the immigration officer Frau Schulz 'in

---

Anerkennungstheorie und Literaturwissenschaft am Beispiel von Abbas Khiders Roman *Die Orangen des Präsidenten*,' in Martin Baisch, ed., *Anerkennung und die Möglichkeiten der Gabe* (Frankfurt am Main: Peter Lang, 2017), 177–95, 185–92.

33   Cf. Zygmunt Bauman, *Strangers at Our Door* (Cambridge: Politi Press, 2016), <https://ebookcentral.proquest.com/lib/ubc/detail.action?docID=4562165>, accessed 25 July 2017.

34   Herrad Heselhaus has pointed out the connection between Khider's narratives and the so-called 'doppelten Biografien' [double biographies] of asylum seekers, forced by the integration process. – Herrad Heselhaus, 'Transnationale Elemente im Flüchtlingsroman', *Studies in Language and Literature* [文藝言語研究] 72 (2017), 47–65, 55 <https://tsukuba.repo.nii.ac.jp/?action=repository_uri&item_id=43525&file_id=17&file_no=1>, accessed 22 March 2018.

35   Moritz Schramm, 'Ironischer Realismus: Selbstdifferenz und Wirklichkeitsnähe bei Abbas Khider', in Søren R. Fauth and Rolf Parr, eds., *Neue Realismen in der Gegenwartsliteratur* (Munich: Fink, 2016), 71–84, 77.

einem viel zu kleinen Raum' [in a room that's far too small] (OF, 10) can be read as a metaphor for the constraints of German immigration policies and the impossibility of cultural exchange, as long as the hegemonic politics of power and sovereignty are applied. Firstly, the narrative frame mimics a torture chamber in a prison with Frau Schulz being the prisoner gagged by an alleged Islamist and unable to speak and respond. Secondly, it is compared to a Christian confessional space or *Beichtstuhl*.[36] Thirdly, it is compared to an interplanetary place where two worlds meet and interact. One is represented as an inhabitant of the Earth and the other as an inhabitant of Mars, and they do not even understand each other when speaking the same language (regardless of being Arabic or German) (OF, 10). Fourth, it is the office of an immigration officer who handles the protagonist's case as asylum seeker number '3873 oder so. Nicht mehr wert als die Nummern, die ich ziehen musste, um zu warten' [3873 or something. Worth no more than the numbers I had to take, and then sit and wait] (OF, 12).

This Kafkaesque situation is not as clear as some of the first critics suggested who seemed to focus on the immigration office as only possible interpretation of the location setting.[37] It seems as though the standpoints of both characters have become interchangeable, mainly for three reasons. Firstly, the roles of asylum seeker and immigration officer are switched, with Frau Schulz being interrogated and held captive rather than Mensy. The interrogation room subsequently becomes a 'space of exception'[38] with the hierarchies of power turned upside down. The reader can never be sure who is in power, who is the insider and the outsider, and who is the *Other*. Secondly, the interrogator is the one who is forced to confess and to re-live the asylum seeker's experiences. Thirdly and most importantly, it is rendered ambiguous as to who is from Earth ('Erdling' [earthling]) and therefore human, and who is the alien, 'Marsianer. Oder umgekehrt' [Martian – or

---

36 'Das hier ist für mich eher wie die christliche Beichte' [This feels more like a Christian confession] (OF, 10).

37 See, for instance, Meike Fessmann, 'Die Blutegel des Unglücks', *Süddeutsche Zeitung* (10 February 2016), <www.sz.de//1.1855838>, accessed 24 August 2017.

38 See the discussion of Georgio's Agamben's and Hannah Arendt's essays, both originally titled 'We Refugees', in Julia Schulze Wessel, *Grenzfiguren: Zur politischen Theorie des Flüchtlings* (Bielefeld: transcript, 2017), 75f., 154–6.

the other way around] (OF, 19). Khider thus raises questions of humanity, humanitarian action and human rights, such as the freedom of action and a refugee's right to freely choose a place for living, all which depend on the politics of belonging, based on hegemonic discourses of power and sovereignty.

Furthermore, and if interpreted as an allegory for the exchangeability of cultural identities,[39] Frau Schulz finally becomes the ultimate *Other* and could even be seen as Karim's alter ego who in the end disappears, just like him, into the dark space of imagination and illegality. But with this endless role play, the symbolic function of the other as *Other* is made visible as alienation effect. The fact that this narrative frame of switching the roles and perspectives of insider and outsider later turns out to be Karim's own imagination while daydreaming at a friend's place opens up many possible perspectives of interpretation. One of them is certainly the fact that the narrator and protagonist Karim speaks and writes in German, what Khider described as an act of alienation itself.[40] By choosing the language of the new society he is forced to live in without being allowed to reconcile with his circumstances, he shares the feeling of alienation with his protagonist. Karim is not only hindered from communicating with Frau Schulz when he speaks his first language, Arabic (OF, 10), but also with all German readers. At the end, they read a text originally written in German that pretends to be a translation. However, by transferring his story into a German context, Karim's narrative produces the feeling of alienation. That this alienation through language mimics an act of othering becomes even more apparent as Karim decides to address Frau Schulz in his own language, Arabic. Through this reverse code switching, the use of Arabic recreates the

39   For a reading of this, albeit timely and spatially limited exchange as a performative role play that turns the power game upside down, see Claudia Zeller, 'Antrag abgelehnt: Eine literarische Case-Study über Bürokratie, Illegalität und Asyl', *Trajectoires: Travaux des jeunes chercheurs du CIERA* 11 (2018), <https://journals.openedition.org/trajectoires/2571>, accessed 9 May 2018, 29ff.

40   'Auch meine eigene Geschichte entdecke ich durch die deutsche Sprache neu: Sie bringt Distanz und Verfremdung hinein, was wiederum ein anderes Verständnis ermöglicht' [I also rediscover my own story through the German language: It adds distance and alienation, which in turn allows for a different understanding]. – Schramm, 'Experimentelle Erkundungen', 189.

culturally exclusive manner of performing *Otherness* on the immigration officer herself. But since the reader, other than Frau Schulz, understands Karim, it is not merely a reversing of binaries, but rather dismantles them.

The novel's last sentence is darkly humorous and blasphemic, as Karim swears by 'Allah und allen Arschlöchern: Irgendwann werde ich Sie erwischen und ohrfeigen' [Allah and every asshole in heaven: when I find you, I'm going to give you an almighty slap in the face] (OF, 220). Metaphorically, this slap goes directly in the face of the imagined German hegemonic society, which Frau Schulz is symbolic of. The clash is due to an imaginative act that is violent in the first place. In other words, if an individual is seen as representative for a whole nation, the society can only be seen as a stereotypic, imagined one. Furthermore, any concept of an imagined nation fails to account for super-diverse communities and identities.[41] Hence, a homogenous cultural identity can only reinforce violence against the individual. It could be seen as an aggressive act, but here, through the blasphemic swearing to 'Allah and every asshole in heaven', the stereotype of the Arab asylum seeker as a potentially aggressive fundamentalist is turned on its head. The sarcastic humour with which Khider retells this clash of cultures renders Huntington's thesis of the 'clash of civilisations' hopeless.[42] In the end, it is Karim's fight against his own imagination of Frau Schulz as the stereotypical *Other* which makes a real clash impossible.

The performed *Slap in the Face* is imaginary, no doubt, but it entails a wake-up call for both the protagonist and society. It furthermore includes the utopian concept of seeing the refugee as an activist who is able to change the host society. As Moritz Schramm has pointed out in Khider's work, the 're-narration' of one's life story also bears the chance of transforming social identity, as well as the social space, and thus, ultimately, the society.[43] For Ilija Trojanow, Khider's protagonist even becomes an example for the refugee as an agent of societal change: 'Der Flüchtling wird wieder Mensch. […] Karim Mensy […] wird zu einem Handelnden, indem er selbst erzählt. Zu

---

41   Cf. Anderson, Benedict R., *Imagined Communities: Reflections on the Origin and Spread of Nationalism* (London; New York: Verso, 2006), 6.

42   Cf. Samuel P. Huntington, *The Clash of Civilizations and the Remaking of World Order* (New York: Simon & Schuster, 1996).

43   Schramm, 'Experimentelle Erkundungen', 191.

einem Widerständigen' [The refugee becomes human again. [...] Karim Mensy [...], by telling his story, becomes an agent. Someone who rises up].[44]

Thus, the protagonist's imagination becomes a telling scene within the cat-and-mouse-play between asylum seekers and the liberal nation state.[45] Mensy, by performing a role play and promoting a change of roles, temporarily turns the hierarchies between refugee and receiving authority upside down. In consequence, the migrants and refugees within German society could be pictured as playing an active part[46] of a European 'Vielheit' [multiplicity],[47] albeit at the cost of never succeeding. In fact, they might even provoke sameness and diversity, which are the crucial antagonistic parts of any postmigrant, super-diverse society. But in that the provocation mimics the construction of cultural identity as an ongoing story of exclusion, it reiterates the Eurocentric history of hegemonic belonging with an alienation effect. As seen in Karim's case, such an ironic take on the Eurocentric politics of belonging can neither be inclusive nor exclusive. But through retelling the history as an individual story, the violent act of imagining the other as *Other* becomes visible. In summary, and as the German sociologist Naika Foroutan asserts for any postmigrant core narrative of a plural society: 'Es darf nicht darum gehen, Geschichte zu verfälschen. Es geht darum, die gleiche Geschichte *anders* zu erzählen, aus einem anderen Blickwinkel zu betrachten, mit anderen Worten zu erzählen' [What should not be at stake, is the falsification of history. What is at stake, is to narrate the same history *differently*, to look at it from a different perspective,

---

44   Ilija Trojanow, 'Wie lange reißt ein Mensch sich am Riemen? Die Erfahrungen des Exils sind voller Widersprüchlichkeiten: Die Romane von Abbas Khider erzählen davon', *Süddeutsche Zeitung* (18 March 2018), 18.

45   Antje Ellermann utilises this analogy from Jane Caplan's and John Torpey's work on *Documenting Individual Identity* (Princeton: Princeton University Press, 2001, 7) to illustrate 'the relationship between the undocumented migrant and the state [...]. This image aptly captures an important aspect of everyday resistance: it rarely succeeds in permanently turning the tables. [...] Instead, migrants are forced to disappear into a life of illegality which at best is free of state interference but in any case falls far short of freeing the individual from her status of social outcast'. – Antje Ellermann, 'Undocumented Migrants and Resistance in the Liberal State', Politics & Society 38/3 (2010), 408–29, 425.

46   See Ludger Pries, *Migration und Ankommen: Die Chancen der Flüchtlingsbewegung* (Frankfurt am Main/New York: Campus, 2016).

47   See Terkessidis, *Nach der Flucht*, 42–5.

and to narrate it with different words].[48] This statement, which also alludes to the aesthetics of literature in general and utilises it for the field of sociology, necessitates the potential of creating *transnational* and *multidirectional memories*, such as finding common narratives of forced migration[49] in order to transform hegemonic societies into super-diverse migrant communities.[50] Khider's novel *Der falsche Inder* can be seen paradigmatic in this regard.

Belonging in a Borderless World: Narrating Exile and Performing Ethnicity in Khider's *Der falsche Inder*

The narrations and 'Erinnerungen' [memories] (FI, 11) of Rasul Hamid, the protagonist of *Der falsche Inder*, begin, not at all coincidentally, with a motto taken from two lines of a poem by Gottfried Benn: 'Es gibt nur zwei Dinge: die Leere [/] und das gezeichnete Ich' [There are two things: emptiness [/] and the I portrayed] (FI, 11).[51] The main narrator, who translates Rasul's manuscript from Arabic to German and publishes it as his own story, finds it when travelling by train from Berlin to Munich (FI, 7). This narrative frame of translating and travelling through cultures mimics Rasul's life and flight from Iraq to Germany. It also encapsulates the idea of an individual who locates himself – without clear orientation – on the

---

48 Naika Foroutan and Dorte Huneke, '"Wir brauchen neue Narrationen von einem pluralen Deutschland": Interview', in Dorte Huneke, ed., *Ziemlich deutsch: Betrachtungen aus dem Einwanderungsland Deutschland* (Bonn: Bundeszentrale für politische Bildung, 2013), <http://www.bpb.de/system/files/dokument_pdf/Dorte Huneke_ Ziemlich_deutsch.pdf>, accessed 20 August 2018, 43–55, 45.

49 Aleida Assmann, 'Erinnerung an Flucht und Vertreibung nach dem Zweiten Weltkrieg' (2016), <https://www.boell.de/de/2016/06/22/erinnerung-flucht-und-vertreibung-nach-dem-zweiten-weltkrieg>, accessed 26 March 2018.

50 See for this aspect, in a wider context, Aleida Assmann, *Auf dem Weg zu einer europäischen Gedächtniskultur?* (Wien: Picus, 2012).

51 For the full poem, see Gottfried Benn, 'Nur zwei Dinge' (1953), in *Sämtliche Werke. Band I: Gedichte 1*. Stuttgarter Ausgabe, ed. by Gerhard Schuster (Stuttgart: Klett-Cotta, 2006), 320. See also Katherine Anderson's intertextual interpretation within this volume, p. 41.

move and in the void. Hence, any place of transit can be turned into a *transitional space*[52] of cultural emptiness.[53] While standing on the platform of Berlin Zoo, a then busy train station, the translator experiences 'das große Nichts um mich herum' [vast nothingness round me] (FI, 7). This 'vast nothingness' symbolises the precarious process of identification through narration, just as the intertextual reference to Gottfried Benn reconstructs the multidirectional memory of an inner exile as an individual search for cultural belonging. The feeling of cultural loneliness in *Der falsche Inder*, however, not only evokes the outsider status of an artist, but can also be interpreted as a spatial metaphor for unrest,[54] migration and flight.[55] As a *transitional space*, the 'nothingness' at the train station Berlin Zoo can further be read as a public zone of neutrality, which is necessary for any individual to define and relate themselves within a plural society. This point is elaborated on by Isolde Charim who states it as a condition of a new 'pluralisierten Individualismus' [pluralised individualism]:

> Es bedarf des öffentlichen Raumes, der Öffentlichkeit als einer neutralen, als einer Begegnungszone […], die nicht nur ein Raum der Gleichen ist – wo Gleichheit sich also nicht über die Ähnlichkeit herstellt […] wo auch Unterschiedliche gleich sein können.[56]

52   Borsò, 'Transitorische Räume', 970–1.

53   Katherine Anderson interprets the emptiness as trauma and the narrative as attempt to overcome it. – Katherine Anderson, 'Von der Wanderung zum Wandel: Die Migration des Abbas Khider in die deutsche Sprache als Traumabewältigung durch Erzählen', in Elke Sturm-Trigonakis, Olga Laskaridou, Evi Petropoulou and Katerina Karakassi, eds., *Turns und kein Ende?: Aktuelle Tendenzen in Germanistik und Komparatistik* (Frankfurt am Main: Peter Lang Edition, 2017), 95–104, 100.

54   Rasul, in the fourth chapter, 'Sprechende Wände' [Talking Walls], also recalls the 'Buchstaben von Feuer' [letters of fire] written on a white wall, from Heine's poem 'Belsazar' [Belshazzar] (FI, 58). – For the full poem, which recites the book Daniel (Dan 5, 25), see Heinrich Heine, 'Belsazar' (1821), in Jost Perfahl und Werner Vortriede, eds., *Sämtliche Werke in vier Bänden*, vol. 1 (Munich: Winkler, 1969), 85.

55   The metaphor of the flight also entails, mainly through the image of a dove, an analogy between fleeing and flying, and thus shows how an English homonym can be utilised within the German-language context. See Hofmann, 'Erzählungen der Flucht aus raumtheoretischer Sicht', 108f.

56   Isolde Charim, *Ich und die Anderen: Wie die neue Pluralisierung uns alle verändert* (Wien: Zsolnay, 2018), 55–6.

[There needs to be a public space, the public as a neutral zone of encounters [...], which is not only a space for the same people - where a definition of the same is not based on similarity [...] where differences can also be the same.]

Rasul, who turns out to be the narrator's alter ego (FI, 153), experiences the same feeling of neutral nothing- or emptiness, but for him, it begins with being expelled into exile. After gradually losing his longing for – and belonging to – his homeland, he pictures how his 'Eintritt ins Exil war eine lange Straße in der Leere [...]. Die Leere aber ist das Einzige, was einem als ewiger Begleiter bleibt' [access to exile was a long path through the emptiness [...]. Emptiness, though, is the one thing that remains, your constant companion] (FI, 72). His emptiness replaces belonging with the endlessness of travelling narratives. In the sense of Edward Said's idea of exile as a 'motif of modern culture',[57] his feeling of being at home nowhere becomes the condition of the narrator's 'play with authorship'.[58] It questions origin as its core concept and creates a polyphonic voice, whereby it is no longer clear for the reader who is the author, narrator or protagonist, and whether *Der falsche Inder* is an autobiographical novel.[59] Rasul's flight increasingly mirrors the life story of the narrator, but at the same time defers the possibility of coming to terms with his own life, authenticity and ethnicity. By transgressing the borders of authenticity, the place of origin also becomes speculative and no longer serves as a fixed point. As Sarah Steidl has shown, Khider thus breaks with the 'Dreieinigkeit von Volk, Territorium und Staat [...]. Das hybride Selbst- und Weltverständnis Rasuls kann als Ausdruck seiner Utopie einer grenzenlosen Welt gedeutet werden' [trinity

---

57 Edward W. Said, 'Reflections on Exile', in Marc Robinson, ed., *Altogether Elsewhere: Writers on Exile* (Boston: Faber and Faber, 1994), 137–49, 137.

58 Sarah Steidl, 'Der Flüchtling als Grenzgestalter? Zur Dialektik des Grenzverletzers in Abbas Khiders Debütroman *Der falsche Inder*', in Thomas Hardtke, Johannes Kleine, and Charlton Payne, eds., *Niemandsbuchten und Schutzbefohlene: Flucht-Räume und Flüchtlingsfiguren in der deutschsprachigen Gegenwartsliteratur* (Göttingen: V&R unipress, 2017), 305–20, 310.

59 As analysed, for instance, by Carola Hilmes, '"Jedes Kapitel ein Anfang und zugleich ein Ende." – Abbas Khiders fiktionalisierte Lebensbeschreibung', in Monika Wolting, ed., *Identitätskonstruktionen in der deutschen Gegenwartsliteratur* (Göttingen: V&R unipress, 2017), 135–46, 141f.

of people, territory, and state [...]. Rasul's hybrid understanding of himself and the world can be interpreted as expressing his utopia of a borderless world].[60] The same de-essentialised hybridity is the case for his birth place, when he describes himself as an offspring of a 'Vereinigung zweier englischer Kolonien' [union of two British colonies]: India and Iraq (FI, 22). His ethnicity, too, becomes a performative construct born from mythical narration more than from genetic heritage:

> Somit habe ich mehrere mögliche Erklärungen für meine dunkle Hautfarbe: Das Feuer der Herrscher und die Bagdader Sonne, die Hitze der Küche und die Glut des Steinofens. Sie sind entscheidend dafür, dass ich mit brauner Haut, tiefschwarzen Haaren und dunklen Augen durchs Leben gehe (FI, 13).

> [So, I have several possible explanations for my dark skin: the rulers' fire and the Baghdad sun, the heat of the kitchen and the stone-oven embers. They're all responsible for the fact that I go through life with brown skin, the darkest black hair and dark eyes.]

Khider, through his narrative of Rasul as an outsider from society even before his flight, whether due to his mother being a 'Zigeunerin' [gypsy] (FI, 15) or not, who also migrated from Turkey to Greece, demonstrates how race is performatively constructed, similarly to Butler's concept of the performativity of gender.[61] It includes the idea of being an 'Inder' [Indian] and coming from India, as well as being called '"Indianer", weil ich aussah wie die Indianer in amerikanischen Cowboy-Filmen' ['The Red Indian' because I looked like the Indians in American Cowboy films] (FI, 14). In trying to find the fitting narrative for explaining his ethnic *Otherness*, which turns out to be constructed by others, Rasul becomes the narrator, and Khider the author of a story of migration, which begins long before his flight.

The title of the novel, *Der falsche Inder*, if literally translated, could accordingly mean 'The Fake Indian', but 'falsch' also alludes to false, wrong, pseudo, insincere and double-faced. It plays not only with the fact that any ethnic identity, especially when assessing refugees, has to be verified, but that

---

60   Sarah Steidl, 'Der Flüchtling als Grenzgestalter?', 317. Steidl also points out that this narrative strategy undermines the proof of identity as condition of being granted asylum.

61   See Mirón and Inda, 'Race as a Kind of Speech Act', 99.

this process might also force asylum seekers to invent their own biographies in order to qualify for asylum. The title classifies any life story, whether autobiographical or not, as being invented. Khider's title further ironises one of the main European narratives of colonial migration when Columbus set out to reach India over the Atlantic and 'discovered' a new continent, as it also comments on the colonial practice of Othering that claims land and people by naming. Khider manages to re-root his protagonist's cultural identity even within the European colonial context of derogatively labelling Indigenous people as 'Indians', since the full German title could also be read as 'The Mistaken Indian' and thus be understood as a decolonial re-translation of the term 'Indianer'. In this sense, the protagonist's ethnic identity is questioned, and in order to narrate his own life, he has to re-invent his own cultural identity. Last, but not least, the full title is a play with words, which is based on the English language, but works only in German. Thus, it could be interpreted as another double alienation effect, as an example of 'ironic realism' within an 'aesthetics of difference',[62] as outline above.

This kind of humorous travelling and counter-narrating between cultures, languages and places can be interpreted as an expression of a 'trans-civic desire', a desire to define one's own identity across colonial civilisations and national languages. It is directed against any monolingual and hegemonic immigration politics.[63] Deniz Göktürk and David Gramling therefore assert Khider's case:

> Treating migration with the aesthetic and political complexity it deserves requires nowadays a scalar attentiveness that takes the national, the supranational, and the transnational seriously at once – understanding how these various scales of practice, policy, and representation intersect minutely in the lives of transnational artists, refugees, postmigrants, and multiethnic communities.[64]

62　Schramm, 'Ironischer Realismus', 77.

63　Brooke Kreitinger in 'Forum: Migration Studies', 216. Her terminology refers to David Gramling, 'The New Cosmopolitan Monolingualism: On Linguistic Citizenship in Twenty-First Century Germany', *Die Unterrichtspraxis / Teaching German* 42/2 (2009), 130–40, <http://www.jstor.org/stable/40608632>, accessed 25 July 2017.

64　Deniz Göktürk and David Gramling, 'Forum: Migration Studies (with contributions by Gizem Arslan, Brooke Kreitinger, Deniz Göktürk, David Gramling, B. Venkat Mani, Olivia Landry, Barbara Mennel, Scott Denham, Robin Ellis, and

Khider's *Der falsche Inder* is neither 'Indian' nor 'Indianer', neither from the East nor the West, neither only from Iraq nor a 'gypsy', neither indigenous to one culture nor just a nomad. He acts outside of geographical, political and national borders, by being in exile and feeling nowhere at home, which allows him to turn the loss of mono-cultural belonging into an aesthetic, narrative quality of performing his ethnicity as borderless and as being in transition.

Cultures and Literatures in Transition: The Aesthetics of Khider's Postmigrant Narratives

As Trojanow and Hoskote have pointed out in *Kampfabsage* [*Confluences*], the history of European migration is itself deeply rooted in cultures and traditions of non-European lands from which most refugees originate. Within this worldview, which goes beyond postcolonialism, culture is imagined as a fluid process of transitions by which ethnic backgrounds are no longer seen as inclusive or exclusive. Or as the authors programmatically state in the subtitle of the revised German edition against Huntington's paradigm of a 'clash of civilisations' that had maintained the idea of cultures as discreet entities, 'Kulturen bekämpfen sich nicht, sie fließen zusammen' [Cultures don't clash, they flow together]. Consequently, cultural identities are seen as always having been connected and intersected, as well as not being 'bound to certain territories'.[65] They are fluid and dynamic and go beyond national boundaries, just as in Khider's *Der falsche*

Roman Utkin)', *The German Quarterly* 90/2 (2017), 212–34, <https://onlinelibrary. wiley.com/doi/full/10.1111/gequ.12033>, accessed 24 September 2017, 218.

65 '[W]ir haben keine Identitäten, sondern dynamische Positionen. Mehr als je zuvor ist Kultur nicht an ein bestimmtes Gebiet gebunden' [We do not have identities, but dynamic positions. More than ever before culture is not bound to a certain territory] (My translation, as this revised part is not part of the English translation, which follows the first German edition from 2007). – Ilija Trojanow and Ranjit Hoskote, *Kampfabsage: Kulturen bekämpfen sich nicht, sie fließen zusammen* (Frankfurt am Main: Fischer, 2016), 172.

Inder, where Rasul transgresses the concept of cultural identity based on territorial belonging.[66]

There is more than just sedentarism and nomadism, when tackling the im/mobilities in an age of mostly forced mass migration. Instead of re-narrating the model of a majority/minority culture, postmigrant narratives depict the migrant society as a super-diverse, relational space, where many cultures intermingle in various ways. A pluralised culture and its postmigrant narratives of super-diversity, such as Khider's, include multiple languages and fluid cultural identities.[67] Societally produced spaces,[68] such as an immigration office in *Ohrfeige* and a train station in *Der falsche Inder*, can become permeable. By decoding the repetitiveness that is inherent to any social space, the hierarchies of power are flipped. Negatively connotated public spaces can be turned into *neutral zones* of social encounters, which are necessary for any individual to define and relate themselves within a plural society. Charim's dictum might be a utopian concept that neglects socioeconomic factors, but it demonstrates that any postmigrant narrative, by creating *transitional spaces*[69]

66   This also happens through the fragmented structure of the narrative form. See Warda El-Kaddouri, ' "Gott, rette mich aus der Leere!" Verlust, Religiosität und Radikalisierung in den Fluchtnarrativen von Abbas Khider und Sherko Fatah', in Thomas Hardtke, Johannes Kleine and Charlton Payne, eds., *Niemandsbuchten und Schutzbefohlene: Flucht-Räume und Flüchtlingsfiguren in der deutschsprachigen Gegenwartsliteratur* (Göttingen: V&R unipress, 2017), 39–52, 41.

67   If cultures today can be defined as fluid networks independent of fixed places, as John Urry did as part of the *mobility turn*, literature also has to be seen as a globally connected system of economic, political, social, and intellectual exchanges beyond national boundaries. – John Urry, *Sociology beyond Societies: Mobilities for the Twenty-First Century* (London: Routledge, 2000), 38ff., <http://www.myilibrary. com?id=35426>, accessed 25 November 2017.

68   Cf. Henri Lefebvre, *The Production of Space* (Oxford/Cambridge: Blackwell, 1991), 16f. and 73ff.

69   By *transitional spaces* in the plural, I here refer not only to public spaces of transit, such as train stations, or to flight and migration as life-changing events and local transitions, but also to any concept of space that goes, as Tim Cresswell suggests, beyond the 'metaphysics of fixity and flow', or beyond sedentarist and nomadic metaphysics. – Tim Cresswell, *On the Move: Mobility in the Modern Western World* (New York: Routledge, 2006), chapter 2. See also Malkki, 'National Geographic', 33 u. 38 (see footnote 9).

in the sense of Trojanow's and Hoskote's *Confluences*, has to shift the
focus away from the hegemonies within and the third space in-between
supposedly binary cultures,[70] towards the people who are and possibly
define themselves outside of geographical, political and national borders
that are still based on a colonial system. Especially the fact that migration
has become a central element of pluralised global societies points to the
necessity of building new relations beyond cultural and ethnic signifiers.

From this point of view, it should also be obvious why Khider's
postmigrant narratives are not necessarily synonymous with transnational
and postcolonial literatures. In describing his protagonists' cultural identities with dynamic signifiers of gender and race as fluid and transgressive,
Khider's aesthetics goes beyond notions of *deterritorialisation*[71] and *displacement*.[72] Thus, the meaning of ethnic identity can be dismantled and
understood as a false assumption of territorial belonging. If understood
in the plural, one's identity has always been multiple and relational. It neither implies the belonging to a culture in just a territorial sense, nor the
belonging to either majority or minority ethnic groups. Constructed in
the plural and relational, one's identity is an ongoing and very dynamic
negotiation between people of multiple cultures and languages, as well
as the ability to perform cultural, gender and ethnic identities as being
always super-diverse and plural, and not just as being caught in-between
any binary politics of colonial, hegemonic and national belonging. By
moving away from ethnically and nationally centred models of narration,

70 This also entails to move beyond what has been labelled as 'minor literature' (Gilles
    Deleuze and Félix Guattari, 'What Is a Minor Literature?', *Mississippi Review* 11/
    3 (1983), 13–33, 16, <http://www.jstor.org/stable/20133921>, accessed 21 August
    2017.), and what has been defined as a culturally hybrid, 'third space of repre-
    sentation which is, just as quickly, reabsorbed into the base-superstructure div-
    ision'. – Homi K. Bhabha, *The Location of Culture* (London/New York: Routledge,
    2004), 221.
71 Deleuze and Guattari, 'What Is a Minor Literature', 18ff.
72 Caren Kaplan, *Questions of Travel: Postmodern Discourses of Displacement* (Durham:
    Duke University Press, 1996), chpt. 1, <http://read.dukeupress.edu/content/ques-
    tions-of-travel>, accessed 15 February 2018.

Khider's literature shifts the focus from a Eurocentric concept of cultural identity and territorial belonging to a postmigrant narrative of multiple cultural and ethnic attachments, connections and confluences. His novels *Ohrfeige* and *Der falsche Inder* show the refugee as a transitional figure of plurality, whose de-essentialised gender and ethnic hybridity allows him to play with the binary paradigms and politics of Othering, belonging, origin, authorship and authenticity.

WARDA EL-KADDOURI

Islam and the Image of God in Abbas Khider's *Der falsche Inder* and *Ohrfeige*

Introduction: Abbas Khider's Muslim Heritage and Islam in Contemporary German Fiction

The following chapter investigates the literary representation of Islam and the image of God in Abbas Khider's novels *Der falsche Inder* (2008) [*The Village Indian*, 2013] and *Ohrfeige* (2016) [*A Slap in the Face*, 2019]. The award-winning German writer has been praised for drawing attention to the fate of refugees in his literary oeuvre. He portrays young male protagonists who are living either as prisoners under Iraqi dictatorship or as refugees attempting to find a more secure life outside their home country. The very nature of forced migration is that it always entails a story of loss and crisis.[1] The insecurity of temporal and spatial disorientation evokes a number of deeply existential and religious questions in Khider's novels such as 'who am I?' and 'where is God?'. In his debut novel *The Village Indian*, the narrator asks himself at the beginning and at the end: 'Where am I? What am I doing here? Where is everyone else?' (VI, 159). The long monologues of the protagonist Rasul – literally meaning 'messenger' or 'prophet' in Arabic – reflect the contemplations of his fate and calling upon an absent God, which recalls the Book of Job. In Khider's most recent novel *A Slap in the Face*, the narrator is a young Iraqi refugee in Germany, Karim. He seeks revenge on the German state and – so my hypothesis – on God for his fate as a refugee by telling his story.

---

1   Cf. Elena Fiddian-Qasmiyeh, ed., *The Oxford Handbook of Refugee and Forced Migration Studies* (Oxford: Oxford University Press, 2014).

At the centre of my analysis is the question of how the protagonists are negotiating their sense of identity in relationship to their Islamic religion and to God in light of their fate as refugees.[2] The basic assumption here is that Islam is an essential part of identity construction for Muslim minorities in a diasporic context.[3] Their migration is not only politically but also religiously loaded as they move from Muslim majority countries to a historically Christian and secular Germany. Today's Muslim presence in Western Europe is, historically speaking, relatively new and is the result of two periods of migration from Muslim majority countries: (1) the post-war labour migration of guest workers from mainly Turkey and the subsequent family reunification; (2) the political migration of refugees as a result of the Iranian Revolution, the Yugoslav Wars and the Gulf Wars.

Sociological studies describe a shift in perception of identity from the ethnic-cultural other ('migrant', 'Turk') to a religious other ('Muslim') in the twenty-first century.[4] This new societal reality is reflected in contemporary German literature. Karin E. Yeşilada has called the increased visibility of Islam as a literary theme the 'Muslim turn',[5] which is part of a broader religious turn of recent years. Instead of writing about Islam from

2   Warda El-Kaddouri, '"Gott, rette mich aus der Leere!" Verlust, Religiosität und Radikalisierung in den Fluchtnarrativen von Abbas Khider und Sherko Fatah', in Thomas Hardtke et al., eds., *Niemandsbuchten und Schutzbefohlene: Flucht-Räume und Flüchtlingsfiguren in der deutschsprachigen Gegenwartsliteratur* (Göttingen: V&R Unipress, 2017), 23–38.

3   Amin Malak, *Muslim Narratives and the Discourse of English* (New York: State University of New York Press, 2005), 4.

4   Werner Schiffauer, 'Enemies Within the Gates: The Debate About the Citizenship of Muslims in Germany', in Tariq Modood, ed., *Multiculturalism, Muslims and Citizenship* (London: Routledge, 2006), 94–116; Dieter Oberndörfer, 'Einwanderung wider Willen: Deutschland zwischen historischer Abwehrhaltung und unausweichlicher Öffnung gegenüber (muslimischen) Fremden', in Thorsten G. Schneiders, ed., *Islamfeindlichkeit* (Wiesbaden: Springer, 2009), 127–42; Frank Peter, 'Welcoming Muslims Into the Nation: Tolerance, Politics and Integration in Germany', in Jocelyne Cesari, ed., *Muslims in the West after 9/11* (New York: Routledge, 2010), 119–44.

5   Karin E. Yeşilada, 'Gottes Krieger und Jungfrauen: Islam im Werk Feridun Zaimoğlus', in Michael Hofmann and Klaus von Stosch, eds., *Islam in der deutschen und türkischen Literatur* (Paderborn: Schöningh, 2012), 175–92, 176.

an outsider perspective in an orientalist tradition, today's German writers with diverse Muslim backgrounds include Islam as a literary topic from within. Theologians Langenhorst and Gellner even speak of 'deutsch-muslimische Literatur' [German Muslim Literature] as a new phenomenon.[6] Such a categorisation can easily function in a reductionist way; a criticism Langenhorst attempts to evade by focussing on the *texts* rather than the *writers* dealing with Muslim themes. The changed perception of Muslims after the terrorist attacks in New York and its social ramifications are briefly addressed in *The Village Indian* and resurface more prominently in *A Slap in the Face*. The discrimination in the labour market as well as the suspicion of Arab migrants with beards are acknowledged several times. In *A Slap in the Face* one character – Ali – even responds to the anti-Muslim sentiments by revitalising and radicalising his religious Muslim identity. Writers with a Muslim background felt the need to express themselves and to challenge the one-sided, negative image of Islam. Frauke Matthes has called this need a form of 'literary outspokenness' and a 'refusal to remain invisible'.[7] Given the historical specificity of the migration of Muslims to Germany, the majority of these authors were originally of German-Turkish origin. However, as the heterogeneity of Muslim communities increases, so too do the number of writers of diverse Muslim backgrounds such as Navid Kermani and SAID, who include Islam in their essayistic and fictional work.

Scholarly research is taking the first steps towards broadening its perspective when analysing religion in literature, as religion no longer exclusively means Jewish or Christian. This article is the first to examine the religious dimensions of Islam in the work of Abbas Khider using a narratological-rhetorical approach. However, by looking into religion and Islam, I do not have the intention of reducing Abbas Khider to a 'Muslim' writer. Rather, I am seeking acknowledgment for the religious and spiritual dimensions of his *texts*. Although Khider does not consider himself a religiously devout person, Islam is an important element of his cultural

6   Christoph Gellner and Georg Langenhorst, *Blickwinckel öffnen: Interreligiöses Lernen mit literarischen Texten* (Ostfildern: Patmos, 2013), 18.

7   Frauke Matthes, *Writing and Muslim Identity: Representations of Islam in German and English Transcultural Literature, 1990–2006* (London: IGRS, 2011), 16.

background, and this is reflected in his novels as characters use religious phrases and practice religious traditions such as pilgrimage and praying.

Khider admitted that becoming a writer was, at least in part, religiously motivated. For Muslims, the Quran is the literal word of God, that is, God is the writer of the holy book.[8] The fact that it is written in an aesthetically elevated and poetically significant language is even a key argument when demonstrating the divine creative power of the Quran.[9] According to Khider, this means that 'jeder Schriftsteller, der ein gutes Buch schreiben will, konkurriert mit Gott' [every writer who wants to write a good book competes with God].[10] The poet portrayed as a creator is reminiscent of the ideal of the genius, who was praised for his divine creativity during the 'Sturm und Drang' period.[11] During the launch of his novel *Die Orangen des Präsidenten* (2011) [The President's Oranges] at the Literaturhaus in Cologne, Khider is said to have shared an anecdote from his childhood that triggered a turning point.[12] As a child, he was very religious and often gushed about the divine beauty of the Scripture. That is, until he discovered a book by American-Lebanese writer and philosopher Khalil Gibran, one of the most important figures in modern Arabic literature. Khider asked himself: 'Wie kann jemand schöner schreiben als

---

8   Wolfert von Rahden, 'Die fremde Sprache bedeutet Freiheit: Ein Dialog mit Wolfert von Rahden über Grenzgänge zwischen Sprachen, Staaten und Kulturen', *Eurozine* (31 July 2012), < https://www.eurozine.com/die-fremde-sprache-bedeutet-freiheit/>, accessed 22 June 2018.

9   Johannes Kleine, 'Navid Kermani's Poetic Hermeneutics of Religious Experiences', in: Thomas Hardtke, ed., *Religious Experience Revisited: Expressing the Inexpressible?* (Leiden: Brill, 2016), 123–36, 128; Navid Kermani, *Gott ist schön: Das ästhetische Erleben des Korans* (Munich: C.H. Beck, 2011).

10   Rahden, 'Die fremde Sprache bedeutet Freiheit'.

11   The eighteenth-century German philosopher and writer Johann Georg Hamann, who is considered a pioneer in the Sturm und Drang era, introduced the idea of God as writer and writer as God into German literature. – Cf. Heinzpeter Hempelmann, *Gott, ein Schriftsteller: Johann Georg Hamann über die End-Äusserung Gottes ins Wort der Heiligen Schrift und ihre hermeneutischen Konsequenzen* (Wuppertal: Brockhaus, 1988).

12   Lewis Gropp, 'Schöner schreiben als Gott', *Neue Bücher Zeitung* (24 May 2011), <https://www.nzz.ch/schoener_schreiben_als_gott-1.10681939>, accessed 2 July 2018.

Gott selbst?' [How can someone write more beautifully than God himself?]. From that moment on, he set out to become a writer: 'Schöner zu schreiben als Gott, das ist das Ziel' [The goal is to write more beautifully than God].[13] Khider's style, however, does not resemble the poetics of the Quran in any way. Rather, the author portrays the hardship of refugees and prisoners with dark humour and irony.

'Gott, rette mich aus der Leere!': Individualised Religiosity as Coping Mechanism for Loss and Disorientation and the Question of Theodicy in *The Village Indian*

The Village Indian tells the story of Rasul's flight from Iraq to Germany through a lost manuscript which is found and read by the narrator in the frame story. The title of the novel already suggests a distorted identity. From the start, Rasul is perceived by his environment as an Indian due to his dark skin and hair, which gives him an 'exotic' appearance. Throughout the novel, the journey through different countries, cultures and languages leads to a sense of temporal and spatial disorientation, adding to the identity confusion of the protagonist: 'What I can't live with is that I don't know who I really am' (VI, 17). In relation to the spatial disorientation, Hanna Maria Hofmann emphasised the identity- and meaning-making function of space for 'das existenzielle Bedürfnis des Menschen nach Selbstverortung' [the existential need of humans for self-positioning].[14] The reorientation of (post-)migrants in a foreign country raises the question of social belonging.[15] Rasul's changing names and false identity cards

13   Gropp, 'Schöner schreiben als Gott'.

14   Hanna Maria Hofmann, 'Erzählungen der Flucht aus raumtheoretischer Sicht: Abbas Khiders *Der falsche Inder* und Anna Seghers' *Transit*', in Hardtke et al., eds., *Niemandsbuchten und Schutzbefohlene*, 97–124, 100.

15   Naika Foroutan, 'The Post-Migrant Paradigm', in Jan-Jonathan Bock and Sharon Macdonald, eds., *Refugees Welcome: Difference and Diversity in a Changing Germany* (New York: Berghahn Books, 2019), 121–42.

during his flight change his 'official' identification constantly, while he remains in fact the same person. He asks himself 'which one of them I really
was. And who they all were' (VI, 102).

Before his flight, the embargo against Iraq renders Rasul's existence
hopeless. In his homeland he feels a 'kind of illness' which he identifies as
being caused by a 'no-one state' and 'a great emptiness', which moves him
to leave the country (VI, 67). The numerous setbacks during his flight, described in the chapter 'Save Me from Emptiness', evoke an ever-increasing
desperation. Each paragraph ends with the explicit and repeated invoca-
tion to God, intensifying each time: 'God, save me from emptiness!' (VI,
68, 69, 71, 76, 78, 85). His prayer includes an anaclasis, that is, the calling
to the addressee of prayer, in this case God, in liturgical language.[16] In
poetic-literary form, however, the anaclasis becomes the stylistic figure of
the apostrophe. The repetition reflects the various attempts of dialogue
between man and God. Since there is no answer, the listening capacities
of God are questioned: 'I slept and thought of my prayer but I had the
feeling, somehow, that God couldn't hear me. Or didn't want to. "What's
wrong with him?" I prayed softly, nonetheless, "God, please, please save
me! Save me from emptiness!"' (VI, 78). The doubt about God's ability
('could') and willingness ('want') to hear the prayer contradicts the general
Islamic image of Allah as an omniscient, omnipotent and merciful God.
Despite his insecurity and despair, Rasul continues to pray. Prayer is ba-
sically a confession of the existence of a divine creature – in this case God.
In other words, Rasul calls upon God through prayer, thereby confirming
faith in his existence. Prayer as communication between man and God is
a direct verbalisation of religiosity and transcendence. In his publication
Spiritual Modalities, William FitzGerald examines the systematic connection between prayer and rhetoric:

> Prayer is *asymmetric* (one-way) discourse that yet unfolds within a scene of *dia-*
> *logic* (two-way) encounter. Even when imagined as a dialogic encounter, prayer's
> asymmetry remains crucial to its operational logic. Whether conceived as speaking,

16   Karl-Heinrich Bieritz, 'Anthropologische Grundlegung', in Hans-Christoph
      Schmidt-Lauber, ed., *Handbuch der Liturgik: Liturgiewissenschaft in Theologie und*
      Praxis der Kirche (Göttingen: Vandenhoeck & Ruprecht, 2003), 95–128, 119.

listening, visualizing, or some other mode, prayer is the human side of any human-divine encounter.[17]

Prayer is characterised by the tension between speech and silence, since it is an act of communication in which the addressee does not respond linguistically. In a way, the silence of God contrasts with the God of Islam, who is portrayed as a revealing God who speaks to his people. However, this does not mean that the silence of God is not broached in religious sources. The mood of God testing His servant in *The Village Indian* draws a clear parallel to the story of Job in the Old Testament, which is also mentioned several times in the Quran. The greatest difference between both versions is that Job's story in the Quran is reduced to that of forbearance: Job does not accuse, but just laments.[18] As Navid Kermani puts it, the dimension of theologically sanctioned protest and his rebellion against God are simply ruled out, with the exception of several Sufi traditions where the Old Testament view of a vengeful God is adopted.[19] Since Job is called a prophet in Islam, a further parallel can be linked to Rasul. In contrast to Job, however, Rasul lacks the longer, more passionate monologues. Moreover, he counters his annoyance about the failed dialogues with humour in which he insults God, even calling him to order. Consequently, he creates an inverted power balance, which is also apparent in the analysis of the later novel *A Slap in the Face*.

In *Die Orangen des Präsidenten*, a similar scene takes place in which the protagonist Mahdi Hamama's hopeless situation leads him to prayer (OdP, 43). Mahdi is the name of the twelfth and yet to appear Imam in Shia Islam, who, as a messianic prophet, is one of the holiest figures. The names Rasul [prophet] and Mahdi [messiah] connect the two characters through the novels. Mahdi is arrested together with his friend Ali after his final exam and thrown into prison, where, in true Kafkaesque fashion, he sits innocently for two years, never finding out what he was accused of in

---

17 William FitzGerald, *Spiritual Modalities: Prayer as a Rhetoric and as a Performance* (Philadelphia: Penn State University Press, 2012), 34–5.

18 Navid Kermani, *Der Schrecken Gottes: Attar, Hiob und die metaphysische Revolte* (Munich: C.H. Beck, 2011), 165.

19 Ibid.

the first place.[20] Ali, outside of Mahdi's knowledge, was active in an opposition group. When Ali is tortured to death by the prison guards, Mahdi seeks comfort in prayer in vain:

> Ich weinte tagelang über Alis Tod. Habe sogar gebetet und Gott mehrere Male gefragt, welchen Sinn dieses Elend haben soll.
> *Allah sieht, was in der Nacht auf dem Land und auf See geschieht.*
> *Nichts auf Erden und in den Himmeln bleibt Ihm verborgen!*
> *Oh Allah, sende uns eine Gnade!*
> Aber Gott schwieg, und Ali kam nicht aus dem Folterreich zurück (OdP, 43).
>
> [I cried for days over Ali's death. Even prayed and asked God multiple times, what the cause of all this misery was.
> *Allah sees what happens at night on land and sea.*
> *Nothing on earth and heaven stays hidden from Him!*
> *Oh Allah, send us your mercy!*
> But God remained silent, and Ali did not come back from the torture realm.]

Although Mahdi identifies himself as non-religious and does not participate in the daily Islamic ritual prayers in prison, he feels the need to connect with God in that moment. The question of theodicy, that is, the justification of God as omniscient and merciful in view of the existence of evil, is raised.[21] Mahdi's supplication contains literal excerpts from various Quran verses which discuss the central concept of *al-ghaib* [the invisible], that is, the conviction that there is a hidden world which we as humans cannot perceive because of the limited abilities of our senses and which only God as the highest being can see. *Al-basir* [the sighted] is one of the ninety-nine names for Allah. Mahdi's question targets the core of the problem: how can God see everything and still not intervene? In the concluding sentences of the novel, Mahdi emphasises his mistrust and anger at God with the following words: 'will ich eigentlich nur auf alles spucken [...]. Und auf Gott, den Faulen, der seinen Hintern nicht

---

20   The names Mahdi and Ali are an explicit reference to the Shia denomination in Islam: Mahdi as the Messiah and Ali as the successor of the Prophet for Shia Muslims. Both names are very common in countries with a Shia majority population.

21   The question of theodicy is also a main topic in Navid Kermani's work. See Kermani, *Der Schrecken Gottes.*

hochkriegt!' [actually I just want to spit on everything [...]. And on God, the lazy one, who can't get his ass up!] (OdP, 155). He subsequently spits on the floor, a non-verbal act that is meant as a public insult to and thus a blasphemy against God. With similar words as those used in *The Village Indian*, God is described as lazy. Laziness is an answer to the absence and silence of God, and on an abstract level, an answer to the question of theodicy. From an Islamic perspective, Allah is a God of justice who acts as *al-adl* [the judge] at the Last Judgement. In Khider's novels, the prison can be read as a replica of the religious legal system, which also encompasses a system of transgressions and punishments. Consequently, the comparison can be interpreted as a critique of the image of God: where is the God of Justice? It suggests that Allah's Last Judgment is or could be similarly unjust.

When Rasul is confronted with the sexual exploitation of women by human traffickers, he reaches the limits of his patience: 'Now, God, no doubt needs my help to save Him! I thought. Why's He not shifting His arse in Heaven? I felt a deep hatred against Him' (VI, 84). God now seems to be in the position where he needs Rasul's help: the power dynamic between God and man is reversed. In contrast to the previous quotation, the personal pronoun 'He' and the possessive pronoun 'His' are written in capital letters. Within the context of the blasphemous statements against the anthropomorphised God, the spelling of those pronouns is to be interpreted as sarcasm. Capital letters usually express reverence and respect for the holiness of God, but here they are reversed so to make a derogatory assessment. The emotional outburst eventually turns into depression: 'I looked up into the bright sky. "God, where on earth are you? Missing already?" ' (VI, 91). Once again, the absence of God is pivotal. Contrary to the usual starting point of modernist authors, his absence does not necessarily mean God is dead, but rather that he is 'missing'.[22] Whether God chose this situation himself remains unclear, but in any case, his absence brings about a void.

The fact that Rasul addresses the absence of a metaphysical instance in his autobiographical manuscript is anticipated in the subtitle. The title

---

22   Gregory Erickson, *The Absence of God in Modernist Literature* (New York: Palgrave Macmillan, 2007), 1.

'Memories' is followed by a fragment from 'Nur zwei Dinge' [Only Two Things, 1957], one of the best-known poems by the German poet Gottfried Benn: 'There are two things: emptiness and the I portrayed' (VI, 6).[23] Benn's poem on the existential question – described in the poem as 'just the eternal question: why?' – concludes with the recognition of an emptiness to which the subject must relate.[24] The emptiness symbolises the absence of a metaphysical authority, forcing the subject, left to its own creative devices, to redesign itself and the world. This corresponds to the final stage of Rasul's writing process.

> To begin with, I simply wrote, thinking that by writing I could capture my feelings in words. [...] Then, I thought I could change the world by writing. [...] Finally, I became persuaded that I could even improve myself by writing.

> When I write, I see everything as if for the first time, I try to empathise, to understand anew. [...] I locked myself in my room, blocked out the external world and plunged deep within to bring, each time, another concealed part of myself to the surface. I discovered myself and the world anew and committed this insight to paper. Is what I write real life? I can't say (VI, 19).

Rasul's writing follows three different phases: from expressive to politically active to introspective. Writing thus becomes an instrument for self-reflection and self-conception, which is symbolised by Rasul's actions: he locks himself in his room, closes the door and 'plunge[s] deep within'. Martin Travers described the relationship between emptiness and Benn's designate self in Benn's poem as 'the relationship between an objective universal emptiness and a subjective experience [...] self-defined by writing'.[25] Here, I would like to draw a parallel between Khider's and Benn's poetology, whereby both try to overcome a metaphysical absence of an omnipotent creature by reshaping themselves and the world through writing. Rasul's physical reaction to the joy and the urge of writing (e.g.

23   David Paisey translated this verse as: 'Only two things exist: blankness and the designate I.' – Gottfried Benn, 'Only two things', in David Paisey, ed. and trans., *Selected Poems and Prose* (Manchester: Fyfield Books, 2013).

24   Ibid.

25   Martin Travers, *The Poetry of Gottfried Benn: Text and Selfhood* (Bern: Peter Lang, 2007), 334.

shivering, faster heartbeat) resembles a status of ecstatic trance. This is similar to Sufi mystics, who try to reach this status through physical meditation (e.g. whirling). In addition to that, Rasul's ascetic withdrawal and the focus on the inner self is typical of Sufi mystics. Like prayer, writing becomes a transcendental and spiritual experience. If we then recall Khider's motivation to become a writer – that is, to write more beautifully than God himself – an analogy occurs. God and artist are thus placed on a similar ontological-epistemological level, since they both have the capacity to create from nothing.

The fifth and sixth chapters of *The Village Indian* each offer an overview of Rasul's repeated setbacks and his moments of bliss. While in the fifth chapter the paragraphs end with a call to God to save Rasul from the void, the paragraphs in the sixth chapter 'The Miracles' all begin with the words 'I swear' (VI, 98, 101, 102, 108, 112, 118, 121, 122). The main character tells about his wondrous experiences during his flight and closes with the following statement:

> I believe in miracles. In those strange moments for which there is no other term. One of life's secrets, as it were. These miracles have much in common with coincidences. But I can't call them coincidences, because a coincidence doesn't happen many times over. A coincidence is just a coincidence, as lame as that might sound. You can talk about a big coincidence in life, two at most, but not more. So there are events that are miracles, not coincidences – that's how I will put it, even if the logic isn't exactly Aristotelian. I'm not a superstitious person, the supernatural and subterrestrial are not for me. In the course of my life I've developed, so to speak, my own religious persuasion, one made to measure for me. Absolutely individual (VI, 98).

At this point, the main character explicitly mentions his belief in miracles. The strongly religiously charged concept 'miracle' differs from chance in that a miracle implies the intended effect of a superhuman force. This explains why the Islamic teaching of predestination does not permit the belief in chance, as it automatically questions the existence of an almighty God. By his own admission, Rasul has developed his 'own religious persuasion'. The personalisation and privatisation of religion is a postmodern phenomenon in which the individual experience of religion is more important than the collective forms of worship and services.[26]

26   Hugh McLeod, *Religion and the People of Western Europe 1789–1989* (Oxford: Oxford University Press, 1997).

The protagonist has invented his own religion, a religion that is 'made to measure for' him and is '[a]bsolutely individual'. This raises the following question: how does individualised religiosity relate to the Islamic world community of the Ummah, which finds its roots in the connection between believers and consequently asserts a collective religious identity? Like other world religions, Islam knows a great religious diversity, which the Quran neither denies nor evaluates negatively. Rather, the Quran recognises religious diversity as well as context-dependent religiosity and tries to find 'unity in diversity' within the idea of the Ummah – which was never meant to be a static concept anyway.[27] Rasul's individualised religiosity is reconcilable with the Ummah and is a reaction to the unsatisfactory answers of Islam as an institutionalised religion during his days as a refugee. *A Slap in the Face* similarly tells a refugee story and a reckoning with God.

Allegorical Reckoning with God Through Imagination and Storytelling in *A Slap in the Face*

Khider worked four years on his novel *A Slap in the Face*. It was ultimately published at a time when the refugee crisis was at its height.[28] The book addresses the marginalised life of a refugee in Germany with painful precision: the difficulties in acquiring a new language, the discrimination, the poverty, the social isolation and the sexual exploitation. *A Slap in the Face* quickly became the 'Buch der Stunde'[29] [book of the hour] and was celebrated as one of the first novels in German-language literature to explicitly

---

27   'Umma', in: Peri Bearman et al., eds., *Encyclopaedia of Islam* (Brill Online, 2013).
28   Bock and Macdonald, eds., *Refugees welcome?*
29   Julia Encke, 'Flüchtlingsroman: Vom Warten wird man immer blöder', *Frankfurter Allgemeine Zeitung* (30 January 2016), <http://www.faz.net/aktuell/feuilleton/buecher/fluechtlingsroman-vom-warten-wird-man-immer-bloeder-14030679.html>, accessed 22 June 2018.

address the current refugee crisis. In contrast to Jenny Erpenbeck's much-discussed novel *Gehen, ging, gegangen*,[30] in which emeritus professor Richard converses with refugees, *A Slap in the Face* puts forward a refugee as both the protagonist and the narrator. Despite the celebration of the topic of Khider's novel, he explicitly distances himself from the role of political commentator and rejects invitations to appear in the media to talk about the situation of refugees in Germany: 'Ich bin kein Instrument, ich bin ein Autor' [I am not an instrument, I am an author].[31] Because of the topicality of the novel's theme, the novel has been translated into other languages such as English and Dutch.[32]

Although the novel was written between 2012 and 2015, the story is set between 2000 and 2003. The protagonist is a young Iraqi refugee, Karim Mensy, who is staying in the refugee camp of the fictitious town of Niederhofen on the Danube. After having lived in Germany for three and a half years, Karim's asylum application is rejected. According to the German authorities, the war in Iraq is over after the Anglo-American invasion and the subsequent fall of Saddam Hussein in 2003. However, Karim is determined not to return to Iraq and, with the help of smugglers, plans his escape to Finland to start all over again. Karim is the narrator of the frame story, in which he tells anecdotes through a first-person perspective.[33] His refugee story is not a prototypical one, because his escape was caused neither by war nor by dictatorship, but by a physical anomaly: Karim developed female breasts during his puberty. It is clear that Khider did not want to fulfil the reader's

30   Jenny Erpenbeck, *Gehen, ging, gegangen* (Munich: Albrecht Knaus, 2015).

31   Christoph Geißler, 'Eine Begegnung mit Abbas Khider: Die deutsche Sprache ist wie eine schöne Frau', *Berliner Zeitung* (27 January 2016), <https://www.berliner-zeitung.de/kultur/eine-begegnung-mit-abbas-khider-die-deutsche-sprache-ist-wie-eine-schoene-frau-23570206>, accessed 2 July 2018.

32   From here on, the page numbers will refer to the German original *Ohrfeige*. Because the English translation was not available at the time of writing, the translations are my own.

33   Khider's use of frame stories in both *The Village Indian* and *A Slap in the Face* is reminiscent of the novella in its original sense, such as Boccaccio's *Decameron* and Chaucer's *The Canterbury Tales*. *One Thousand and One Nights*, however, is one of the earliest examples of this and has influenced the classical Arabic literary tradition, with which Khider is undoubtedly familiar as well.

expectations by creating a character seeking political asylum. In addition to the literary effect of surprise and humour – which is typical of Khider's style – he has produced a socially critical message about the generalisation and stereotyping of refugees: 'Nicht für alle finden wir Schubladen wie "politischer Flüchtling" oder "Wirtschaftsflüchtling". Es gibt unendliche Gründe, warum Menschen ihre Heimat verlassen, eben auch Geschlechtsprobleme' [We don't find pigeonholes like 'political refugee' or 'economic refugee' for everyone. There are infinite reasons why people leave their homeland, including gender issues].[34] Out of fear of social rejection and isolation, Karim eventually decides to flee. The novel begins and ends with the image of a slap in the face, creating a circular structure borrowed from the title. The novel concludes with the following words: 'Ich schwöre bei Allah und allen Arschlöchern des Himmels: Irgendwann werde ich Sie [Frau Schulz] erwischen und ohrfeigen' [I swear to God and all the assholes in heaven: one day I am going to catch you [Frau Schulz] and slap you in the face] (OF, 220).

A Slap in the Face is in fact a revenge fantasy staged in the form of a monologue with the civil servant Mrs Schulz as a silent listener in the frame story. Such a setting is reminiscent of prayer with a silent partner in dialogue. Mrs Schulz's forced silence is significant because it implies a hierarchy in the narrative discourse. In a conversation with the Bosch Foundation on the occasion of receiving the Chamisso Prize, Khider said that his intention was to give the refugee the central stage in his book: 'Es gibt keine Romane in der deutschen Literatur, in diesem Bereich, wo die Hauptfigur ein Asylbewerber ist. Ein Asylbewerber, der selbst redet. Ich war tatsächlich überrascht. Sogar in der Literatur sind sie noch nicht angekommen' [There are no novels in German literature in this field, where the main character is an asylum seeker. Asylum seekers who speak for themselves. I was truly surprised by this discovery. They haven't even arrived in the literature yet].[35]

34   Kaspar Heinrich, 'Wir sollten nicht plötzlich alles infrage stellen', *Planet Interview* (11 May 2016), <http://www.planet-interview.de/interviews/abbas-khider/48826/>, accessed 2 July 2018.

35   Tobias Krohne, 'Chamisso-Literaturpreis für Abbas Khider', *Deutschlandfunk Kultur* (9 March 2016), <https://www.deutschlandfunkkultur.de/letzte-ehrung-dieser-art-chamisso-literaturpreis-fuer-abbas.1013.de.html?dram:article_id=380946>, accessed 3 July 2018.

The starting point here is that narrative and power are connected. In this context, according to Foucault, it is even more appropriate to use the word 'domination' instead of power: while power and power structures exist everywhere and always, domination means the unequal distribution of power of people by people. In this concrete case, it is achieved through narrative constructs.[36] In this novel, only the refugee speaks and the German civil servant Mrs Schulz cannot take the floor once, thereby creating an inverse relationship of domination. The silence is not voluntary but forced upon her. It is not only narratively depicted since she never utters a word as a character, but also explicitly visualised: she is tied to an office chair and her mouth is taped.[37] Karim's action is an act of resistance that is also physically portrayed: he stands and looks down on her. Khider has commented on this narrative construction: 'In dieser Redesituation steckt auch das Gefühl: Ihr Deutschen, ihr habt so viel geredet, lasst jetzt mal die anderen reden' [This speech situation also echoes the distinct feeling: you Germans, you have talked so much, now let the others speak].[38] The anticipated dialogue with Mrs Schulz that turns into a monologue can be read on a second, allegorical level as addressing God. Karim's revenge fantasy not only reckons with German bureaucracy, but also with the unjust role of God in the refugee story.

At first, Karim compares Mrs Schulz with God, since he only addresses her with her surname: 'Es ist, als würde ich Gott einen Vornamen geben. Wenn Allah einen Vornamen hätte, wäre er auch weniger einschüchternd. Amir Allah oder Wilma Allah klingt schon wesentlich sympathischer, finden Sie nicht?' [It is as if I would give God a first name. If Allah would

---

36   Michel Foucault, *Dispositive der Macht: Michel Foucault über Sexualität, Wissen und Wahrheit* (Merve: Berlin, 1978). Although Foucault used power and domination as synonyms in earlier works, he differentiated the two concepts here.

37   This image contains a disturbing gender imbalance in terms of physical status (the woman is sitting down and is tied, the man is looking down on her and is free to move around) as well as the ability to speak (the woman is forced into silence, the man can speak freely). However, in this particular scene, the dynamics between the marginalised refugee and the institutionalised governmental power is more urgent here.

38   Encke, 'Flüchtlingsroman: Vom Warten wird man immer blöder'.

have a first name, he would also be less intimidating. Amir Allah or Wilma Allah sounds significantly more likeable, don't you think?] (OF, 9–10). The absence of a first name adds to her mysterious and divine character, abstracting her and turning her into a symbol. Moreover, the name 'Schulz' is not only one of the most common German surnames, but is etymologically derived from the Middle High German word 'Schultheiß', which means 'official' or 'judge'.[39] In Islam, judge is also one of the ninety-nine names for God. As is also the case in Judaism and Christianity, the Islamic image of God is strongly influenced by the eschatological worldview of the Last Judgement. God – like Frau Schulz – acts as a judge who pronounces a final verdict. In the following long excerpt, the depiction of the civil servant as a divine figure becomes even clearer:

Sie, Frau Schulz, gehören zu jenen, die hier darüber entscheiden, auf welche Weise ich existieren darf oder soll. Stellen Sie sich umgekehrt mal vor, in meiner Position zu sein. Würden Sie nicht gern wissen, wie diese gottesgleiche Figur mit Vornamen heißt? Jene Person, die Ihr Leben nach eigenem Gutdünken paradiesisch oder höllisch gestalten kann? […] Da sind Sie. Hilflos. Verschnürt wie ein Paket. In Ihrem teuren schwarzen Lederstuhl. Sie waren eine Göttin. Eine Naturgewalt, die Macht über andere Menschen hat. Ich war Ihnen ausgeliefert. Aber wie ein mythischer Held habe ich mich erhoben und den Olymp erstürmt. Und ich werde Sie bald zurücklassen in Ihrem kleinen Beamtenstübchen. Dann sitzen Sie hier, einsam wie ein Schöpfer, dessen Kreaturen ihn vergaßen. Ein Gott, an den keiner glaubt, existiert nicht. Das gilt auch für Göttinnen (OF, 11).

[You, Ms. Schulz, belong to those who decide in which way I should, can or may exist. Imagine it the other way around, being in my position. Wouldn't you like to know the first name of this godlike character? This person who can shape your life into paradise or hell at his own discretion? […] There you are. Helpless. Tied up like a package. In your expensive black leather chair. You were a Goddess. A force of nature, who had power over other people. I was surrendered to you. But like a mythical hero I rose up and overthrew Olympus. And soon I will leave you in your little office. Then you will be sitting here, lonely like a Creator whose creatures have forgotten about him. A God in whom nobody believes does not exist. The same is true for Goddesses.]

39   Daniel Kroiß, 'Schulz', *Digitales Familiennamenwörterbuch Deutschlands*, <http://www.namenforschung.net/id/name/9/1>, accessed 18 July 2018.

Mrs Schulz – and in a broader sense, the German state – is similar to a God in her status as a civil servant: her decision-making power greatly affects the lives of the human beings at her mercy. The description of life with religiously charged insinuations emphasises Mrs Schulz's divine character. Karim also compares himself to a mythical hero who resists an almighty in the House of Gods on Mount Olympus from Greek mythology. The expensive black leather armchair in which she is tied up is a power symbol for corporate governance. The image evoked suggests that refugee politics are conducted the same way large companies are run, with refugees being subjected to a cost-benefit analysis. Through his act of resistance, Karim reverses the balance of domination. The condition of existence for God introduced in the quotation also changes the dependence: God only exists if people believe in him. A similar reversal of power dynamics can be found in *The Village Indian*. Karim chooses to 'leave behind' Mrs Schulz – and on a second, more abstract level, also God. In the light of the fate of refugees, Karim's address to Mrs Schulz can be interpreted as an appeal to God. By turning to a different figure (God) than the previously addressed one (Mrs Schulz) as he speaks, Karim's speech is transformed into an apostrophe, more specifically an apostrophe interiectio [interjection]. He reverses the roles and preaches to God.

In his texts, Khider draws comparisons with God that evoke the Quranic image of God, who is judging and punishing towards the unrepentant. The implicit blasphemy is associated with the aforementioned language taboo and with cultural self-censorship. An example in *A Slap in the Face* is the curse 'Charab Allmanya', which literally translated means 'Scheiß auf Deutschland' [Shit on Germany] (OF, 112). According to Karim, the expression is based on an unfortunate coincidence, because the word 'Allmanya' sounds similar to 'Allah'. This way, a blasphemous condemnation of God can be avoided in the Iraqi-Arab colloquial language: 'Man wolle eventuell vermeiden, Gott zu beleidigen, wenn man wütend sei' [One would like to avoid potentially offending God when one is angry] (OF, 114). Replacing swear words with phonologically similar words is a well-known euphemism tactic, thus bypassing potential blasphemy. Another rhetorical tactic for implicit blasphemy is that of comparison. When talking about Iraqi bureaucracy, Karim dismisses it as 'so chaotisch und bürokratisch […]

wie eine göttliche Strafe, die keine Gnade kennt' [so chaotic and bureaucratic like a divine punishment that knows no mercy] (OF, 75). An angry
image of God appears through comparisons and associations with dictatorship and oppression, not only in *A Slap in the Face*, but also in Khider's other
novels. In *Die Orangen des Präsidenten*, for instance, the transformation
of a fellow prisoner into a cruel prison guard is compared to a punishing
God: 'Abu-Zainb benahm sich seitdem wie ein Gott, er verwandelte unser
höllisches Leben in eine noch höllischere Hölle' [Since then Abu-Zaid acted
like a God; he transformed our hellish lives into an even more hellish hell]
(OdP, 48). Moreover, Saddam Hussein is also depicted as a holy figure in
another novel by Khider, *Brief in die Auberginenrepublik* (2013) [Letter
to the Aubergine Republic]: 'Der Himmel leuchtete rot bis bräunlich,
und Saddam lächelte im silbrigen Mond, um sein Gesicht eine Aureole
aus Licht. Wie ein heiliger, ein weiser Prophet' [The sky glowed red to
brownish, and Saddam smiled in the silver moonlight, around his face a
halo of light. Like a holy, wise prophet] (BiA, 82–3). By comparing God
to a brutal, punishing prison guard and the prophet to a political dictator,
the suggestion is made that God and prophets are not as just or righteous
as they are believed to be.

Conclusion

Both *The Village Indian* and *A Slap in the Face* are refugee narratives addressing the question of theodicy without fully renouncing God. Rasul
is portrayed as a seeker struggling to come to terms with his identity and
with his religion. The sense of disorientation and existential crisis caused
by the setbacks during his flight and the loss of his manuscripts lead him
to questioning the role of God with intertextual parallels to the story
of Job. Rasul attempts to overcome the feeling of metaphysical absence
or 'blankness' – as Benn would describe it – by the act of writing and
thus by creating a new fictional world and a new self. The reckoning with
God in *A Slap in the Face* is much more subtle, using metaphors and alle-
gories instead of prayer. Through an imaginary act of revenge in form of a

monologue, Karim is able to tell *his* story and to express his frustrations of injustice towards the German state and towards God. By introducing an Iraqi asylum seeker in Germany as protagonist and only narrator, Khider makes a clear statement about power dynamics by emphasising the emancipatory nature of storytelling. Both novels make use of humour to reverse power dynamics. Despite the blasphemy through cursing, swearing and verbal actions such as spitting, the protagonists still call upon God. Paradoxically through absence, God becomes present, albeit in a passive role. This is especially the case in *The Village Indian*. In *A Slap in the Face*, the suggestion is that Karim rejects the god-like figure due to its unjust behaviour, to which he reacts by renouncing God and taking his fate in his own hands, by taking over control: not only physically, but also by telling his own story on his own terms.

CAROLIN MÜLLER

The Transience of Prisoners' Memoirs in Abbas Khider's *Die Orangen des Präsidenten*

A life in prison is often one in the shadows; it unfolds in spaces that are doomed to non-existence and places that require incredible human perseverance. Through an array of techniques of control and punishment, the panoptic system of discipline and surveillance works to diminish individual bodies and voices. The multifold structure of prisons restricts memory-keeping and the way that individuals can reclaim their humanity in this space and beyond. A life in prison is, thus, a life in a space where walls are the borders beyond which voices cannot escape. At the same time, the imprisoned sometimes carve secret inscriptions into the very same walls as an act of rebellion. Shadows of a past existence, the words on the walls bear witness to torment and become testimonials to torture and suffering.[1]

On the one hand, the penal institution is a closed space[2] that aims to limit expressions of agency. Michel Foucault described how the totalising

1   For an overview on the impact of the prison environment on the emotional well-being of the incarcerated, see Ben Crewe et al., 'The Emotional Geography of Prison Life', *Theoretical Criminology*, 18/1 (2014), 56–74, <https://doi.org/10.1177/1362480613497778>, accessed 6 January 2020.

2   This understanding of 'closed space' relies on Doreen Massey's reading of Ernesto Laclau's usage of the 'spatial'. Space in his sense refers to a 'close and self-determining system [...]', in which the possibility of change from outside the governing system is absent. Massey notes that 'the spatial, because it lacks dislocation, is devoid of the possibility of politics'. Space within the penal system, as the term's usage is attributed in this essay, is determined by the structures of the panoptic carceral. By its definition, change to its dynamics is impossible. The penal panopticon is characterised 'by closure and immobility, as containing no sense of the open, creative possibilities for political action/effectivity'. Doreen Massey, 'Politics and Space/Time', *New Left Review*, 196 (1992), 65–84, 69.

institutions and structures of the prison panopticon control time and space that people occupy.[3] Constant control and observation through hegemonic powers deprive imprisoned individuals of any form of security and constitute multiple layers of surveillance.[4] The prison complex strips individuals off the right to participate in the social and political acts and reduces their bodies to 'bare life',[5] 'exposed and abandoned to violence'.[6] Ben Crewe et al. argue that the prison organises the social according to the 'internal geography of the regime'[7] that manages the emotional world of the incarcerated by mapping zones for permitted and restricted social interaction.[8]

3   Michel Foucault, *Discipline and Punish: The Birth of the Prison*, trans. Alan Sheridan (New York: Random House, 1977).

4   Gresham M. Sykes, *The Society of Captives: A Study of Maximum Security Prison*, Revised Edition (Princeton: Princeton University Press, 2007).

5   Giorgio Agamben discusses the term 'bare life' in his critique of the treatment of political prisoners at Guantánamo Bay. He explains how a perpetual state of exception has emerged as the political paradigm, drawing on accounts of political prisoners in Auschwitz and more recently President George W. Bush's order from 13 November 2001, issuing 'indefinite detention' for captured Taliban after the 9/11 attacks on the US. Agamben warns that if such interventions and suspensions of regulated power apparatuses, like the Geneva Convention, along with an increase in power given to military authority, interfere with the organisation of the civic sphere, 'the physical elimination not only of political adversaries but of entire categories of citizens who for some reason cannot be integrated into the political system' becomes evident. – Giorgio Agamben, *State of Exception*, trans. Kevin Attell (Chicago: University of Chicago Press, 2005), 2. – Puspa Damai explains that '[the] biopolitical threshold of the exception is the extreme zone of intensity wherein law remains but its application is deactivated'. – Puspa Damai, 'The Killing Machine of Exception: Sovereignty, Law, and Play in Agamben's State of Exception', *The New Centennial Review*, 5/3 (2005), 255–76, 256. The conditions of the state of exception would '[produce] a legally unnamable an unclassifiable being', otherwise referred to as 'bare life'. – Agamben, *State of Exception*, 45.

6   Derek Gregory, 'The Black Flag: Guantánamo Bay and the Space of Exception', *Geografiska Annaler: Series B, Human Geography*, 88/4 (2006), <https://www.jstor.org/stable/4621537>, accessed 8 January 2020, 406.

7   Bettina van Hoven and David Sibley, '"Just Duck": The Role of Vision in the Production of Prison Spaces' (2015), <https://journals.sagepub.com/doi/10.1068/d5107>, accessed 8 January 2020.

8   Ben Crewe et al., 'The Emotional Geography of Prison Life'.

Such spatial rendering of social life in this confined environment produces different scripts that oppressive forces use to act on vulnerable bodies.

Conversely, prisoners also develop their own scripts with which they initiate 'free places' that allow limited expressions of agency.[9] In their study of identity transformation in maximum security prisons in the US, Thomas Schmid and Richard Jones observed that 'conscious identity work' can be a strategy used by incarcerated people to counteract the ascribed prison identity.[10] Managing emotional reactions can take different forms, and Abbas Khider's *Die Orangen des Präsidenten* (2011) [The President's Oranges] presents writing on walls as one of them. The semi-autobiographical account of political prisoner Mahdi Muhsin, who unexpectedly finds himself in a maximum security prison in Iraq's Nasiriyah desert, illustrates the effects that the prison space has on the emotional state of its incarcerated people. It also shows how that restrictive spatial relationship brings about resistances to the annihilating function of the carceral complex and yields spaces in which prisoners can appear to each other.[11]

Framing his protagonists' narratives in relation to their social experience of space is a common thread throughout Khider's writing. By turning liminal spaces, like prisons, into stages, Khider's stories shed light on the mechanisms of control over and the struggles of displaced and erased characters. Outlining the ambiguous territory of the in-between space between prisons and the outside world introduces the potential for new meanings, social relations and identities to be visible.[12] His novels provide his

---

9   Erving Goffman's analysis of asylum points to the presence of 'free places' in so-called totalising institutions to highlight the places in which limited movement and expressions are possible. Erving Goffman, *Asylums: Essays on the Social Situation of Mental Patients and Other Inmates* (Garden City/NY: Anchor Books, 1961).

10   Richard Jones and Thomas Schmid, *Doing Time: Prison Experience and Identity Among First-Time Inmates* (Stamford/CT: Jai, 2000).

11   This chapter relies on Hannah Arendt's notion of the 'space of appearance' which describes a state 'where I appear to others as others appear to me, where men exist not merely like other living or inanimate things, but to make their appearance explicitly'. – Hannah Arendt, *The Human Condition*, 2nd edn (Chicago: University of Chicago Press, 1998), 198–9.

12   This chapter refers to Homi Bhabha's notion of 'third space' which describes the realisation of in-between spaces through language in which oppressed

readers with fascinating insights into the equivocal nature of borders in *Der falsche Inder* (2008) [*The Village Indian*, 2013], the vital significance of letters in border zones in *Brief in die Auberginenrepublik* (2013) [Letter to the Aubergine Republic] and the implicit detrimental hierarchies of refugee accommodation centres in Germany in *Ohrfeige* (2016) [*A Slap in the Face*, 2019]. Throughout Khider's novels, the spatial quality of the environment is in dialogue with experiences of borders, captivity, displacement and migration.

Part and parcel of the liminal spaces portrayed in *Die Orangen des Präsidenten* are the prison walls that encapsulate the bodies of political detainees and other members of the lower social strata. References to what appears on and disappears from the walls give witness to interactions between prisoners and wardens, the poor conditions of prison life and the endless cycle of mutual suspicion and inconceivable tortures. Walls serve the novel as a narrative feature that reflects the complexities and ambiguities of prison life. Incarcerated persons memorialise their carceral experiences on prison walls through writing, carving, etching, scratching and chiselling words into the concrete. Walls become the canvases onto which struggles of survival are cast.

Literary accounts like *Die Orangen des Präsidenten* engage in the ambiguities of the penal complex. The narrative trope of inscribed reflections of experience on concrete can elucidate how characters identify their subject positions in relation to prisons' spatial identity.[13] Captivity narratives,

---

individuals can engage socially. – Homi Bhabha, *The Location of Culture* (London/ New York: Routledge, 1994), 55.

13   On earlier writings on walls in prisons, see the Tudor and Stuart inscriptions into the walls at the Tower of London in Brian A. Harrison, *The Tower of London Prisoner Book: A Complete Chronology of the Persons Known to Have Been Detained at Their Majesties' Pleasure, 1100–1941* (London: Trustees of the Royal Armouries, 2004). Wall inscriptions in the carceral complex are elsewhere also referred to as 'prison graffiti'. On the linkage between incarcerated humans to the confining environment, see Eleanor Conlin Casella, 'Enmeshed Inscriptions: Reading the Graffiti of Australia's Convict Past', *Australian Archaeology*, 78/1 (2014), 108–12, <https://doi.org/10.1080/03122417.2014.11682006>, accessed 7 January 2020. On prison wall literature in the People's Republic of China by authors such as Zhang Xianliang and Cong Weixi, see Philip F. Williams and Yenna Wu, *The Great Wall of Confinement: The Chinese Prison Camp through Contemporary Fiction and*

like those from inside the panoptic complex, share descriptions of engraved quotations as narrative features to allude to different experiences and themes that are otherwise not visible.[14] The spatial keepers of individuals' memory, prisons' concrete boundaries record accounts of both endurance and resistance.

This chapter shows how *Die Orangen des Präsidenten* employs a narrative structure that unveils the segmented geography of carceral experiences. Detailed descriptions of the gaze of prison's environment that bereaves its inhabitants of their humanity reflect how the heterogeneous workings of power deconstruct identities and personal histories. Permeated with different 'epigraphs' that embellish the protagonist's narrative onto the very framework that signifies confinement, the novel evinces a layered recollection of futility, madness and ingenuity. *Die Orangen des Präsidenten* presents silenced voices on multiple terrains. Mahdi's account of prison life reveals how he and the characters are shaped by the spatial geography of the carceral complex, how the unique environment manages access to forms of expressions and how in turn graffiti serves as one of the avenues of resistance to being disappeared.

Trauma in *Die Orangen des Präsidenten*

Die Orangen des Präsidenten centres on young protagonist Mahdi Muhsin's first-person account of the conditions in Iraq between the 1970s

---

Reportage (Berkeley/Los Angeles/London: University of California Press, 2004), 154–88.

14   See Esmail Nashif's ethnography of captivity narratives by Palestinian political captives in Israeli prisons in Esmail Nashif, *Palestinian Political Prisoners: Identity and Community* (New York: Routledge, 2008). On the social function of narratives about life in captivity in England during the Reformation, see Ruth Ahnert, 'Writing in the Tower of London during the Reformation, ca. 1530–1558', *Huntington Library Quarterly*, 72/2 (2009), 168–92, <https://www.jstor.org/stable/10.1525/hlq.2009.72.2.168>, accessed 7 January 2020.

and 1990s that result in his imprisonment, displacement and eventual status as a refugee. In fifteen chapters, Mahdi narrates different episodes of his life that delineate the development of his character into a writer. After losing his parents to war and sickness, Mahdi finds himself caught up in a raid by Saddam Hussein's military police who is accusing him of co-conspiracy and membership in the Iraqi Communist Party. Thrown into jail at a time when he was supposed to start his life at university, Mahdi's reality is turned upside down. In response to how prison reality changes his character and life, Mahdi weaves the stories of his life into a tapestry of tales.

The written word plays a crucial role throughout Mahdi's life. He is first introduced to different authors and the beauty of language by his friend and mentor Razaq Mustafa while living with his uncle Jasim in Nasiriyah. Recollecting his engagement with literature from that time provides Mahdi's narrative a space to not just tell his own life story but also those of his friends. As the novel progresses, it becomes evident that these spaced anecdotes construct the posthumous histories of Razaq and family members who died before being able to tell their own biographies. Channelling their histories through Mahdi's narrative reveals a common tradition in contemporary Arabic fiction, which seeks to reconstruct the lost Iraqi identities and histories that have been destroyed by systemic violence and trauma.[15] For example, after escaping from prison, Mahdi receives a letter from Razaq that contains details of the suffering that family and friends endured during this absence. It states the death of his close friend Sami Salman, news that his uncle Jasim was unable to convey to him personally (OdP, 136). There is a certain reluctance among community

---

15   Haytham Bahoora identifies that 'the violent post-2003 national landscape is a constitutive thematic concern of [Iraqi writers' and artists'] artistic production'. Due to a lack of political accountability to the events during and leading up to the crisis, fiction has played a central role in reconstructing 'a history and experience of structural violence'. – Haytham Bahoora, 'Writing the Dismembered Nation: The Aesthetics of Horror in Iraqi Narratives of War', *The Arab Studies Journal*, 23/1 (2015), <https://www.jstor.org/stable/44744904>, accessed 8 January 2020, 184–208, 188.

members to speak of the horrors and, thus, written accounts of that experience become the only point of reference for Mahdi.

Set in italics, these letters are presented in the novel as autonomous voices that accompany and complement Mahdi's narration. Interweaving stories about his own life with the biographies of others is conducive to overcoming the trauma of being erased by oppressive forces. The novel's presentation of these stories spaced throughout the text visualises the diverse connections between characters and places and the impacts of structural violence on humans' lives. This narrative framework produces a nuanced portrayal of everyday life in Iraq in the late twentieth century and rewrites the history of his community, evincing the silenced voices of its members.

Overcoming trauma through what Jones and Schmid have termed 'conscious identity work' is pervasive throughout Mahdi's recollection of torture and surveillance in prison.[16] Part of that is showing how the emotional geography of the carceral complex regulates and suspends the expression of emotions and agency. Crewe et al. explain that prisoners' awareness of institutional control, surveillance and torture influences how and how much of their emotional conditions they present to others.[17] The extended internal monologues through which Mahdi mirrors what he experiences give insight into the way in which the space shapes how he perceives his own identity and his interactions with others.

In prison, reality is under constant scrutiny and distortion. The Kafkaesque tone in Mahdi's voice reflects the ambivalence of that experience. For the sake of political gain and control, the cartography of the prison depicted in *Die Orangen des Präsidenten* seeks to transform and deconstruct the pre-prison identities of incarcerated people. It highlights how 'the determining force of space is not just physical or architectural, but resides in the ways that places carry meanings, harbour and cultivate particular practices and sentiments, are devised for specific activities, and are populated by certain personnel'.[18] That kind of biopolitics produces Mahdi and other incarcerated people as 'legally unnameable […] unclassifiable

---

16   Jones and Schmid, *Doing Time*.
17   Crewe et al., 'The Emotional Geography of Prison Life', 56–74.
18   Ibid., 71.

[beings]' that lack any control or power over their own life and environment.[19] Interactions follow discriminatory scripts with which wardens aim to destabilise prisoners' identities. Mahdi struggles to identify between sincerity and deceit. Even though the wardens acknowledge his innocence, Mahdi stays imprisoned. Their false promise of release upon closing the case of the Communist Resistance group becomes a powerful tool for further enfeebling his will power. Recounting the endless wait, Mahdi states, 'Every day I waited for someone to come and tell me "Get out!" But nobody came' (OdP, 45).[20] Unsure of what to believe anymore, his mind weakens.

Mahdi's thought spirals into a dream sequence that resounds with the intimidating qualities of the space:

> conspicuous creatures grinned nastily at me. Some come through the walls or the floor. They have no faces but black ropes and long fingernails like daggers. One jumps onto me and screams. All of a sudden Ali is there. [...] Everything begins to fade away suddenly [...] All of a sudden the room is gone. Fog rises. I am flying through the air. I am beginning to feel dizzy. I fall onto the floor. [...] Where is Ali now? [...] Someone grabs my arm and yells: 'Get up!' The door opens. [...] It was Ali. [...] 'Did Ali know of your organisation?', asks the grey-haired one. 'No. He had no idea.' [...] Since then I never saw him again (OdP, 27–9).

The torturous constancy of the spatial inscription of power causes Mahdi's mind to tremble and nebulises his thought so that he imagines a conversation with his arrested accomplice Ali. Worried for his safety, Mahdi cries out, but Ali remains out of reach. This dream serves as the first indicator of Mahdi's survival at the expense of Ali's life who is tortured to death after confessing the crime and confirming Mahdi's innocence. The multi-layered structure of this experience bears witness to the boys' friendship and reveals that Ali has agency even if being the reason of Mahdi's incarceration.

Different from other prisoners, Mahdi is redeemed early on in the narrative. As the survivor of this situation, he lives on to tell the stories of the unnamed and forgotten, bringing them back to the surface. Bearing the weight of collective suffering, Mahdi's storytelling can be understood as a

19   Agamben, *State of Exception*, 4–5.
20   All translations in this chapter are the author's unless otherwise noted.

practice of bringing to life what is deemed to die. Eliciting the grotesque, he communicates the collected experiences of torture and violence that have been disembodied from the disappeared by lending his own narrative as a space to capture them again. Giving language to the unspeakable through depicting the afterlives of horror is a gothic literary element that '[has] appeared in Iraqi fiction precisely at the historical moment of Iraq's possible fragmentation as a state [...] to give voice to silenced or buried historical narratives, and to expose the historical genealogies of the present'.[21] The voices of past trauma, although restricted to the memories of those left behind, haunt the present and refuse to be silenced.

Walls as Bearers of Knowledge

Die Orangen des Präsidenten presents a corpus of testimonies embedded in Mahdi's first-person account. The narrative feature of wall graffiti serves as a prominent soundboard against which different carceral voices appear to the protagonist. These additional layers reveal the multiple ways of how the silenced incarcerated people's accounts come to light. Mahdi's discovery of different quotations and narratives of his fellow prisoners on walls alludes to these characters' recalcitrant practice of writing themselves into a space that is designed to dehumanise and make disappear.[22]

---

21   Bahoora, 'Writing the Dismembered Nation', 205.

22   Wall writing is a recurring theme in different literary works that address carceral experiences, displacement and other forms of oppression. See Ananya Jahanara Kabir's evaluation of Grace Nichols in Ananya Jahanara Kabir, 'Diasporas, Literature and Literary Studies' in Kim Knott and Sean McLoughlin, eds., *Diasporas: Concepts, Intersections, Identities* (London: Zed Books, 2010), 145–50. – See also Jaine Chemmachery's analysis of Rudyard Kipling, in whose work 'destabilising voices [...] often appear in the literal margins of Kipling's short stories'. – Jaine Chemmachery, 'Spatial, Temporal and Linguistic Displacement in Kipling's and Maugham's Colonial Short Stories: The Disrupting Power of the "Colonial" in Modern Short Fiction', *Journal of the Short Story in English*, 64 (2015), 47–65, 53. – Assia Djebar also uses epigraphs in *Le Blanc De L'Algerie* as devices to mediate the voices of writers. See Alexandra Gueydan-Turek, ' "Homeland Beyond Homelands": Reinventing Algeria Through A Transnational Literary

Carefully engraved, a range of epigraphs attest to the agony and suffering inflicted on the prisoners' bodies and minds, evincing not only violence but also the space into which the emotional reactions of its victims are cast. The walls hold the reanimated corpses of nightmarish experiences to remind the living of perpetual suffering. For example, when Mahdi describes a period in prison during which he feels the deteriorating force of hunger, he draws attention to an epigraph that was carved into the wall by Dhalal, the head of an alternative counter-movement: 'Hunger could bring the truth of a person to the surface, whether for the rotten smells or aromatic fragrances' (OdP, 50). Desperate for more food, prisoner Abu-Zainb stages a coup against Adnan, the eldest of the cell. For collecting faeces, Adnan received an extra loaf of bread that he shared with his helper Mahdi. After losing his privileges, both men are forced to starve even further until the reign is revoked again. Mahdi describes that for three months, 'our hellish life transformed itself into an even more infernal hell' (OdP, 49).

Die Orangen des Präsidenten embeds the notion of how the carceral complex choreographs social life into Mahdi's personal historiography. Jens Jesser places the work in the 'Lagerroman' genre, explaining that Khider utilises narrative features that are known from works reflecting on the impacts of totalitarian regimes like Fyodor Dostoyevsky's *The House of the Dead*.[23] It begs the question whether and if so, how, it is possible to recover from torture. This is a question to which essayist and Holocaust-survivor Jean Améry famously responded:

Community: Assia Djebar's "Le Blanc De L'Algérie"', *Cincinnati Romance Review* 31 (2011), 85–102. – On prison graffiti in Kuala Lumpur's Pudu Jail see Khairul Azril Ismail, 'Pudu Jail's Graffiti: Aesthetics Beyond the Walls of the Prison Cells', in *Proceedings of ISEA2008: The 14th International Symposium on Electronic Art*, Isea Archives (2008), 248–50, <http://www.isea-archives.org/docs/2008/proceedings/ISEA2008_proceedings.pdf>, accessed 8 January 2020.

23   Jens Jesser, 'Was den Erniedrigten schützt', *Zeit Online* (5 May 2011), <https://www.zeit.de/2011/19/L-B-Khider>, accessed 9 January 2020. – Fyodor Dostoyevsky, *The House of the Dead* (Mineola/NY: Dover, 2004).

> Whoever has succumbed to torture can no longer feel at home in the world. The shame of destruction cannot be erased. Trust in the world, which already collapsed in part at the first blow, but in the end, under torture, fully, will not be regained.[24]

Mahdi's elaborate descriptions of his carceral experiences show the struggles of trying to make sense of prison's peculiarly cold and inhumane environment. He has to draw on the cues that the walls provide. By way of addressing the impact that the physical features of the space have on prisoners' bodies and minds, Mahdi makes legible the space's cartography. The arrangement of epigraphs throughout his narrative show how individual characters rely on the 'free places' on the wall to curate them with their testimonies as a way to work against forgetting their identities and experiences. As Erving Goffman argues, '[e]very total institution can be seen as a kind of dead sea in which little islands of vivid, encapturing activity appear. Such activity can help the individual withstand the psychological stress usually engendered by assaults upon the self'.[25] While the recurring references to the appearance and spatial dimensions of the prison cell and the corridors and interrogation rooms recreate the physical conditions of his captivity in writing, the narrative also embeds wall writing as a reparative practice of coming to terms with and giving testimony to traumatic experiences.

There is an ambivalence to walls as spaces of both disappearance and appearance. Ironically, while prisoners use writing as a subversive tool, wardens employ it as yet another means of psychological abuse. Above Mahdi's cell door, wardens engraved 'salvation lies in honesty' (OdP, 27). Officers use the engraving to encourage prisoners to betray each other. In a terrifying simultaneity, the saying calls to ethical morality and, at the same time, conveys its subversion in the setting of torture. The conflict at hand is weighing out the implications of moral conscience and punishment.

Mahdi's first experience in pretrial detention, in a one-square-metre small cell, introduces another face of the concrete that surrounds him. As

---

24   Jean Amery, *At the Mind's Limits: Contemplations by a Survivor on Auschwitz and Its Realities*, trans. Sidney Rosenfeld and Stella P. Rosenfeld (Bloomington: Indiana University Press, 2009), 40.

25   Goffman, *Asylums*, 68.

a sounding board, these walls reveal the presence of human experiences in this dehumanising setting that haunt the space, wanting to be read. The walls of the cell hold names, dates, quotations and drawings. Inscriptions are each weathered through the strong humidity and dense air. Like 'menacing frescos', Mahdi says the writings convey a threatening notion, yet at the same time are forebearers of reparative action (OdP, 27). The narrative function of such epigraphs reiterates Doreen Massey's understanding of the relationship between space and history. She explains that 'the spatial is integral to the production of history, and thus to the possibility of politics'.[26]

By turning to Massey's understanding of the multiplicity of space-time in this reading, it becomes possible to explore the practice of writing on walls as reinscribing the possibility of speech and action into a space from which it was stripped. The motif of walls can be recognised as the interstitial space that allows the novel's characters to practice and recognise each other's experiences; to become active within and at the same time beyond the enclosing constructions of the prison. Inscribing anecdotes, poems and surah into the materiality of the space alters the voids and raises the question of how the imprisoned characters preserve their memoirs to be seen by others. The work by comparative literature theorist Mireille Rosello becomes useful to locate 'the reparative in [these] narratives'.[27] Reconstituting the physicality and materiality of spaces of torment brings about a productive tension in the novel that reveals how the evolution of the narrator's identity is entangled with his relationship to the space that restricts him. Mahdi's stories respond to the panoptic complex and its disciplinary structures by including how the interrelated topoi of control and punishment stretch into every aspect of prison life and restrict the expression of life and individuality in every configuration of place. In the panoptic system, power works on an array of levels and affects the way prisoners eat, communicate, dream and sleep.

26   Massey, 'Politics and Space/Time', 84.
27   Mireille Rosello, *The Reparative in Narratives: Works of Mourning in Progress* (Liverpool: Liverpool University Press, 2010), 1.

Appearing in Narrative

Khider's insertion of epigraphs as a narrative trope makes the point that, despite all restrictions, prisoners find ways to disrupt the politics of the prison panopticon. In other words, wall inscriptions function as liminal spaces that provide incarcerated people with the opportunity to act and make their mark. Engraved traces of prisoners' experience construct walls into the keepers of their testimonials. Homi Bhabha uses the term 'third space' to describe the location of such a 'site of the witness – the work of witnessing'.[28] Bhabha discusses the act of witnessing as the process that recognises the existence of human beings and their agency. He emphasises that a just recognition of subjectivity demands the presence of a witness that assures others of his existence.

Mahdi's narrative witnesses the ambivalence of the carceral complex's spatial composition. The penal cartography produces innumerable conditions of torture that yield emotional responses from prisoners but for which there is only limited space to express. Embedding them into his own coming-of-age story, Mahdi assumes agency and claims space for the lost stories in his own. *Die Orangen des Präsidenten* proves the significance of storytelling in coming to terms with the horrors of Iraq's unacknowledged past. Mahdi, as the narrator of this tale, carries the delegative duty to record the realities and names of those who were disappeared. He is both embedded in and a witness to the trauma.

The process of creating records of life in the cell includes the prisoners' collective assemblage of historical and religious texts that maps an archive of past and present knowledge (OdP, 61). The inscribed surahs are important reference points for prayer practice. Especially after the death of prayer leader Ahmed, who took a shower too cold (OdP, 85), the graffiti secures the continuance of religious practice even if Ahmed's voice is absent from the space. The continuity of religious practice beyond death signifies the continuity of life. Filling the voids in the walls with Quranic

28　Homi Bhabha, *Our Neighbours, Ourselves: Contemporary Reflections on Survival* (Berlin: De Gruyter, 2011), 6.

phrases maps places that enable the enfeebled prisoners the opportunity to express their humanity by way of creating a space for a relation with God. That kind of engagement reroutes the intended emotional geography of the prison space and creates places for the expression of agency. At the same time, the walls become a memorial site for lost knowledge bearers.

Recognising the existence of history in this space of torment is crucial for understanding the protagonist and his fellow incarcerated people as survivors and not just victims. This argument is in line with Bhabha's notion that 'speech and action in the realm of alterity might sound irredeemably abstract but it is a crucial site of ethical and equitable recognition'.[29] Surrounded by the totalitarian devices of domination, writing for Mahdi provides an opportunity to act. As Hannah Arendt explains, the dwellings of horror and the institutions of totalitarianism have at their core the interest to make those who were merely apparent at first instance disappear.[30] The narrative function of writing and reading signifies an act of 'appearing'. Arendt utilises this concept to argue that something is only then considered recognisable when it appears to all, and through this act of appearing comes into being. Even the slightest and most silent way of resistance can, according to Arendt, be understood as an act of exerting power because power is not stable or measurable, but instead a potential that 'springs up between men when they act together and vanishes in the moment they disperse'.[31] It is through power that a space of appearance remains in existence between 'acting and speaking' humans.[32] Arendt notes that 'the *polis* [...] is the organization of the people as it arises out of acting and speaking together, and its true spaces lie between people living together for this purpose, no matter where they happen to be'.[33] *Die Orangen des Präsidenten* presents imprisoned characters who map their stories on the walls. Interwoven in Mahdi's narrative, they come to light and emerge as a polis and resist their disappearance.

29   Bhabha, *Our Neighbours, Ourselves*, 11.
30   Hannah Arendt, *The Origins of Totalitarianism* (Cleveland/NY: Meridian Books, 1958), 442.
31   Arendt, *The Human Condition*, 200.
32   Ibid.
33   Ibid., 198 (emphasis in original).

Reparative Speech of Survivors

The reparative function of this interconnected narrative is most visible in chapter nine. Central to this chapter are the suicides by Ahmed and another cell mate Shruq Fridon. Accompanying Mahdi's descriptions of each of these characters is his emphasis on their unique contributions to the communities inside and outside the prison. Mahdi points out how Ahmed's beautiful singing voice leads the cell community to identify him as the knowledge bearer of the Quran. Ahmed's artful enunciation of surahs filled the cell with life that could only be reconstructed through the writing on the walls after his passing. Shruq, on the other hand, was a skilled poet. He used writing as a way of coming to terms with the turbulences of his personal history. As a Kurd, he underwent excessive beatings and torture that he was only able to take for three months. In an effort to write his memory to live beyond his body, Shruq carved a lengthy poem entitled 'The Life of Lanterns', a devotional text to resistance, into the wall above the cell door (OdP, 90). Mahdi encounters it as he learns of his death and recovers Shruq's account to situate it in the novel's narrative framework:

> A wall like the southern forests,
> like the loneliness of a city after the war,
> like a long row of mountains made from knife-sharp stone.
> Excuse me, how was the wall, my son?
> Was it wet language, wet carpet,
> Moisture of life that is hanging from the ceiling fan?
> Excuse me, wet was the heart from water
> of the ghosts.
> Wet was the world [...]
> What a life that was that on the corner
> Of the prison cell
> And hung onto the floor? (OdP, 90–1)

Speaking of the walls that are as foreign and thick as the impenetrable southern Iraqi forests, Shruq illustrates the hopelessness that he experiences, and the solitude that cuts like a knife into his existence. The wetness of the walls functions as a metaphor for the underground conditions and sparse quality of life, which is decimated even more by the wardens, the 'ghosts', who steal the remaining strength from his heart. Shruq feels swallowed by those walls and the water that he describes running down on them. The inescapable suffocation that the threat of moisture poses drowns the voices captured on the wet concrete, the bodies hanging from it and his entire world. Eventually, even Shruq's inscription will weather away. A life in this situation is one not worth living for him, but one worthy of reflection.

In this intertextual encounter with Shruq's past, Mahdi learns more about Shruq, who was a Kurdish rebel. Shruq's poem is addressed to his son whom he lost during his fights against the Baathists on the Iranian-Iraqi border. He describes his suffering and the torments his body and soul endured. Shruq's poem also speaks to an audience outside the walls within which he chose to end his life. His words ask for forgiveness for his betrayal of his family and people. With regard to the space within which this narrative is conceptualised, Shruq's writing can be read both as an act of trying to redeem himself as well as an act of resistance. He is leaving an imprint of his soul as a testimony of his suffering on the cold surfaces that restrict his freedom. While his suicide can be understood as a loss of the power of his words, Shruq's words traverse the boundaries of the walls into Mahdi's re-narration by citing it more seamlessly in the larger narrative. Shruq's voice impacts Mahdi, who memorises the poem and recites it in his own survivor testimony after the prison's liberation by Iraqi civilians.

As Mahdi embeds different testimonials in the narrative framework of his own story, he bridges the gap between the human and deceptive characteristics of the individuals in his cell, whose inner selves remain otherwise hidden. Although interpersonal spaces and notions of collectivity are continuously disrupted by the workings of the prison panopticon, the constructed liminal communicative spheres that epigraphs represent are not devoid of the possibility of politics. Instead, they refer to a space of possibility, a space that lies between individuals and in which recognition is practiced to acknowledge the experiences of the oppressed. The markings on the walls provoke, as Bhabha puts it, 'an interstitial moment produced through the negotiation of contradiction and ambivalence'.[34] In Rosello's terms, this form of intertextual narrative works within Mahdi's reparative approach to recover his own voice so it can bring to light the lost ones around him. Jean-Pierre Boulé reflects on Rosello, stating that in reparative reading 'one ultimate form of silence is ironically replaced by words that will scrutinize and try to come to terms with other forms of narrativized silences'.[35] According to Rosello, 'the reparative is an energy, a process, a specific set of narrative choices that propose to offer a conscious or unconscious strategy to a double process of recapturing and recovering'.[36] The reproduction of the characters and the physicality that shapes Mahdi's accounts contribute to a process of identifying and coming to terms with the events and shape this literary narrative to articulate what can otherwise not be put into words.

Conclusion

As this analysis has shown, Khider's work can be situated among other fiction and semi-autobiographical accounts that use liminal spaces as settings to represent prisoners and others oppressed not as victims, but as survivors of the panopticon of horror and torture. Those that live on carry the burden of having to do the reparative work of 'narrating the silenced, repressed, and untold experiences of Iraqis'.[37] Mahdi's narrative demonstrates the insurgent impacts of the physical space of the prison complex on expressions of agency by the political prisoners. The gradual deterioration of the mind, which Khider makes visible in his writing, allows readers a glimpse at the conditions under which solidarity, collectivity and spirit are passed on in this community through sharing experiences in writing.

34   Bhabha, *Our Neighbours, Ourselves*, 6.
35   Jean-Pierre Boulé, 'Writing Selves as Mourning and *Vita Nova*: Abdellah Taïa's *Un Pays Pour Mourir*', *Contemporary French Civilization*, 41/1 (2016), 25–47, 34.
36   Rosello, *The Reparative in Narratives*, 22.
37   Bahoora, 'Writing the Dismembered Nation', 198.

While the walls restrict the everyday actions of the prisoners, they echo the voices, personalities and stories of those incarcerated. The imprisoned men pass their time in conversation, prayer and silence. In movements, their bodies occupy the cold and devastating space of the cell. Inscriptions on the walls reiterate their actions. Metaphors, surahs and descriptions duplicate the torment that their bodies endure. In congruence, the restricted and free spaces compose the complex emotional geography of the Nasiriyah prison. Crewe et al. argue that '[recognizing] a multitude of normative and emotional domains [...] could describe the transitional moments [of the penal experience] from one to another' and expressions of selfhood and existence become momentarily possible.[38] Knowing that one is still alive is crucial for staying alive in a space whose structures work to deconstruct and destroy bodies and humanity. The prisoners have been stripped naked of their dignity, left to rot in a cell too small to hold their bodies. Their collective suffering is all that connects their randomly assembled community. The system of constant and penetrating torture and fear indoctrinates a lack of human value into them. Storytelling, then, becomes the only occupation through which the men reassure themselves of their own humanity. Mahdi's narrative from the dark side of the world is infused by the memoirs of those living with him in captivity and of those whose bodies face ultimate destruction. Providing these memoirs with a space of their own in his personal account elevates their significance for Mahdi's own journey. The inscription of these statements into his own memoir, therefore, signifies how those words live on, far beyond the walls that are meant to confine them.

38   Crewe et al., 'The Emotional Geography of Prison Life', 71.

SABINE ZIMMERMANN

Refuge and Refuse: Waste Imagery in Abbas Khider's *Die Orangen des Präsidenten* and *Ohrfeige*

The many direct references to waste in Khider's texts expose dehuman-ising political structures, thus giving a voice to the marginalised: inno-cent detainees held in dictatorial systems, and powerless migrants such as asylum seekers and refugees whom Zygmunt Bauman cynically refers to as 'that human waste of distant parts of the globe unloaded into our own backyard'.[1] The use of waste imagery in Khider's texts is worth ex-ploring; it is through this medium that Khider reiterates the questions posed by Judith Butler, namely 'Who counts as human?' and 'Whose lives count as lives?'[2] This essay demonstrates how Khider, with his 'un-pretentious and succinct style that touches on the absurd and the gro-tesque, thereby lending a bizarre tone to serious content', employs waste imagery in order to expose how power relations in various political sys-tems denigrate others and turn them into 'trash'.[3] My analysis aims to show that Khider's waste imagery provides an effective tool for enabling the 'politics of literature', which Jacques Rancière suggests 'makes vis-ible what was invisible; it makes audible as speaking beings those who were previously heard only as noisy animals'.[4]

1 Zygmunt Bauman, *Wasted Lives: Modernity and Its Outcasts* (Cambridge/ Malden: Polity Press, 2004), 56.

2 Judith Butler, *Precarious Life: The Powers of Mourning and Violence* (London/ New York: Verso, 2004), 20.

3 'Sprache, die unprätentiös und lakonisch wirkt, immer wieder aber auch das Absurde und die Groteske streift und damit dem ernsten Inhalt eine skurril-komische Note zu verleihen vermag.' – Michael Hofmann and Julia-Karin Patrut, *Einführung in die interkulturelle Literatur* (Darmstadt: WBG, 2015), 82.

4 Jacques Rancière, *The Politics of Literature* (Cambridge/Malden: Polity, 2011), 4.

This study of Khider's waste imagery is based on his *Die Orangen des Präsidenten* (2011) [The President's Oranges][5] and *Ohrfeige* (2016) [*A Slap in the Face*, 2019]. *Die Orangen des Präsidenten* is a literary meditation on life in Iraq during the 1980s and early 1990s; it has been praised by critics for its 'miraculously economical narrative style' that effectively portrays life in Iraq during that time.[6] *Ohrfeige*, on the other hand, skilfully narrates 'an emotional catastrophe' experienced by an Iraqi asylum seeker who is able to reach a Western democracy.[7] Characteristic for Khider's writing is that it does 'interact aesthetically with German and European asylum and migration law', thereby treating migration with the 'aesthetic and political complexity it deserves'.[8] Khider manages to do justice to the complexity of migration with his relatively short but powerful works that are related to his own life's experiences. As a survivor of imprisonment in a dictatorial system and as an asylum seeker who faced the cold-hearted bureaucratic machinery in a Western liberal democracy, Khider has developed a distinctive narrative style which bluntly exposes faults in interlinked systems and power relations.[9] I will explain a key feature of waste before discussing

5   All translations from both works are my own unless otherwise noted.

6   Meike Fessmann, 'Lachen unter der Folter', *Süddeutsche Zeitung* (19 April 2011).

7   Katharina Granzin, 'Abbas Khider *Ohrfeige*: Der Mensch im Durchgangsland', *Frankfurter Rundschau* (5 February 2016). – Surprisingly Fessmann, who praised *Die Orangen des Präsidenten*, argues that *Ohrfeige*'s success is linked mainly to its timely publication: 'Weder Autor noch Verlag konnten die Ereignisse vorhersehen. Verständlich, dass sie den aktuellen Stoff schnell auf den Markt werfen wollten' [Neither the author nor publisher could have foreseen these events. Of course, they wished to quickly throw this timely material onto the market]. – Meike Fessmann, 'Die Blutegel des Unglücks', *Süddeutsche Zeitung* (10 February 2016). – Critic Ijoma Mangold (2016) even labels Khider as a 'speed-writer' with 'calculating motives'. – Ijoma Mangold, 'Ein guter Burger', *Zeit Online* (18 February 2016), <http://www.zeit.de/2016/06/ohrfeige-abbas-khider>, accessed 17 September 2018. – In contrast, critic Fatma Aydemir praises *Ohrfeige* as it resonates with readers because it 'directly weighs on their conscience'. – Fatma Aydemir, 'Eine Sachbearbeiterin wird gefesselt', *TAZ* (29 January 2016).

8   Deniz Göktürk and David Gramling, 'Forum: Migration Studies', *The German Quarterly* 90/2 (2017), 217–9, 218.

9   Cf. Fessmann, Meike, 'Die Freiheit, sein Leben noch einmal zu erzählen: Laudatio auf Abbas Khider', *Sinn und Form*, 66/4 (2014), 705–11, 708.

waste creation in *Die Orangen des Präsidenten*'s portrayal of various interlinked systems and ill-conceived solutions that actually perpetuate waste.
Subsequently, I will present an analysis of *Ohrfeige*'s illustration of the
motifs of *redundancy* and *disposability* associated with waste, and how
these are applied to humans.

Waste and Malleability

Waste is typically not an isolated occurrence but the by-product of a systematic ordering and classification of any matter, be it biological, material
or informational.[10] We are faced with the concept of waste through managing it daily in our personal, communal and societal lives.[11] Societies produce trash, not only of things but also of people. Theorist John Knechtel
elaborates as follows: 'The concept of trash is the Midas touch inverted,
and its malleability allows it to convert any thing or any one into garbage.
People themselves [...] can be made into trash.'[12] A key feature of trash
then is its *malleability*, the capability of being controlled or shaped by
outside forces. According to philosopher Richard Rorty, 'extraordinary
malleability' is also a key attribute of human action. He argues: 'We
have come to see that the only lesson of either history or anthropology
is our extraordinary malleability.' Since there are many 'ways of excluding
[others] from true humanity', regardless of where one lives, Rorty sees inhumane tendencies in all of us 'paradigmatic humans'.[13] We are indeed
malleable beings. This characteristic allows us to adapt to our environment and to be creative when transforming it. We are in essence constantly

10   Gay Hawkins, *The Ethics of Waste: How We Relate to Rubbish* (Lanham: Rowman
      & Littlefield, 2006).
11   Mary Douglas, *Purity and Danger: An Analysis of the Concepts of Pollution and
      Taboo* (New York: Routledge, 2002).
12   John Knechtel, ed., *TRASH* (Cambridge, MA: MIT Press, 2007), 8.
13   Richard Rorty, 'Human Rights, Rationality, and Sentimentality' in Christopher
      Voparil and Richard Bernstein, eds., *The Rorty Reader* (Hoboken, NJ: Wiley-
      Blackwell, 2010), 351–65, 352–3.

being shaped while providing shape at the same time. However, due to inhumane tendencies in all of us, the outcomes of these provisions are often problematic, leading to the marginalisation of others, and even worse, at times to physical violence towards some.

Interlinked Systems and Waste Creation

Rorty's insight can be connected to the fate of Mahdi Hamama, the protagonist in *Die Orangen des Präsidenten*. Mahdi is an ordinary Iraqi adolescent whose life unravels as he is facing various interlinked systems. When potent outside forces intervene in Iraq, the sheltered and rather spoiled boy loses his father, a soldier who dies in the Iran-Iraq war in the early 1980s (OdP, 36). Khider laconically points out that various geopolitical forces have influenced this war which was more than just a local conflict: 'Also führte der Irak Krieg gegen den Iran, aber im Grunde war es der Krieg der halben Welt gegen den Iran. Die Iraker schickten Soldaten an die Front, die Unterstützer Geld, Waffen und Autos' [Therefore, Iraq went to war against Iran, but this was actually a war of half the world against Iran. The Iraqis sent soldiers to the front, while the supporters sent money, weapons and cars] (OdP, 36). Geopolitical forces contributed to the outbreak of a war that is wasting the life of Mahdi's father and many others, while severely impacting the living conditions of all survivors.

Beyond the direct deprivations caused by the war, Mahdi falls victim to the ruthless politics of a totalitarian regime, a complex interlinked system that disregards human rights. The text illustrates the deplorable state of human rights in Iraq during the years of Saddam Hussein, whose personality cult and authoritarianism, according to political scientist David Malone, was 'extreme even by Middle Eastern standards'.[14] Since Europe has its own list of brutal dictators, Malone's assertion displays a rather Orientalising

---

14   David Malone, *The International Struggle Over Iraq: Politics in the UN Security Council 1980–2005* (Oxford: Oxford University Press, 2006), 5.

take. At any rate, on their last day of high school, Mahdi and his friend Ali are arrested by the secret police and kept without trial as political prisoners under Hussein's dictatorial system (OdP, 17). Both are accused of being 'communists' (OdP, 43), which Mahdi finds difficult to understand, since he is not even aware of the existence of such a political movement. The guards treat their political prisoners like waste by trampling on their backs while referring to themselves as 'Wölfe' [wolves] and to the prisoners as 'Schafe' [sheep] and 'Würmer' [worms] (OdP, 72–3). Ali soon dies from the effects of torture, whereas Mahdi survives the abuses but is not freed from his underground cell until two years later when Saddam's regime is overthrown (OdP, 109). Khider's illustrations of the cramped underground cells in the Nasrijah desert, lacking proper sanitation systems and forcing over twenty inmates to sleep in one tiny room (OdP 41; 57), should not be viewed as an exaggeration. The blunt description of this atrocious locale that is also infested with bedbugs, incessantly torturing the detained men, serves as an indirect appeal to human rights. Such appeals may be fuelled by what sociologist and philosopher Jürgen Habermas calls 'the outrage of the humiliated at the violation of their human dignity'.[15] In Iraq's façade democracy during this time, human rights covenants officially existed but were ignored. Abuses of political prisoners and dissenters are routinely criticised by the UN. However, Khider's vivid accounts of the ongoing acts of torture and of the appalling space where too many people are kept as prisoners indirectly question the effectiveness of such official rhetoric. Despite human rights initiatives that have numerous supporters, albeit mostly at the rhetorical level, countless powerless detainees remain 'invisible', as portrayed by protagonist Mahdi and his friend Ali. An international community that stands by and only changes the volume of its human rights rhetoric from time to time is completely ineffective in the dismantling of such an interlinked system.

Die Orangen des Präsidenten realistically renders an authoritarian system as a powerful complex, constituted by many technical and social

15 Jürgen Habermas, 'The Concept of Human Dignity and the Realistic Utopia of Human Rights', in Claudio Corradetti, ed., *Philosophical Dimensions of Human Rights: Some Contemporary Views* (2012), 63–79, 65.

interlinkages including institutions, such as underground prisons, and related occupations, like agents of the secret police and prison guards. The underground cells where Mahdi is kept as a political prisoner bear a strong resemblance to a concentration camp, a system which philosopher Giorgio Agamben labels as 'the most absolute biopolitical space ever to have been realized, in which power confronts nothing but pure life, without any mediation'.[16] What Agamben means by this is that in such a space, even basic life functions are structured by naked power. Agamben's view is illustrated by *Die Orangen des Präsidenten*, as Khider emphasises the direct and humiliating effects of biopolitics on a detained and tortured body. For example, when tortured with electroshocks for the first time, Mahdi wets his pants: 'Ohne es zu wollen, pinkelte ich in die Hose' [I could not help it, but I had to wet my pants] (OdP, 24). As time passes, even his body's natural waste production in the form of passing stool is attempting to adapt to the effects of torture and insufficient nutrition; however, the passing of bodily waste becomes more and more painful for him (OdP, 50).

The image of the impacted bodily waste production emphasises that on the cursor of biopolitics, an authoritarian political system ensures that its detainees steadily move away from being 'kept alive' towards 'letting them die'. Mahdi is unable to remove himself physically from this space where he encounters such extreme biopolitics. Unlike the doves which he raised as a teenager, he cannot simply fly away. The only time Mahdi rises above his bodily pain is the instance when he breaks into an 'uncontrollable type of laughter' while he is beaten by the short guard who reminds him of comedian Charlie Chaplin. This laughter lets Mahdi briefly forget his pain, fears and desperation (OdP, 6) and is thus a symbol of hope, indicating that despite having to endure extreme biopolitics in this system, the self instinctively attempts to survive. The outbreak of laughter is illustrative of the human body as the turning point between a person's interiority and exteriority.[17] In short, the laughter is the symbol for human experience,

16   Giorgio Agamben, *Homo Sacer: Sovereign Power and Bare Life*, trans. Daniel Heller-Roazen (Stanford: Stanford University Press, 1998), 110.
17   All human experience is influenced by 'a lived or subjective body and as a living or objective body', according to psychiatrist and philosopher Thomas Fuchs (2018: *v*). – Thomas Fuchs, *Ecology of the Brain* (Oxford: Oxford University Press,

pointing to reflection and consciousness which are important contributing factors to human malleability.

At various instances during his imprisonment, Mahdi's conscience reacts by conceiving fantasies of revenge against the guards and against Saddam Hussein himself (OdP, 71). After the regime's fall, he actually resists a strong desire to beat one of the guards when a concrete opportunity arises: 'Doch etwas in meinem Inneren befahl mir, es nicht zu tun' [Yet something inside of me commanded that I did not do it] (OdP, 137). The innocent ex-detainee's decision against violent revenge is based on a complex process driven by human reflection, namely that 'chance' contributed a great deal to the young policeman's situation in life: 'Dieser junge Polizist ist genauso zufällig in seine Position und Situation hineingeraten, wie ich ins Gefängnis geworfen wurde. Es ist nur ein Zufall, wohin wir im Leben geraten' [This young policeman has come into his position and situation by chance, just as I got thrown into prison. Chance determines where we end up in life] (OdP, 138). While chance may determine that one has to live *in* a particular setting, *Die Orangen des Präsidenten* suggests, by describing Mahdi's internal struggles, that reflective deliberation decidedly impacts how one lives *through* a situation. If Mahdi had taken revenge on the young former guard, the cycle of wasting lives through ongoing marginalisation would have continued.

Die Orangen des Präsidenten includes another level of complexity regarding human reflection. For example, when a guard named Salim provides an inmate with an additional bread ration and even an egg, this guard is beaten by his colleagues (OdP, 105). Obviously, the guard named Salim wishes to break the inhumane prison rules, but he is subsequently punished by other individuals with agency in this authoritarian system. This situation underscores how systems are not in fact faceless. In contrast to Salim, another guard named Sufian makes apologetic remarks to the prisoners as soon as the Allied Forces are on their march towards Bagdad: 'Aber ich schäme mich. [...] Ich will sagen, wir sind, ich meine wir Wärter, nur kleine Beamte' [But I am ashamed. [...] I want to say, I mean, us guards,

---

2018). Fuchs further clarifies that human experiencing is brought about by the tacit functioning of the body and conscious attention at the same time (281).

we are only lowly civil servants] (OdP, 105). Sufian's apology is not sincere but driven by fear of punishment from the Allied Forces. This fake apology indicates, as author Ilija Trojanow rightly observes, that '[s]elbst in einer Diktatur sind Machtverhältnisse brüchiger als man meint' [even in a dictatorial system, power relations are more fragile than one presumes].[18] Because of the fragility of such power relations, Khider's writing highlights that human reflection, followed by concrete action, could actually change the balances of power.

Flawed Solutions and Perpetuation of Waste Creation

Human malleability implies a resourcefulness that may change an environment for the better. However, such creativity may not lead to betterment but instead to waste creation. *Die Orangen des Präsidenten* connects two related grounds where waste is created despite good intentions: first, with the inclusion of a small, yet significant detail concerning plastic cutlery sets that will inevitably go to waste, the novel problematises the adverse effects of humanitarian interventions on those who are theoretically being aided. Second, with Mahdi being confined to a refugee camp, the text exposes a significant flaw of the global refugee system, which political scientist Alexander Betts and economist Paul Collier elaborate on in detail, calling for a 'more effective refugee system, fit for purpose in the twenty-first century'.[19]

The seemingly minor detail of sturdy but useless plastic cutlery sets that are handed to civilians who are attempting to survive a bombing raid challenges the stereotypical provision of humanitarian interventions. When Mahdi and other civilians march towards the border between Iraq and Kuwait, they encounter soldiers of the Allied Forces who are advancing in

18   Ilija Trojanow, 'Wie lange reißt ein Mensch sich am Riemen? Laudatio auf Abbas Khider', *Frankfurter Allgemeine Zeitung* (18 March 2017), 18.
19   Alexander Betts and Paul Collier, *Refuge: Rethinking Refugee Policy in a Changing World* (Oxford: Oxford University Press, 2017), xiii.

tanks. The soldiers, wearing headphones and listening to music, only briefly stop their vehicles but do not engage in conversation with the fleeing Iraqis (OdP, 149). The distraught Iraqi civilians are shouting out for help, yet in response, the soldiers simply throw small aid bags filled with 'bread, sausage, chocolates, matches, chewing gum, plastic cutlery sets and a handkerchief' (OdP, 149). The inclusion of these plastic cutlery sets in the humanitarian aid bags is peculiar, given that all edibles in these bags could very easily be consumed without cutlery. The non-degradable plastic cutlery sets undoubtedly end up as permanent litter in the Iraqi landscape, revealing an 'impressive thing' about most trash – 'how well made it is'.[20] Thus, Khider's writing not only questions the conception, the timing and scope of such interventions but also their long-term effects. According to anthropologist Liisa Malkki, humanitarian interventions in essence 'tend to silence refugees'.[21] Malkki's chief concern is that the refugee is not expected to have a voice. She contends that the refugee is 'commonly constituted as a figure who is thought to speak to us in a particular way: wordlessly'.[22] Khider's description of the Allied Forces soldiers wearing headphones and refusing to talk to the Iraqi civilians, while other segments of the same forces are carrying out the bombing of Iraqi cities, effectively illustrates Malkki's concerns (OdP, 153). The soldiers' refusal to engage in dialogue as well as the senseless inclusion of the plastic cutlery sets in these aid bags is symbolic of how once dominant colonial powers still contribute to waste generation in faraway locales.[23]

---

20 Barry Allen, 'The Ethical Artefact: On Junk', in Knechtel, ed., *TRASH*, 198.

21 Liisa Malkki, 'Speechless Emissaries: Refugees, Humanitarianism, and Dehistoricization', *Cultural Anthropology* 11/3 (1996), 377–404, 378. Malkki does not wish 'to dismiss humanitarian interventions as useless'. However, she is critical of the 'substantially standardized way of talking about and handling "refugee problems" among national governments, relief and refugee agencies'. Ibid., 379, 386.

22 Ibid., 390.

23 Philosopher Bernhard Waldenfels similarly points to the effects of actions by former colonial powers which are destroying local infrastructures and blocking developments, while their own weapons exports have contributed to dire situations in entire continents. – Bernhard Waldenfels, 'Flüchtlinge als Gäste in Not', *Deutsche Zeitschrift für Philosophie*, 64/1 (2017), 89–105, 104.

Underscoring the image of refugees being viewed as 'residual waste' that must be quarantined in a faraway location, Khider intentionally does not invent a 'dream country' willing to offer Mahdi resettlement. The novel emphasises how becoming a refugee in a territorially bounded nation-state system leaves a person in a very vulnerable legal state. To that regard, political scientist Seyla Benhabib describes the difficulty that individuals within 'the state-centric international order' encounter when crossing borders and trying to receive recognition as a member by another polity.[24] Without legal status, recognition in a state-centric system is impossible. Not surprisingly, recognition is denied to Mahdi as he transitions from the category of an *internally displaced person* to that of a *refugee* as soon as he crosses the border from Iraq into Kuwait. Mahdi cannot simply demand resettlement from any of the Western liberal democracies. In fact, as Betts and Collier point out, 'less than 1 per cent of the world's refugees will be lucky enough to get that lottery ticket'.[25] Thus, Mahdi's only option is to wait in the Kuwaiti camp: 'Ich zähle Sandkörner, bis mir vielleicht irgendein Traumland Asyl gewährt. Wann das sein wird? Ich habe keine Ahnung, aber der Sand wird mir nicht ausgehen. Es gibt Tausende hier, die mit mir darauf warten' [I am counting grains of sand until maybe some dream country will grant asylum to me. When might that be? I have no idea, but there is definitely enough sand. There are thousands here with me; all are waiting for the same] (OdP, 8). The current international refugee system relies on camps, but a camp clearly does not constitute a political community willing and able to offer a future to those who have reached it. As philosopher Hannah Arendt warns, without a 'community willing and able to guarantee any rights whatsoever', a person is 'deprived, not of the right to freedom, but of the right to action'.[26] Political scientist Josef Koudelka accentuates Arendt's

---

24 Seyla Benhabib, *The Rights of Others: Aliens, Residents, and Citizens* (Cambridge: Cambridge University Press, 2004), 55. Benhabib clarifies that '[…] in a 'state-centric' international order, one's legal status is dependent upon protection by the highest authority that controls the territory upon which one resides and issues papers to which one is entitled' (ibid.).

25 Betts and Collier, *Refuge*, 8.

26 Hannah Arendt, *The Origins of Totalitarianism* (London/New York: Harcourt, 1973), 296–7.

view by explaining that international agreements 'state that refugees have the right to seek and enjoy asylum, but they do not impose a correlative obligation upon the states. [...] There is no effective enforcement which could guarantee protection'.[27] *Die Orangen des Präsidenten* underscores these views because the final scene presents Mahdi as a refugee without access to legal recognition, which makes him not much better off than the political prisoner he was before.

Of course, there are differing views concerning this summation. For example, Moritz Schramm reads *Die Orangen des Präsidenten* differently concerning the legal recognition for refugees.[28] Schramm analyses in particular the two instances when an orange is given to Mahdi as a gift (the first time, he receives an orange while in prison, and the second time while he is fleeing to Kuwait) and concludes that the second orange given by an Allied Forces soldier symbolically connects Mahdi's identity as a refugee with his prior identity as a prisoner. Schramm contends that neither a detainee nor a refugee has a chance at self-determination, but he argues that 'being a refugee means that one is not completely without legal recognition'.[29] Perhaps the tone and setting of *Die Orangen des Präsidenten*'s beginning and ending support my less optimistic summation: since those housed in a camp cannot make demands on any nation-state to hear their claims for asylum, guaranteed legal recognition remains out of their reach. Anthropologist Michel Agier holds a similar view regarding legal recognition for those who manage to reach a camp, since he argues that a camp is a location that puts a person in the group of the 'victims and guilty, vulnerable and undesirable – all incompatible with those of the subject and citizen'.[30]

---

27   Josef Koudelka, 'The Refugee Regime and Its Weaknesses: Prospects for Human Rights and Kant's Ethic', *Human Affairs*, 26 (2016), 356–70, 360.

28   Moritz Schramm, 'Experimentelle Erkundungen: Überlegungen zum Verhältnis von Anerkennungstheorie und Literaturwissenschaft am Beispiel von Abbas Khiders Roman *Die Orangen des Präsidenten*', in Martin Baisch, ed., *Anerkennung und die Möglichkeiten der Gabe* (Frankfurt a. M.: Peter Lang, 2017), 177–95, 180, 186.

29   Ibid., 186.

30   Michel Agier, *Managing the Undesirables: Refugee Camps and Humanitarian Government* (Cambridge/Malden: Polity Press, 2011), 215.

Similarly, in reference to Agier, Bauman more sharply reiterates that camps are in essence places to store 'wasted humans'. Bauman writes: 'Camps will no longer be used to keep vulnerable refugees alive, but rather to park and guard all kinds of undesirable populations.'[31]

In *Die Orangen des Präsidenten*, Mahdi becomes the personification of political dirt. First, the text skilfully employs waste rhetoric to highlight human rights abuses suffered by countless invisible detainees held by totalitarian regimes. Second, based on a clear reference to avoidable waste in the form of useless plastic cutlery sets, the text is urging a review of humanitarian missions for internally displaced persons. And third, with the imagery of Mahdi 'counting grains of sand', Khider points to the chronic disorder that characterises the global refugee system. The lack of resettlement options available to Mahdi is illustrative of the situations which many refugees today are forced to endure, since waiting endlessly in camps does not represent a 'normal form' of life. Similarly, in *Ohrfeige*, Khider employs references to *waste*, illustrating how marginalised individuals are declared 'redundant' which forces them to live in a state of limbo and inaction, even if they physically manage to reach a Western liberal democracy.

Redundancy of Waste: *Ohrfeige*

Waste is redundant matter that needs to be disposed of intermittently. 'Redundant humans', too, are removed akin to disposables. Bauman portrays their disposal process as follows:

> The others do not need you; they can do as well, and better, without you. There is no self-evident reason for your being around and no obvious justification for your claim to the right to stay around. To be declared redundant means to have been disposed of *because of being disposable* – just like the empty and non-refundable plastic bottle

---

31   Zygmunt Bauman, *Strangers at Our Door* (Cambridge/Malden: Polity Press, 2016), 90.

or once-used syringe, an unattractive commodity with no buyers, or a substandard or stained product without use thrown off the assembly line by the quality inspectors.[32]

Ohrfeige's protagonist, Iraqi asylum seeker Karim Mensy, is the embodiment of redundancy. Karim leaves his birth country around the year 2000 (OF, 39), secretly hoping to undergo an operation abroad to correct his severe gynecomastia (enlargement of male breast tissue). Ashamed of his body's shape since his teenage years (OF, 78), Karim even considered suicide as an adolescent (OF, 91), yet managed to keep this bodily disfigurement a secret even from his family. Already viewing his own body's shape as abnormal, Karim experiences that in Germany, his presence is viewed as 'unwanted'. Karim's sentiments soon resemble those of other refugees who have taken migratory routes towards Europe in the fall of 2015. Author Navid Kermani, who has written extensively about refugees arriving in Germany, summarises their feelings as the 'hopes and fears, the shame and anxiousness to please, and also the depression or anger when, even if they reach their destination, they find no future there'.[33] Similarly, Karim finds out that there is no future for him in Germany.

Shortly before his ordered deportation, Karim fantasises about tying up his caseworker, Frau Schulz, then slapping her in the face, and forcing her to listen to his story: 'Heute bin ich mit der Absicht zu Ihnen gekommen, mich einfach mal mit Ihnen von Mensch zu Mensch in aller Ruhe zu unterhalten. Worüber? So genau weiß ich das selbst nicht' [Today I have come to you in order to talk, face to face, without haste. About what? I really do not quite know] (OF, 12–3). Karim's fantasy of this dialogue illustrates that humans want to attain meaningfulness, which they may, according to Arendt, 'only because they can talk with and make sense to each other and to themselves'.[34] Through telling his story, or at least imagining that he is telling it to this interlocutor who never wanted to listen to him, Karim

32   Bauman, *Wasted Lives*, 12.

33   Navid Kermani, *Upheaval: The Refugee Trek through Europe* (Cambridge/ Malden: Polity, 2017), 78.

34   Hannah Arendt, *The Human Condition* (Chicago: University of Chicago Press, 1998), 4.

retraces the various steps that characterise the German nation-state's final application of the label 'redundant' to his presence in Germany.

The motif of *redundancy* is illustrated in *Ohrfeige* by referring to bodily waste in the form of vomiting. When initially held in a detention cell in Bavaria, Karim is stripped of his clothes and has to endure the penetration of his anal body cavity (OF, 44–5). His body reacts soon after: 'Dreimal kotzte ich in die Toilettenschüssel, obwohl ich seit einer Ewigkeit nichts mehr gegessen hatte. Als wollte mein Magen zusammen mit meiner Seele aus meinem Körper ausbrechen' [I vomited three times into the toilet bowl, although I had not eaten anything for a what seemed like an eternity. As if my stomach, together with my soul, wanted to escape from my body] (OF, 47). This bodily excretion foreshadows Karim's rejection from the orderly system of another nation-state which did not invite him in. The text includes another moment of foreshadowing, again using the action of vomiting: when taken on a bus to an asylum seekers' centre, Karim watches how another young migrant named Hasan also throws up violently 'mitten auf den Gang. Anschließend hob er den Kopf, gelbe Galle tropfte von seinem Mund. "Ich wollte nur ausdrücken, was ich über unsere jetzige Situation denke"' [right in the middle of the aisle. Lifting his head, he was dropping yellow gall from the corners of his mouth. 'I just wanted to express my thoughts about our current situation'] (OF, 55). These two explicit references to vomiting by undocumented migrants who left behind their respective community memberships in search of legality, residence and rights in a liberal democracy, effectively symbolise their status as 'unwanted'. Both will be 'disposed of' akin to garbage. Indeed, after the 'official end' of the Iraqi civil war has been declared, Karim soon receives a letter that confirms his unwanted status in Germany (OF, 31). Neither his human achievements during his three-year residency, such as learning German and carrying out hard physical labour, nor his emerging social ties can prevent the host nation's decision to commence the disposal process. Even the 'borrowed story' of Meki, Karim's high school friend back in Iraq, who was killed by the Saddam regime for making a joke about the dictator and his wife, is rendered 'useless' by the German rejection letter (OF, 109). Meki's true account had been decisive for Karim's own asylum hearing, and by borrowing it, Karim temporarily gained the right to stay in Germany (OF, 107). However, his Iraqi friend's sad fate is also a form of foreshadowing for Karim's own fate in Germany, as this country will dispose of him after revoking his asylum seeker's temporary legal status. Although in the short term, Karim may partake in German civil society through work, as an asylum seeker he has no access to representation. Karim embodies one of the 'guests at the mercy of others' who are confined to a place which philosopher Bernhard Waldenfels calls 'Ort der Schwelle' [threshold].[35] These uninvited guests are powerless petitioners who are not allowed to leave this threshold; they are neither in nor out, and no longer there where they came from, and neither have they really arrived at the place they escaped to. Even the fact that Karim receives a two-year temporary residency permit for Germany, along with a 'blue travel passport for stateless persons', does not give him the right to make any legal or political demands (OF, 156).

Disposability of Waste

It is no coincidence that Karim works at a recycling plant for a number of weeks while he is awaiting the outcome of his claim for asylum. A recycling plant is tied to the idea of 'waste as stored energy', which is containing in itself 'the seeds of its own transformation'.[36] The ethics of resourcefulness, in terms of recycling and reusing, is integrated into the concept of a recycling plant, or the German term 'Wertstoffhof', which is an important part of modern German waste culture. The concept of residual waste opposes the idea of waste as stored energy. Residual waste spells *permanence*, an expression used for waste that will stay as it is, with no ready-to-implement solutions to recycle or to rehabilitate it into other forms. This type of permanent or residual garbage 'embarrasses and

35 Waldenfels, 'Flüchtlinge als Gäste in Not', 39.
36 Greg Kennedy, *The Ontology of Trash: The Disposable and its Problematic Nature* (New York: SUNY Press, 2007), 5.

shames us because it confronts us with a reflection of our own shortcom-
ings'.[37] The motif of residual waste spells negativity, and Khider skilfully
employs it to foreshadow the outcome of Karim's struggles for legal and
political acceptance by the receiving society.

Karim's brief tenure at this 'Wertstoffhof', where elderly clients reward
him with generous tips for carrying heavy boxes, offers him insight into
Germany's garbage recycling system (OF, 153). In his so-called 'integration
job' at the recycling plant, Karim is allowed to earn 80 marks per month, a
rather laughably small amount that is determined by the asylum laws (OF,
151). The asylum seeker displays a resourcefulness and finds value in waste
by rescuing 'trashed' items that still function, such as a cassette recorder
and a TV set (OF, 154). However, he is shocked that despite German effi-
ciency, this society still generates high levels of 'Restmüll' [residual waste]
(OF, 153). This image of residual waste points to Karim being drained of
his energy and becoming 'trash' which Germany wishes to dispose, like a
private household would at regular intervals.

Before being declared 'disposable', Karim clearly contributes to German
society in various short-term positions that pay no more than the minimum wage. According to philosopher Thomas Nail, migrants do play an
underacknowledged role in society since it is 'constantly being modified
through the cleaning and maintenance of labor' while it only 'appears to
be the relatively static place'.[38] Karim is an important modifier of German
society: after his tenure at the recycling plant, he works in a physically
demanding position at a metal-cutting factory, followed by monotonous
assembly-line work at a shampoo factory, and finally by a position as a
janitor, when he is cleaning a hospital and various offices for ten hours
daily (OF, 178). Apart from earning minimal wages, Karim does not receive
decent treatment for his valuable societal modifications. On the contrary,

37 Ibid., 4.
38 Thomas Nail, *The Figure of the Migrant* (Stanford: Stanford University Press, 2015),
    12. Nail illustrates that 'every day our cities must be maintained, remade, built up,
    torn down, and cleaned. Our office buildings and homes are cleaned and main-
    tained while we are away by an underground and largely invisible reproductive
    labor force disproportionately composed of migrants' (ibid.).

he lives in constant fear of being deported as soon as Germany will declare that Iraq's civil war is over.

Karim's situation indeed urges a consideration in favour of a statute of limitations, which already exists in Germany's civil and criminal law, but not for undocumented migrants who have been long-term residents. Political Scientist Antje Ellermann contends that 'in the absence of a statute of limitation on illegal entry, the deportation of settled migrants constitutes an arbitrary act of state power'.[39] Her view represents a valid political objection against deportation. As for *Ohrfeige*, a statute of limitation could have aided Karim, who at the end of the novel refers to himself as 'Müll' [garbage]: 'Ich bin wie eine unerwünschte Reklame, die immer wieder in Briefkästen geworfen wird, obwohl ganz deutlich Aufkleber angebracht sind. STOPP! KEINE WERBUNG BITTE! WIR VERMEIDEN MÜLL!' [I am like unwanted advertisement flyers, repeatedly being inserted into mailboxes even though there are stickers which clearly say STOP! NO FLYERS PLEASE! WE MINIMIZE GARBAGE!] (OF, 39). The laconic tone used by the author to describe Karim's existential crisis is also found in his illustration of Germany's decision regarding the protagonist's deportation to Iraq: 'Seit die Amerikaner die Diktatur von Saddam Hussein beseitigt hätten, sei die Situation im Irak besser geworden' [Since the Americans abolished Saddam Hussein's dictatorship, the situation in Iraq is said to be better] (OF, 31). Of course the situation is not 'improved', and regardless of Karim's considerable accomplishments and his having played a role in societal modifications, the German government exercises its state power and then determines that his plea for permanent resettlement is unnecessary. The disposal process to eject him, once set in motion, cannot be stopped. As a secondary result of being declared 'disposable', Karim fails to secure the highly desired elective surgery to correct his physical abnormality.

39   Antje Ellermann, 'The Rule of Law and the Right to Stay: The Moral Claims of Undocumented Migrants', *Politics & Society*, 42/3 (2014), 293–308, 293.

Refuge and Refuse

Khider's novels make the struggles of marginalised humans visible. He portrays Mahdi in *Die Orangen des Präsidenten* as an abandoned individual who is living through a nightmare, first as a political prisoner and then as a refugee. Initially, Mahdi cannot remove himself from a two-year abandonment in a totalitarian regime's prison cell, which is followed by his confinement to a refugee camp in the desert. The young refugee ends up as 'toxic human waste' – there are no countries interested in offering him a chance to make long-term plans for his life. The novel's tone and setting emphasise that those stored away in a camp are akin to 'trash', kept separate since trash has a fluidity that 'may be seen as a threat to be contained'.[40] Such storage practices of redundant humans are unlikely to change since the 'very idea of asylum, once a matter of civil and civilized pride, has been reclassified as a dreadful concoction of shameful naivety and criminal irresponsibility'.[41]

Karim in *Ohrfeige* has also become redundant, based on political decisions that he cannot influence. Having to live through his unexpected arrival in (and ultimate rejection from) Germany, not quite knowing where to go next, he is the embodiment of 'disposability'. His presence is unwanted, akin to residual waste, or *Restmüll*. Notwithstanding any potential moral claims for legalisation or naturalisation, the rejected asylum seeker must be transported around the planet in trucks, 'like beef or imported bananas' (OF, 216). In addition, Karim is forced to come to terms with not being able to secure elective surgery which would correct a physical deformity that causes him severe emotional stress. While he can easily obtain the information about the medical procedure, he cannot get the desired relief, simply because the costs are out of his financial reach, and because his host country denies him more time to save the required funds.

---

40 Maurizia Boscagli, *Stuff Theory: Everyday Objects, Radical Materialism* (London: Bloomsbury, 2014), 228.
41 Bauman, *Wasted Lives*, 57.

With his waste imagery, Khider makes the voice of the *refused* audible: political prisoners, asylum seekers and refugees, and those who cannot
obtain elective medical procedures available to others living within the
same geographical region. Such imagery effectively exposes the disinterest
to intervene on behalf of political prisoners held by authoritarian regimes,
the flaws of the global refugee system and the adverse effects of humanitarian missions that create almost as much harm as good. Political systems
that marginalise powerless groups or individuals in essence declare them
as redundant. Khider's texts indeed give the 'refused' a voice and urge a
review of entrenched systems of power and control that have blurred the
boundaries between marginalised people and trashed things.

JARA SCHMIDT

'[W]enn die anderen rausbekämen, dass ich eine Mannfrau bin':[1] Grotesque Physicality and Carnivalesque Subversions in Abbas Khider's *Ohrfeige*

Introduction: In Times of Flight

Abbas Khider's fourth novel *Ohrfeige*, which tells the story of Karim Mensy and his friends, all of them asylum seekers, was proclaimed as the 'novel of the hour' when it was published in 2016. As with his previous novels, the author confronts topics such as displacement, flight, the status of marginalised members of society and the fight for agency.[2] But in this text, Khider – unlike other authors whose novels often end with the arrival in the new country – focuses on the *attempted* arrival in Germany, namely a problematic process that is no less difficult than the prior flight to and through Europe.[3] In *Ohrfeige*, the protagonist Karim no longer wants to remain 'Asylant 3873 oder so' [asylum seeker 3873 or so] (OF, 12),

---

1   'If the others found out that I am a man-woman' – Abbas Khider, *Ohrfeige* (Munich: Random House, 2017 [2016]), 101. All quotes are from this edition. Unless otherwise noted, all translations are mine.

2   Cf. Hubert Spiegel, 'Ein Schutzwall aus Worten gegen Gewalt, Not und Elend: Abbas Khiders "Rache des Poeten"', *Chamisso. Viele Kulturen – eine Sprache* 16 (2017), 4–9, 7.

3   Cf. Ulrike Schneider, 'Darstellungsweisen von Fluchtprozessen in der Gegenwartsliteratur am Beispiel von Merle Kröger und Abbas Khider sowie den Reportagen von Wolfgang Bauer und Navid Kermani', *Argonautenschiff: Jahrbuch der Anna-Seghers-Gesellschaft Berlin und Mainz e.V.* 25 (2017), 82–92, 83.

but needs to reclaim his own story by telling it from his perspective and by forcing an authority figure to listen.

Khider once called himself an 'annalist of his time'.[4] The particular time he refers to in this novel is one of flight and migration. Currently, massive movements affect almost seventy-one million people, and a constantly increasing percentage of the world's population does not live in its country of birth.[5] The author himself was born in Bagdad in 1973 and fled from Iraq in 1996. Khider then lived as an undocumented refugee in Egypt, Libya, Tunisia, Italy, Turkey and Greece before the police in Germany apprehended him in 2000.[6] So far, all of his novels depict young male Iraqi protagonists and deal with the experience of flight and exile. The dictatorship of Saddam Hussein, 9/11 and the Iraq War in 2003 build the historic context for *Ohrfeige*[7] – a chaotic background which has in common with the time of carnival that it leaves room for a redefinition of norms and regulations.

According to the literary theorist Mikhail M. Bakhtin, the historical carnival is a public event that comprises all carnivalesque festivities, traditions, and forms, which can become a literary phenomenon once they are transferred into literary texts.[8] Bakhtin establishes four categories for the identification of carnivalesque literature: the familiar, which replaces the hierarchical; the eccentric, which makes room for what is usually suppressed; the carnivalesque mésalliances, which allow contact between

---

4   Spiegel, 'Ein Schutzwall aus Worten gegen Gewalt, Not und Elend', 4.

5   Cf. homepage of the United Nations, <https://www.un.org/en/sections/issues-depth/refugees/>, accessed 17 July 2019.

6   Cf. Warda El-Kaddouri, ' "Gott, rette mich aus der Leere!" Verlust, Religiosität und Radikalisierung in den Fluchtnarrativen von Abbas Khider und Sherko Fatah', in Thomas Hardtke, Johannes Kleine and Charlton Payne, eds., *Niemandsbuchten und Schutzbefohlene: Flucht-Räume und Flüchtlingsfiguren in der deutschsprachigen Gegenwartsliteratur* (Göttingen: V & R unipress, 2017), 39–51, 39–40. After his arrest, Khider had to stay in Germany and could not apply for asylum in any other European country. He later studied literature and philosophy in Munich and Potsdam; he now lives and writes in Berlin.

7   Cf. Spiegel, 'Ein Schutzwall aus Worten gegen Gewalt, Not und Elend', 4.

8   Cf. Mikhail M. Bakhtin, *Literatur und Karneval: Zur Romantheorie und Lachkultur* (Frankfurt am Main: Fischer, 1990 [1969]), 47.

people of all classes; and the profanation, a semantic field of blasphemy and parody.[9] Hence, the carnivalesque stands for abolished boundaries, for change and renewal of the world order; everything and everyone becomes subject to modification.[10] Yet, as the historical carnival as a folk festival only lasts for a specific time span and eventually comes to an end, so do the modifications.[11] During the festivities, the reversal of the social power is acted out by the dethronement of the (carnival) king and the coronation of the fool in his place – but once the folk festival is over, the old order in re-established. Thus, solely during the carnival's time frame does the possibility exist of a radical structural reversal of society, which offers a new perspective on the given world order. Nevertheless, what remains after the festivities are over is a utopian idea of how (lasting) change could look like.

Carnivalesque laughter (as laughter in general cannot be claimed by a dominant power) is universal and aims at superior social and institutional instances that will be degraded and at the given world order that is about to change for the duration of carnival.[12] Yet the laughter is ambivalent and also includes those who are usually socially weaker but celebrate their gained 'power' during carnival; it simultaneously stands for mockery and negation as well as triumph and affirmation.[13] In contemporary literature, the carnivalesque elements can be applied to characters and narrator-protagonists that are marginalised by the social majority, as is often the case in intercultural novels on migration or flight. In those stories that are told from the perspective of the marginalised, the dominant culture becomes subject to ridicule and consequently, the given norms are implicitly renegotiated. Social boundaries are questioned and the characters

9   Cf. Renate Lachmann, 'Vorwort', in Mikhail M. Bakhtin, *Rabelais und seine Welt: Volkskultur als Gegenkultur* (Frankfurt am Main: Suhrkamp, 2015 [1987]), 7–46, 31.
10   Cf. Bakhtin, *Literatur und Karneval*, 50.
11   Ibid., 56.
12   Ibid., 54.
13   Ibid.

use carnivalesque as well as picaresque strategies for self-empowerment and self-positioning.[14]

This also applies to Khider's *Ohrfeige*, in which Karim wants his story to be heard and he therefore confronts Ms Schulz, the person responsible for him at the Alien Registration Office. By forcing her to listen, Karim creates a carnivalesque reversal of the usual power dynamics; the boundaries between them are dismantled for the duration of Karim's narrative. However, in this encounter he also opens up about the real reason for his flight – his 'female' breasts and grotesque physicality, which are linked to the carnivalesque as well: as a body that symbolises the transgression of boundaries and constant renewal. In the following, this article will focus on the novel's applications of carnivalesque elements, such as profanation and ridicule, as a means of offering an alternative perspective on society by depicting a heterotopic microcosm for asylum seekers through the picaresque and on its use of the grotesque to point to an ongoing global metamorphosis. In this context, the exiled serves as a bearer of social criticism and as a symbolic figure.

Profanation: Ridicule and Reversed Power Positions

Karim tries to win back some control over his life by constraining Ms Schulz to her office chair and gagging her. He claims that he simply wants to talk to her 'von Mensch zu Mensch' [from human to human], implying that he does not feel treated with human dignity and equal rights. Yet, the whole situation contradicts his claim for equality (OF, 12). Not only is Ms Schulz unable to respond because of the gag, she also does not understand his words as he speaks to her in Arabic. Karim's German would not suffice for the monologue that is to follow: his life story. But he asserts that language is not the only barrier in their communication.

14   Cf. Jara Schmidt, *Literarische Narreteien: Karnevaleske Strategien in deutsch- und englischsprachigen Migrationsromanen der Gegenwart* (Würzburg: Königshausen & Neumann, 2019).

Karim claims that even if Arabic was Ms Schulz' native language, she still would not understand him because: 'Sie stammt aus einer ganz anderen Welt als [er]' [She is from a completely different world than [he is]] (OF, 10). Being the one who makes significant life decisions for him, she is to Karim a 'gottesgleiche Figur' [God-like figure] (OF, 11); her last decision was to revoke his residence permit. So, in an act of profanation and carnivalesque reversal, Karim, the socially inferior asylum seeker, further degrades her by blowing cannabis smoke in her face and finding her a first name because, according to the protagonist, surnames create too much distance between people. As she cannot answer, he guesses names – forcing a carnivalesque mésalliance – and asserts: 'Es ist, als würde ich Gott einen Vornamen geben' [It is as if I would give God a first name] (OF, 10–1). The protagonist states that he has not felt this alive in a long time and is very content observing Ms Schulz:

> Da sind Sie. Hilflos. Verschnürt wie ein Paket. In Ihrem teuren schwarzen Lederstuhl. Sie waren eine Göttin. Eine Naturgewalt, die Macht über andere Menschen hat. Ich war Ihnen ausgeliefert. Aber wie ein mythischer Held habe ich mich erhoben und den Olymp erstürmt (OF, 11).

> [There you are. Helpless. Tied up like a package. In your expensive black leather chair. You were a goddess. A force of nature with power over other people. I was at your mercy. But I rose like a mythical hero and took Olympus by storm.]

She is forced to listen to one of the many whom she treated as nameless numbers, not as human beings. But just as Karim represents a certain group of people – thousands of refugees in Germany – so too does Ms Schulz. Because the readers read in German what Karim speaks in Arabic, only they are able to understand his words. The readers therefore take the place of the official person addressed in the novel; the 'Ohrfeige' [slap in the face] is meant for them (OF, 9). Consequently, they feel both sympathetic towards Karim yet identify with the humiliation of Ms Schulz. In this framing storyline, Karim is at the same time speechless (with his lack of German) and possesses the power of speech due to his newly gained position of power at that very moment.[15] There is no common ground

---

15   Cf. Eduard Haueis, ' "Charab Al ..." – Fluch(t)punkt Sprache im Roman *Ohrfeige* von Abbas Khider', *OBST. Flucht_Punkt_Sprache* 89 (2016), 53–6, 54.

for understanding between him and Ms Schulz,[16] and the readers take a mediating position in this *Wutrede*.[17]

As the author never knew Iraq as a peaceful place, it is typical for Khider's novels to lack nostalgia or a longing for his country of origin. In order to handle his own experience with oppression, torture and jail, Khider in his autofictional texts subverts the power of official authorities, for example, the secret police, prison guards, political leaders or, as in *Ohrfeige*, representatives of the bureaucracy, by ridiculing them. Humour, according to Khider, functions as criticism as well as a coping strategy.[18] But what is most healing to him, and at the same time an act of revenge, is his writing:

> Ich verstehe die Literatur als eine Kritik an der Realität. Wenn ich der Folter eine ganz eigene sprachliche Form entgegenstelle, dann entsteht ein Raum, den die Folterer nicht antasten können. Der Vorgang selbst wird dann banal und lächerlich. Ich entferne mich davon. Ich löse mich aber auch von der Geschichte, die ich erzähle. Die gehört plötzlich nicht mehr nur mir selbst. Dadurch wird alles viel leichter. [...] Ich würde es eher eine Dämonenaustreibung nennen. Und eine Rache an denen, die mir Schmerz zugefügt haben. Eigentlich sind alle meine Romane eine Art Rache. Am Ende bin ich es, der zurückschlägt. Ich triumphiere mit den Mitteln der Literatur.[19]

> [I understand literature as a criticism of reality. If I oppose torture with a very distinct linguistic form, then a space originates that cannot be touched by the torturers. The process itself then becomes mundane and ridiculous. I distance myself from it. I free myself from the story that I am telling. Suddenly it no longer belongs to me alone. That makes everything easier. [...] I would rather call it an exorcism. And a revenge on those who caused me pain. Actually, all my novels are a kind of revenge. In the end, I am the one who strikes back. I triumph with the means of literature.]

---

16   Ibid., 55. According to Haueis, this constant communicational bondage is symbolised by the character Hayat, Karim's childhood love, who is deaf-mute.

17   Ibid., 56.

18   Cf. El-Kaddouri, '"Gott, rette mich aus der Leere!"', 39–40.

19   Ronald Düker, 'Literat Abbas Khider: "Ich stelle der Folter eine sprachliche Form entgegen"', *Cicero: Magazin für politische Kultur* (15 March 2013), <https://www.cicero.de/kultur/abbas-khider-auberginenrepublik-ich-stelle-der-folter-eine-sprachliche-form-entgegen/53874>, accessed 3 November 2018.

Another way for Khider to distance himself from and at the same time approach his traumatic past is the decision to write his novels in German.[20] While writing in German, he can simultaneously keep up and cross a protective boundary. In the new language, Khider found a barrier to the language of his haunting past, which he can metaphorically cross with his storytelling.[21]

In *Ohrfeige*, the strategy to use laughter as a means of overcoming becomes very evident after 9/11, when things get more difficult for the asylum seekers. When society finally pays attention to them, it is the wrong kind of attention, and in a grotesque climax, they now not only suffer from social marginalisation, but also become victims of racial profiling. Due to their appearance, refugees like Karim face increased racism and suddenly all of them become suspects: 'Nach diesem verdammten Tag wurde der wichtigste Ausdruck für uns Araber in Deutschland: verdächtig' [After this damn day, the most important expression for us Arabs in Germany became: suspect] (OF, 164). But while the carnivalesque stance of the novel allows the migrants' perspective on the social clashes to be the dominant one and to dismantle racist stereotypes,[22] the narrator's overall humorous tone makes the conflicts seem more bearable. Thus, the novel's carnivalesque and humorous subversions function as means of defence that point out the absurdities the asylum seekers encounter. For example, when the so-called 'War on Terror' begins, it is very difficult for Karim and his friends to take

20   Cf. Katherine Anderson, 'Von der Wanderung zum Wandel: Die Migration des Abbas Khider in die deutsche Sprache als Traumabewältigung durch Erzählen', in Elke Sturm-Trigonakis, Olga Laskaridou, Evi Petropoulou and Katerina Karakassi, eds., *Turns und kein Ende? Aktuelle Tendenzen in Germanistik und Komparatistik* (Frankfurt am Main: Peter Lang, 2017), 95–104, 95.

21   Ibid., 99.

22   Systemic as well as individual racism is exposed, for example, when Karim uses a 'Tarnung als Lesender' [disguise as a reader] (OF, 14) and carries a daily newspaper with him because he knows that this way he will escape racist police checks, as anyone who can read and seems to be eager to learn does not correspond to the image that the German police have of undocumented migrants. Also, Karim is not allowed into any of the city's four clubs (OF, 139), which suggests that only people of a certain phenotype are welcome, and when thefts occur in the city, the police always first turn up at the refugees (OF, 143).

a clear position because they are both anti-war and anti-dictatorship: 'Wir stecken in einer absurden Zwickmühle. Entweder ertragen wir weiterhin eine beschissene Diktatur, die unsere Seelen zerstört. Oder wir ziehen mit den USA in einen beschissenen Krieg, der unser Land zerstört. Wir sollen plötzlich wählen zwischen Scheiße und Scheiße' [We are stuck in an absurd predicament. We either keep enduring a shitty dictatorship, which destroys our souls. Or, we go along with the Americans, off to a shitty war that destroys our country. We are suddenly supposed to choose between shit and shit] (OF, 194).

According to Khider, only humour keeps you alive, even in the most critical situations.[23] It is therefore hardly surprising that besides the protagonist's vengeful visit to Ms Schulz, another strategy of the novel to oppose the bureaucratic insanity, which Khider calls 'babylonische, bürokratische Demütigungen' [Babylonian, bureaucratic humiliations], is humour.[24] Plays on words in particular can be found in *Ohrfeige*, for example, when it comes to Karim's job hunt. The protagonist is lucky enough to receive his two-year residence permit shortly before 9/11, because after the attacks, the German public authorities stop issuing permits. The protagonist can now finally move freely and plans to improve his German and

23   Cf. Hubert Spiegel, '"Wenn ich auf Arabisch schreibe, handelt alles von Leid. Das Deutsche hält mich auf Distanz": Abbas Khider wird für seinen Debütroman ausgezeichnet', *Chamisso: Viele Kulturen – eine Sprache* 4 (2010), 10–3, 11.

24   Abbas Khider, 'Zum Dort verflucht', opening event of *Tage des Exils* 2018, <https://www.koerber-stiftung.de/mediathek/zum-dort-verflucht-1642>, accessed 9 November 2018. Khider was the patron of *Tage des Exils* 2018; at the opening event, he gave a speech and was afterwards interviewed by Daniel Kaiser (Norddeutscher Rundfunk). According to Khider, the waiting and with it the boredom were the biggest problems – not knowing whether you could stay or not. But Khider was granted asylum rather quickly because he could prove that he had been in prison in Iraq after he was caught selling forbidden books (e.g. by Shiites or Iraqi communists). When he fled from Iraq in 1996, he absolutely wanted to return. So he did in 2003 – but only for a year because his dream had been destroyed. In Iraq he was 'ein Mann ohne Träume' [a man without dreams]. War had turned the country into hell, everything was destroyed. He then decided to go back to Germany and make a new start in a country where he has the freedom to write about anything he wants (ibid.).

to find a proper job. When he learns that he first has to work for a whole year and has to pay taxes before he can start a German course, Karim wonders how he is supposed to find a job while hardly speaking any German. At the employment office, he is told that he can begin with an easy job and is offered employment at Burger King: 'Sie sind krankenversichert, verdienen etwas Geld und können langsam ein guter Bürger werden' [You have health insurance, earn some money and can slowly become a good citizen] (OF, 157). For the placement officer, being a good citizen is obviously connected to being economically productive. Shaped by a neoliberal thinking which defines society as an all-encompassing economic market and not as a civil society, his image of citizens is one of profit and loss. Karim however is not sure how to interpret the offer on a more basic, linguistic level. Due to his lack of German, he is unable to tell the difference between 'Burger' and 'Bürger' – which causes a comic relief for the readers. The placement officer corrects Karim: 'Nicht Burger, Bürger! Bürger. Bewohner des Landes. Bürger. Mit Umlaut. Also Staatsbürger. Deutscher. Bei Burger King. Arbeit. Dann. Bürger' [Not burger, citizen! Citizen. Resident of the country. Citizen. With an umlaut. Thus, state resident. German. At Burger King's. Work. Then. Citizen] (OF, 158).[25] But the joke remains on the officer and the bureaucratic, neoliberal system. Karim's friend Rafid later jokes about being a 'guter Bürger im Burger King' [good citizen at Burger King's], and the pun evokes carnivalesque laughter. The social outsider, the exiled, is humorously questioning the bureaucracy and its ideal of being a good citizen only if one has work [Arbeit. Dann. Bürger / Work. Then. Citizen]. Even if it means working for minimum wage (or less) at a fast food company – a job many Germans would decline (OF, 158).

The use of profanity and the break-down of social hierarchies are carnivalesque traditions which can be found in the novel in another word play: the curse *Charab Allmanya*, which the protagonist uses so often that his friends start calling him 'Karim Charab Allmanya', humorously aims at a secular and a divine authority at the same time. The protagonist explains to Ms Schulz:

25   Obviously, the pun does not work in a direct translation.

Charab Allmanya!, liebe Frau Schulz, ist eine im Irak weitverbreitete Wendung und überhaupt nicht ungewöhnlich. Wenn ein Iraker schlecht drauf ist, verteufelt er die Deutschen stellvertretend für alles Schlechte auf der Welt. Der Iraker macht das von ganzem Herzen. Alternativ sagen einige auch 'Chara be Allmanya!', was ungefähr einem 'Scheiß auf Deutschland' nahekommt (OF, 112).

[Charab Allmanya!, dear Ms Schulz, is a wide-spread phrase in Iraq and not at all special. When an Iraqi is in a bad mood, he curses the Germans as representatives for all the bad in the world. The Iraqi does this with all his heart. Alternatively, some say 'Chara be Allmanya!', which roughly means 'fuck Germany'.]

Karim's friend Rafid thinks that cursing Germans is not due to a historic context but rather because 'Allmanya' sounds similar to 'Allah' – so cursing Germans is a substitute for blasphemy. It is a pun that aims at the degradation of the divine through the cursing of Germans. By substituting the reference to Allah, the divine is only implicitly ridiculed and subverted. The explicit curse aims at the Germans who also, like Allah, keep the refugees in line. Their carnivalesque laughter thus serves as a means of overcoming rules and restrictions.

Home for Asylum Seekers as Heterotopia

In *Ohrfeige*, Khider's protagonist uses his storytelling – his monologue which forms the story-within-the-story – to make his audience aware of the problems that refugees have to face after their flight. Karim is exhausted by the ongoing questions concerning his past – no one seems to recognise his present difficulties: 'die Schwierigkeiten mit der Aufenthaltserlaubnis, die Folter in der Ausländerbehörde, die Schikanen des Bundeskriminalamtes, [...] die Peinlichkeiten des Bundesnachrichtendiensts oder die Banalitäten des Verfassungsschutzes. Und warum fällt niemandem die Tatsache des Polizeirassismus auf?' [the difficulties with the residence permit, the torture at the Alien Registration Office, the bullying of the Federal Criminal Police Office, [...] the embarrassment of the Federal Intelligence Service or the banalities of the protection of the constitution. And why does no one notice the fact of police racism?] (OF, 19). Besides the bureaucratic harassment and the racism they have to cope with, the refugees are also always kept at a distance from the rest of society. To Karim and his friends, the other citizens are like 'Fabelwesen aus einem fernen Märchenland' [mythical creatures from a faraway fairyland] (OF, 121). They live in a microcosm for asylum seekers that offers them everything they need in their restricted normalcy and that makes contact to the 'world outside' allegedly obsolete:

> Alles, was mit Asylbewerbern zu tun hat, findet sich auf dem Gelände: die Büros des Bundesamts für die Anerkennung ausländischer Flüchtlinge, eine Polizeidienststelle, eine Niederlassung der Caritas und eben die Behausungen der Asylanten. Der Komplex liegt am Stadtrand und war früher wohl mal eine Kaserne, vielleicht aber auch ein Gefängnis oder ein Seuchenhaus (OF, 59).

> [Everything that has to do with asylum seekers is on the premises: the offices of the Federal Office for the recognition of foreign refugees, a police office, a branch of Caritas and the homes of the asylum seekers. The complex is in a suburban area and probably once used to be a barracks, maybe even a prison or an infirmary.]

The protagonist compares these grounds to a jail and a plague house and thereby points out their restrictiveness and sickening atmosphere. The complex is depicted as a heterotopia, a place contrary to the rest of society, which questions the legitimacy of the latter's structure.[26] The carnivalesque reversal of power dynamics, which Karim creates in the framing story of his narrative, serves as a counter-action and resistance to this feeling of being trapped and kept at bay. Yet at the same time – as carnival (or here, more specifically, the carnivalesque narrative) only lasts for a limited time and the heterotopic microcosm for asylum seekers can be ignored by the majority society – both serve as some kind of safety valves that maintain the structures and norms of the German society. Norms and structures are questioned and criticised, but are not permanently disturbed.

Due to the so-called 'Residenzpflicht' [residence obligation], the refugees in the novel have to stay close to their grounds and are not allowed to

---

26   Cf. Michel Foucault, *Die Heterotopien: Der utopische Körper. Zwei Radiovorträge* (Frankfurt am Main: Suhrkamp, 2005 [1966]), 19.

move further than 30 km away from them. While Karim and his friends are still waiting for their residence permit, which will allow them to learn German and find work, they try to satisfy their 'Sehnsucht nach Normalität' [longing for normality] (OF, 66) by going to a shopping mall and watching the other people go about their business: 'Zu gern wollten wir sein wie sie. [...] Wir standen mittendrin und doch waren wir meilenweit von all dem entfernt. Die Einheimischen gingen shoppen, wir wärmten uns an ihrem Leben' [We wanted to be like them so badly. [...] We stood right in the middle and were still miles away from all of it. The locals went shopping, we warmed ourselves on their life] (OF, 66–7). But although Bayreuth, where they are located, feels like a thirty square kilometre jail, Khider's characters do not long for their home country, the 'Kampfarena der Weltmächte und Verrückten' [fighting arena of the world powers and the insane] (OF, 32). Their country of origin is upside down. Yet, instead of a carnivalesque power reversal, the chaos' potential of renegotiating norms and regulations results in a fight for power that leaves the citizens in fear for their lives. Thus, Karim's humorous storytelling is a way of coping with this frustrating situation and the (non-)choice between 'jail' and a 'fighting arena'.

Khider has made his experience with war and its consequences his literary focus. Since he started publishing thirteen years ago, his approach to narratives on flight and exile have won him several prizes and scholarships; Khider also had two lectureships at German universities.[27] His texts are at the same time poetic and laconic, tragic and comic[28] – and he says they free him because art and literature are limitless.[29] Yet this freedom should not fall victim to romanticising. In a laudation for Khider, the speaker Meike Fessmann claimed:

---

27   Detailed information can be found on the author's homepage: <http://abbaskhider. com/seiten/biografie.html>, accessed 3 November 2018.

28   Cf. Meike Fessmann, 'Die Freiheit, sein Leben noch einmal zu erzählen: Laudation auf Abbas Khider', *Sinn und Form. Beiträge zur Literatur* 66/4 (2014), 705–11, 706.

29   Cf. Khider, 'Zum Dort verflucht'.

Wer seine Heimat verläßt, muß vieles hinter sich lassen. Doch er gewinnt auch etwas: die Freiheit, sein Leben noch einmal neu zu erzählen, ein bißchen bunter womöglich, ein bißchen spannender, vielleicht auch waghalsiger, mutiger. Für Schriftsteller ist das ein ideales Terrain.[30]

[Whoever leaves home has to leave a lot behind. But he also gains something: the freedom to tell his story anew, a bit more colourful maybe, a bit more exciting, maybe more daring, braver. For writers this is an ideal terrain.]

This observation is disputable at the least, considering everything the refugees have to leave behind and the losses they have to face. The flight itself takes a lot of courage and is an 'adventure' they never asked for. The odds of reapproaching your life through literature are better described by Khider himself: 'Man versucht, Lösungen zu finden, der Leere eine Bedeutung zu geben, das Exil als Projekt zu gestalten. Man ist andauernd damit beschäftigt, die Fremde zu verfremden, um nicht seelenverwundet zu bleiben' [One tries to find solutions, to give meaning to the emptiness, to make exile a project. One is always preoccupied alienating the other in order to not stay harmed in one's soul].[31] In order to realise this literarily, Khider endows his protagonist with picaresque humour and allows him to critically reflect in a carnivalesque manner on the othering he is confronted with and the heterotopic demarcation he experiences.

According to Khider, the only advantage that living in exile offers is the appealing illusion to have a task[32] – and this turns out be true for his protagonist Karim Mensy as well. He desperately wants to change his grotesque physicality. Yet precisely because Karim's grotesque body defies the norms, it gains a carnivalesque and universal meaning.

---

30   Fessmann, 'Die Freiheit, sein Leben noch einmal zu erzählen', 707.

31   Abbas Khider, 'Zum DORT verflucht: Grußwort', *Hamburger Abendblatt,* four-paged special *Tage des Exils* (12 October 2018), 2.

32   Ibid.

The Grotesque Body

While on his way from Iraq to Paris, Karim gets caught by the police in Dachau.[33] When they bring him in for inspection, they witness the actual reason for Karim's flight:

> Die beiden schauten mich an. In ihren Augen konnte ich sehen, wie sehr mein Oberkörper sie zugleich anekelte und faszinierte. Ja, Frau Schulz, sie sahen etwas, wofür ich mich bis heute zutiefst schäme. Sie sahen den wahren Grund meiner Flucht. Seit Jahren und vor allen Menschen versuche ich, ihn zu verheimlichen (OF, 44).

> [Both of them looked at me. I could see in their eyes how much my torso disgusted and at the same time fascinated them. Yes, Ms Schulz, they saw something for which I am still deeply ashamed. They saw the real reason for my flight. I have tried to hide it for years and from all people.]

What the police officers see, after they asked the protagonist to undress, is that he has full breasts, usually attributed to women. Karim is so ashamed about his unusual body that he never talked to anybody about it and finally fled from his home country to avoid a seemingly inevitable confrontation: the duty to military service and with it the risk of being exposed. He even considered suicide until his father gave him enough money to flee the country and study abroad. Yet Karim's main plan was a different one – he wanted to get to Europe to have aesthetic surgery: 'Ich wünschte mir nichts sehnlicher als eine wundervoll glatte Männerbrust. Ich wollte mich endlich wieder vollwertig fühlen. Über Suizid dachte ich keinen Augenblick mehr nach' [I longed for nothing more than to have a wonderful, flat male chest. I finally wanted to feel adequate again. I no longer thought about suicide] (OF, 91–2). This reason for Karim's flight, his longing for a flat male chest and for feeling adequate, has hardly been

---

33   The first thing that Germans associate with this city is the concentration camp Dachau, which was established in 1933 and lasted until 1945. Khider's protagonist, caught by the police in this historically loaded place, serves as an allusion to the horrific way Germans treated those who were unwanted in their society. Karim says that his heart would probably have stopped if he had known about the concentration camp on his arrival in Dachau (OF, 46).

taken into account by critics and academics. Moreover, it has often been downplayed in reviews. The reviewer Ursula März, for instance, does not name the protagonist's problem, but simply states that it is rather intimate.[34] She even reads it as one of Khider's strategies to make the novel less overtly political – thereby calling his breasts a humorous attribute. Friedrich Christian Delius specifies the reason for Karim's flight, but calls it a deformation.[35] A third critic even seems to doubt that the reason for Karim's flight is credible and calls it 'truly abstruse'.[36] But, in fact, Karim's body and shame are political, and calling breasts a deformation – even on a man's body – or degrading them to a joke speaks volumes about still prevailing restrictive and binary gender politics leading to social ridicule, structural discrimination or even violence and death.

But the novel gives a common explanation – hormonal imbalance: 'Gynäkomastie. Dabei handele es sich um eine Vergrößerung der Brustdrüsen. Das sei eigentlich eine häufige Erscheinung, bei über sechzig Prozent aller Jungen in der Pubertät trete sie auf' [Gynecomastia. It is an enlargement of the mammary gland. It is actually a common phenomenon that occurs in over sixty per cent of all boys during puberty] (OF, 92). What is uncommon is that Karim's breasts remain beyond puberty. They become a grotesque element of the novel and an existential problem to the protagonist.[37] They turn Karim's body into a grotesque body in the

34   Cf. Ursula März, 'Abbas Khider: *Ohrfeige*. Die Wutrede eines abgelehnten Asylbewerbers', *Deutschlandfunk Kultur* (30 January 2016), <https://www.deutschlandfunkkultur.de/abbas-khider-ohrfeige-die-wutrede-eines-abgelehnten.950.de.html?dram:article_id=343983>, accessed 3 November 2018.

35   Cf. Friedrich Christian Delius, 'Die deutsche Verlogenheit', *Süddeutsche Zeitung* (9 March 2017), <https://www.sueddeutsche.de/kultur/preisrede-die-deutsche-verlogenheit-1.3412260>, accessed 4 November 2018.

36   Simon Welebil, 'Monolog für mehr Verständnis: In seinem neuen Roman *Ohrfeige* feuert Abbas Khider eine Breitseite auf das europäische Asylsystem ab', *FM4* (27 March 2016), <https://fm4v3.orf.at/stories/1768692/index.html>, accessed 5 November 2018.

37   Cf. Katharina Granzin, 'Der Mensch im Durchgangsland: Die Katastrophe des Nie-irgendwo-ankommen-Dürfens. Abbas Khider erzählt in seinem neuen Roman *Ohrfeige* die Geschichte eines ewigen Flüchtlings', *Frankfurter Rundschau* (5 February 2016), <http://www.fr.de/kultur/literatur/abbas-khider-ohrfeige-der-mensch-im-durchgangsland-a-372313>, accessed 5 November 2018.

carnivalesque sense, into a body which tries to transcend its own range and metaphorically reaches out into the world in order to take it in and at the same time be devoured by it. It is a symbol of transgression and change. The grotesque body is never completed, but always nascent. It represents a collective rather than an individual, as it is constantly expanding and renewing.[38] The opposition of the collective and the individual is dissolved in the metaphysical, grotesque and universal body; the collective becomes individualised and vice versa.[39] Karim as a 'universal body' can therefore be understood as representing a range of refugees, male and female all the same. Even if there is, of course, a great diversity among refugees, Karim's experience and suffering are not a singular case, but are common.

Karim is insecure because of his unusual physicality, which limits his daily life. He avoids spas and locker rooms, stops playing soccer and spends most of his time inside the house, especially in the summer when it is hot. He is afraid how others might react if they find out and he has also internalised the societal norms around masculinity and femininity himself. This becomes evident by Karim's urgent desire for surgery to 'correct' his body. The protagonist comes up with his own explanation for his 'grotesque' appearance:

> Manchmal, Frau Schulz, glaube ich, Hayat wollte mich für den Rest meines Lebens begleiten und deswegen schenkte sie mir aus dem Jenseits einen Teil ihres Körpers. Deshalb wurde ich so ein seltsames Wesen. Einerseits mit einem prächtigen Penis ausgestattet, andererseits mit einem wohlgenährten Frauenbusen (OF, 87).

> [Sometimes, Ms Schulz, I believe that Hayat wanted to keep me company for the rest of my life and therefore, from the beyond, gifted me with a part of her body. This is why I became such a strange creature. On the one hand equipped with a splendid penis, on the other hand with a well-fed female bosom.]

Hayat is Karim's childhood love, who was raped and killed when she was still a young girl. Because her name means 'life', for Karim, life itself is

---

38   Cf. Bakhtin, *Literatur und Karneval*, 16–8.
39   Cf. Ute Brylla, 'Die Maske des Unmaskierten: Eine Zusammenschau von Bruno Schulz und Michail Bachtin', in Elfi Bettinger and Julika Funk, eds., *Maskeraden: Geschlechterdifferenz in der literarischen Inszenierung* (Berlin: Erich Schmidt Verlag, 1995), 307–22, 317.

always linked to murder and death.[40] This ambiguity of life and death also links Hayat to the grotesque figure of the 'pregnant death' which, according to Bakhtin, is a symbolic figure that connects new life and death and thereby displays the ambivalent processes of the body: its constant metamorphosis and decay as well as its transitory state.[41] Karim, who says that he is 'zur Hälfte eine Frau' [half a woman] (OF, 87) and that Hayat is always with him, not only symbolises a grotesque body that reaches out into the world, but also a renewal of the world order, in which more and more people now defy norms and boundaries. The exiled becomes a symbolic figure for global change, even if he himself feels stuck and helpless and wants to stop defying this particular norm around masculine bodies.

But temporarily, for Karim, who got his asylum granted before 9/11, life seems to become more normal. He finds a one-room apartment and a job at a temping agency. After one year of working, he is finally allowed to participate in a German-language course. There he meets Lada, a married woman from Belarus with whom he falls in love. She is also the first woman Karim has sex with. Again, his breasts hinder him from a normal (sex) life and he has to come up with a lie once more. Karim pretends to have torture scars on his body and claims that because of them he does not want to completely undress in front of Lada. In an absurd mixture of historic events and personal experience, Karim's complicated sexual awakening is intertwined with the cruelties of war:

> Dort fiel eine Bombe. Hier wurde Wodka getrunken. Dort starb ein Mensch. Hier wurde eine Unterhose ausgezogen. Dort wurde ein Kind verletzt. Hier hatte ich einen Orgasmus. Es war skurril. Alles fand gleichzeitig statt. Und alles schien gleichzeitig in mir stattzufinden (OF, 197).

> [Over there a bomb came down. Here one drank vodka. Over there a person died. Here one took off one's underpants. Over there a child got hurt. Here I had an orgasm. It was bizarre. Everything happened at the same time. And everything seemed to happen simultaneously inside of me.]

40　Cf. Haueis, '"Charab Al …"', 55.
41　Cf. Mikhail M. Bakhtin, *Rabelais und seine Welt: Volkskultur als Gegenkultur* (Frankfurt am Main: Suhrkamp, 2015 [1987]), 76.

This particular, disconcerting amalgamation combines and mixes the grotesque elements of war and an intimate struggle within Karim's body. Once again, the symbolic meaning of his grotesque body becomes evident: its collective representation of all those traumatised, exiled and reaching out into the world.

In the end, Karim is never able to have breast surgery. He was neither able to earn enough money, nor would his health insurance have supported his request. And not only did he receive a negative answer from his health insurance, but he also received a repeal of his granted asylum. During the last few months before his visit to Ms Schulz, Karim spent most of his time inside. Since he lost his residence permit, he was in constant fear of the police and only went outside to do illicit work. But mostly, he was disappointed because the reason for his flight was still unsolved: 'Auf einen Schlag war jede weitere Hoffnung dahin. Und jetzt habe ich noch immer diese Brüste. Schauen Sie mal. Liebe Frau Schulz, ich habe meine Heimat verlassen, weil ich davon träume, ein normaler Mann zu werden. Das ist alles' [In one swoop, all hope was gone. And now I still have these breasts. Take a look. Dear Ms Schulz, I left my home because I dream of becoming a normal man. That is all] (OF, 93). Karim decides to flee to Finland before he can be deported. He wants to free himself from the 'nicht enden wollenden deutschen Qual' [German agony that doesn't want to end] (OF, 35), but first he pays Ms Schulz a visit in the 'allmächtigen Behörde' [almighty authority] (OF, 31) – and thereby initiates his critical and humorous counternarrative.

Picaresque Writing

The act of writing itself, which has above been defined as a healing act and as a form of taking revenge, is always present in Khider's novels. In *Der falsche Inder* (2008) [*The Village Indian*, 2013], the whole story revolves around a refugee's autobiographic manuscript, in *Die Orangen des Präsidenten* (2011) [The President's Oranges], inmates write on prison walls, and *Brief in die Auberginenrepublik* (2013) [Letter to the Aubergine

Republic] is about a secret love letter that is smuggled to Iraq.[42] In *Ohrfeige*, Karim's friend Rafid, who is a writer, barely has the means to produce texts and in the end, when he suffers from mental illness, disposes of all his manuscripts. Hence, it seems that writing also always serves as an empowering act of the characters, who are reclaiming their own story – or are at least trying to do so.

Khider's literature is critical, yet aware of the subjectivity of the reality it portrays.[43] That there are different versions of reality, which depend on one's approach and perspective, becomes especially clear in his award-winning, autofictional debut novel *Der falsche Inder*. Just as the novel's protagonist Rasul Hamid always comes up with new approaches during his flight from Iraq, so does the story itself. Rasul's manuscript, which forms the story-within-the-story, gives eight different accounts of his flight, and each version has a different focus and mood. Thus, Khider draws on the genre of the picaresque novel, in which the narrator tells a quasi-autobiographic story with a very subjective version of reality. The narrator always maintains sovereignty while depicting the events yet proves to be unreliable – which in *Der falsche Inder* becomes most evident through the eight different versions of events.

Due to their autobiographical elements, Khider's novels never lose their link to reality, but by using a subjective, selective and unreliable perspective, they also subvert it.[44] Moritz Schramm therefore places the realism in Khider's works somewhere between a postmodern irony, reflecting discursive constructions of reality, and a new form of realism, which offers a literary approach to reality.[45] Schramm defines Khider's writing as ironic realism, which claims and simultaneously challenges a reference to reality. It asks for an ironic distance to self and circumstances and is required for

---

42　Cf. Moritz Schramm, 'Ironischer Realismus: Selbstdifferenz und Wirklichkeitsnähe bei Abbas Khider', in Søren R. Fauth and Rolf Parr, eds., *Neue Realismen in der Gegenwartsliteratur* (Paderborn: Wilhelm Fink, 2016), 71–84, 73.

43　Ibid., 84.

44　Ibid., 74–5.

45　Ibid., 72.

critical thinking.[46] By using a framing story in each of his novels, Khider also generates a certain distance to the narrator and the created self.[47] This strategy of ironic distancing is a typically picaresque stance that gets the readers involved and asks them to make up their own minds. In a carnivalesque reversal of power dynamics, the migrant characters, whose point of view the stories take on, gain the authority of what is narrated and how it is narrated. This allows them to speak critically about the dominant culture and its practices. By mixing their criticism with humour and irony, it seems less accusatory to the readers, whose critical thoughts are prompted and who are implicitly asked to reconsider certain structures, stereotypes and prejudices.

In *Ohrfeige*, too, Khider's writing is not only an act of protest, revolt and provocation,[48] it also shows a picaresque reclaiming of one's own story. His narrator-protagonist at times exaggerates certain events, reflects on them in his favour or even lies to achieve his goals. This becomes most obvious when the protagonist and his friends have to testify for their asylum requests. Karim, who wants to keep the true reason for his flight a secret, decides to come up with a 'Lebensgeschichte [...], die das Gesetz anerkennen würde' [a life story [...] that would be recognised by law] (OF, 75). In order to have his asylum request granted, he steals the story of Meki, a friend from school, who joked about Saddam Hussein and his wife, and vanished without a trace. Now in Germany, Karim and his friends pretend to be more political than they ever were when they lived under Saddam's dictatorship (OF, 72–3). Back home, Karim knew not one real antagonist to the oppressive regime; they all cursed the system but never took action against it. Yet ironically, 'im Asylantenheim wimmelt es jetzt plötzlich vor Revolutionären' [in the home for asylum seekers it is suddenly now swarming with revolutionaries] (OF, 72).

46   Ibid., 79.
47   Ibid., 81–2.
48   Cf. Schneider, 'Darstellungsweisen von Fluchtprozessen in der Gegenwartsliteratur', 91.

Conclusion: Dominant Power Re-established

As outlined above, Abbas Khider's novel portraits the difficult fate of refugees in Germany with the use of different carnivalesque elements, such as profanation and ridicule directed at higher authorities, the display of a heterotopic demarcation of asylum seekers which at the same time questions and maintains the majority society's structure, a grotesque, universal body which symbolises common suffering and a picaresque writing as means of reclaiming agency. Yet eventually, the given structures remain, and the end of the novel coincides with two other endings: firstly, the Iraq war is declared over and the German institutions start to issue asylum repeals – and Ms Schulz sends Karim his documents. The protagonist feels like his life in Germany ends even though it never really started. After more than three years, he still has not reached his dream and is left with nothing:

> Drei Jahre und vier Monate habe ich hier gelebt. In Dachau, in Zirndorf, in Bayreuth, in Niederhofen an der Donau und in München. [...] Noch immer bin ich kein normaler Mann, noch immer habe ich die verdammten Brüste. [...] Hätte ich früher angefangen schwarzzuarbeiten, hätte ich die Operation vermutlich längst finanzieren können. Aber ich bin eben doch ein aufrichtiger Trottel. Alles, was ich erreicht habe, ist ein gigantisches Nichts (OF, 218).

> [I have lived here for three years and four months. In Dachau, in Zirnsdorf, in Bayreuth, in Niederhofen on the Danube and in Munich. [...] I am still not a normal man, I still have these damn breasts [...] Had I started earlier to do illegal work, I probably would have long since been able to pay for the surgery. But I am an honest fool. Everything that I have achieved is a gigantic nothing.]

Secondly, according to the basic rules and traditions of the historical carnival as a folk festival, it only lasts for a specific time span and eventually comes to an end. For the plot of *Ohrfeige*, this means that the carnivalesque reversal of power dynamics also comes to an end when Karim awakens from a cannabis-induced dream: '*Ich sitze in Salims Wohnung. Wo ist Frau Schulz?* [*I am sitting in Salim's apartment. Where is Ms Schulz?*] (OF, 220). Only now, the readers realise that the framing narrative at the Alien Registration Office and the confrontation with Ms

Schulz were merely a dream or hallucination. Thus, Karim turns out to be an unreliable narrator, who told his embedded life story hallucinating under the influence of drugs.[49] It becomes evident that Ms Schulz is not actually constrained, gagged and smacked – she is still the one 'restraining' the protagonist. This plot twist combined with Karim's allegedly frail masculinity leads the journalist and novelist Fatma Aydemir to the conclusion that the portrayal of the protagonist helps to change a prejudiced perception of Arab men: 'So ist Karim so etwas wie der Gegenentwurf zu dem, was dem Zeitungsleser seit Silvester als "der arabische Mann" präsentiert wird: verschüchtert, unsicher, durchweg passiv' [Thus, Karim is something like an alternative model to 'the Arabic man' that newspaper readers have been presented with since New Year's Eve: intimidated, insecure, always passive].[50] Aydemir's interpretation of a shy and passive protagonist can only be agreed on to a limited extent. At least in his dream, Karim presents himself as resistant, and even after he awakes, up to the last sentence – 'Irgendwann werde ich Sie erwischen und ohrfeigen' [At some point I will catch you and slap you] (OF, 220) – also as being prepared to use violence. Nevertheless, the humorous tone dominates in the narrative, and despite all the criticism the protagonist voices, he always remains dependent on higher authorities who push him into a rather passive role.

What sticks with the reader is the insight into the daily struggles refugees have to face in a bureaucratic system that always keeps them at

---

49 Cf. Carola Hilmes, '"Jedes Kapitel ein Anfang und zugleich ein Ende": Abbas Khiders fiktionalisierte Lebensbeschreibung', in Monika Wolting, ed., *Identitätskonstruktionen in der deutschen Gegenwartsliteratur* (Göttingen: V & R unipress, 2017), 135–46, 146.

50 Fatma Aydemir, 'Eine Sachbearbeiterin wird gefesselt: Sein Roman *Ohrfeige* dreht sich um den Wahnsinn im Alltag eines Asylbewerbers in Deutschland. Eine Begegnung mit Abbas Khider', *taz* (29 January 2016), <http://www.taz.de/Roman-Ohrfeige-von-Abbas-Khider/%215270464/>, accessed 5 November 2018. Aydemir here refers to the many cases of sexual harassment that took place in Cologne on New Year's Eve 2016. Allegedly, most of the suspects were from Tunisia, Morocco and Iraq.

a distance from the rest of German society. Also, even though the story's carnivalesque power reversal is temporary, the given structures are undermined more substantially through a remaining idea of radical change – a utopian vision of how lasting change could look like if one would look at the world through the lens of the marginalised. In addition, there is an implicit appeal for more humanity, a call for awareness directed at the readers; as Aydemir explains:

> In einer Diktatur erwartet man ja, dass Menschenleben zerstört werden. Aber in diesem Roman geschieht das innerhalb einer offenen Gesellschaft, einem demokratischen Land. Das wird für einige Leser sicher schmerzhaft sein. Aber Kunst muss manchmal auch wehtun – wenn es denn nötig ist.[51]

> [Under a dictatorship, one expects human lives to be destroyed. But in this novel, it happens within an open-minded society, a democratic country. This will surely be painful for some readers. But sometimes art also has to hurt – if it is necessary.]

Therefore, Khider uses grotesque elements as well as carnivalesque and humorous strategies to point to a restrictive, degrading system within an allegedly free country. He displays that 'die Bundesrepublik seit Jahrzehnten ein Einwanderungsland ist, aber kein Einwanderungsland sein will' [the Federal Republic [of Germany] has been a country of immigration for decades, but does not want to be a country of immigration].[52]

51   Ibid.
52   Delius, 'Die deutsche Verlogenheit'.

BEATE BAUMANN AND CORINNE PUGLISI

'German Is My New Tongue': The Role of (Foreign) Language in the Construction of Identity[1]

Abbas Khider's biography and literary production are deeply rooted in a context of migration. With countless other people, he shares the fate of having had to leave his homeland and his family because of traumatic and life-threatening circumstances and having to go through further dramatic experiences before he was granted asylum in Germany, after years of wandering. It goes without saying that such extreme life situations have a profound impact on someone's identity, but also the confrontation with the new living environment, which is inevitably marked by a change in language and culture, affects a person's linguistic and cultural identity.

The topic of this contribution must be seen against this background, as well. The aim of this chapter is to shed light on the role of language and identity-related elements in Khider's novels, especially in relation to the genre of autofiction. These central aspects and their intrinsic relationship to one another will be presented and examined by means of selected examples, which will allow conclusions to be drawn about the characters' and also the author's identity formation processes.

---

1   All translations are our own unless otherwise noted. Pages 157 and 181–182 of this contribution are by both contributors, pages 158–171 and 178–181 are by Beate Baumann, and pages 171–177 are by Corinne Puglisi.

Migration, Language(s) and Identity

There have always been migration processes, but transcontinental migration flows across the Mediterranean Sea heading to Europe have seen a huge increase in the last few years. The leading causes as to why people are forced to leave their living environment are attributable to climate change, water and food shortages. On the other hand, the continuing state of war in the Near and Middle East and the resulting political and economic instability have generated migration waves and forced people to flee.

It is not just Khider's biography that must be placed in this context, but also his literary works, in which themes such as violence, escape and the desire for a new, safe life are key. In this regard, Khider's texts are autofictional in nature, since they are 'not autobiographies, [and] not exactly novels'.[2] They simply are a 'fiction of purely real events and facts'[3] which necessarily have strong implications for identity as Khider himself – with reference, for example, to his traumatic experiences in prison – clearly expresses: 'When you leave prison behind or when you are released, you carry prison within you. You are psychologically not the same anymore.'[4]

Khider's difficult years on the run through several North African countries and his life as a refugee, which is likewise characterised by violence and imprisonment, came to an end in 2000 when he arrived in Germany. Originally Germany was just a transit country for Khider, as his actual destination was Sweden. The reason seems, at first, to be mainly practical, but

2   'nicht Autobiographien, nicht ganz Romane'. – Serge Doubrovsky, 'Nah am Text', *Kultur & Gespenster: Autofiktion* 7 (2008), 123–33, 126. Cited in Martina Wagner-Egelhaaf, 'Einleitung: Was ist Auto(r)fiktion?', in Martina Wagner-Egelhaaf, ed., *Auto(r)fiktion: Literarische Verfahren der Selbstkonstruktion* (Bielefeld: Aisthesis, 2013), 7–21, 10.

3   'Fiktion strikt realer Ereignisse und Fakten'. – Doubrovsky, 'Nah am Text', 123.

4   'Wenn man das Gefängnis hinter sich lässt, oder wenn man entlassen wird, man trägt das Gefängnis in sich mit. Psychisch ist man nicht mehr der alte', Interview in ARD-alpha (14 March 2017), <https://www.youtube.com/watch?v=8KyI1d8UB-0> (09:24–09:33/44:54), accessed 25 July 2018.

at the same time, it points to the importance that Khider attributes to language, or more accurately to a foreign language: in Scandinavian countries like Sweden, asylum-seekers received – unlike in Germany at that time – some financial support from the government to attend a language course which would enable them to learn the national language and also to study at university.[5] Khider saw this as a chance to make his desire and dream of an education come true, something which was denied to him in Iraq.

It goes without saying that foreign/second language acquisition plays a central role in the achievement of this personal goal. From the perspective of the host countries, the acquisition of the official national language constitutes a key instrument in light of the 'Integration-durch-Sprache-Diskurses' [integration-through-language-discourse], which guarantees a (supposed) linguistic and cultural homogeneity through which the stability of the national identity and of the prevailing value system should be secured.[6] In this respect, Uli Linke points out that '[t]hrough the medium of language, and its strategic deployment, in citizenship and immigration, the nation state seeks to engraft a linguistic memory of national belonging'.[7] Consequently, people who want to integrate have on the one hand an obligation to fulfil this duty, while on the other hand the acquisition of the host country language means for them confronting a new linguistic and cultural context, which has an impact on their identity formation.

Language shapes our way of thinking, our culture and our identity, as George Herbert Mead pointed out in *Mind, Self, and Society*, which provides the basis for the theory of symbolic interactionism, namely, the notion that individuals construct their identity through communication.[8]

5   Interview in ARD-alpha (12:22–12:47/44:54).

6   Brigitta Busch, *Mehrsprachigkeit* (Wien: Facultas, 2013), 115.

7   Uli Linke, 'Language as Battleground: "Speaking" the Nation, Citizenship and Diversity Management in Post-unification Germany', in Jan-Jonathan Bock and Sharon Macdonald, eds., *Refugees Welcome? Difference and Diversity in a Changing Germany* (New York/Oxford: Berghahn, 2019), 41–66, 53.

8   George Herbert Mead, *Mind, Self, and Society: From the Standpoint of a Social Behaviorist* (Chicago: University of Chicago Press, 1934). Blumer, Mead's disciple, delves deeper into the connection between the individual and social dimension and the role of language in the identity construction processes. – See Herbert Blumer, *Symbolic Interactionism: Perspective and Method* (Englewood Cliffs, NJ: Prentice-Hall, 1969).

In these inter-individual exchanges, the individual takes on a role and ne-gotiates rules and meanings by assuming – even unconsciously – the role of the interlocutor and develops, in this way, his own self in the symbolic interaction through language. Hence, the self is essentially social in nature.

The theoretical assumptions of the symbolic interactionism became fundamental for subsequent studies, especially in the domain of social and psychological sciences. All theories underline the fact that no indi-vidual is born with a predetermined identity. Rather, identity is constructed through communication in the social context. Individual identity is thus to be considered always and only as the fragile and temporary result of the individual interacting with himself/herself and others.[9] It is not a stable entity but a dynamic and changeable one, which is able to adapt to the various situations and stages of life the individual goes through. Besides, identity is not homogenous in nature, but can instead appear as fragmen-tary and contradictory.

Starting from the assumption that our societies are increasingly char-acterised by structural dynamics such as individualisation, pluralisation, flexibility and mobility – which influence the lives of today's individ-uals – postmodern studies have developed new concepts that highlight the pluralistic nature of identity. Social psychologist Heiner Keupp intro-duced the concept of patchwork identity, describing a construct made of several elements, which at first glance do not seem to fit together well but are actually connected to each other and complete each other, creating the whole. This patchwork identity is the result of a construction process that the individuals carry out continuously, which entails real work on identity, an 'Identitätsarbeit' that the individual fulfils through each action he/she performs.[10] Wolfgang Welsch also uses the term 'patchwork identity' which, according to the German philosopher, characterises not only the people who have gone through the experience of migration but all young people

9   Jürgen Straub, 'Identitätstheorie, empirische Identitätsforschung und die "postmoderne" armchair psychology', *Zeitschrift für qualitative Bildungs-, Beratungs- und Sozialforschung* 1 (2002), 167–94, 171.

10   Heiner Keupp et al., *Identitätskonstruktionen: Das Patchwork der Identitäten in der Spätmoderne* (Reinbek: Rowohlt, 2006), 215.

as well, because today's individuals are increasingly 'in sich transkulturell' [transcultural in themselves].[11]

Participation in social and cultural practices, which is crucial for identity construction, is thus achieved through interaction, namely through the use of language (including paraverbal and non-verbal language). In the case of migrants, the goal of becoming part of a new linguistic and cultural community demands learning a new language which allows them to build, define and negotiate interpersonal relationships and to be part of a 'community of practice'.[12]

In this regard, Bonny Norton's works on the construction of identity in a context of migration, which are based on sociocultural theories, have led to meaningful conclusions. Norton defines identity as 'how a person understands his or her relationship to the world, how that relationship is constructed across time and space, and how the person understands possibilities for the future'.[13] Individuals negotiate their self by learning a new language through the interpersonal confrontation with their social environment so that identity development becomes a 'site of struggle'.[14] At the same time, language is not predominately a means to exchange information, but instead it helps learners develop self-concepts, negotiate their relationship to the social environment and, in so doing, construct their identity.[15]

Identity is, therefore, not stable or homogeneous, but is non-uniform, multiple, dynamic, variable and socially constructed. This is also clearly shown in the centrality of agency in language learning because '[t]hrough human agency, language learners who struggle to speak from one identity

11 Wolfgang Welsch, 'Was ist eigentlich Transkulturalität?', in Lucyna Darowska, Thomas Lüttenberg and Claudia Machold, eds., *Hochschule als transkultureller Raum? Beiträge zu Kultur, Bildung und Differenz* (Bielefeld: transcript, 2003), 39–66, 42.

12 Bonny Norton and Carolyn McKinney, 'An Identity Approach to Second Language Acquisition', in Dwight Atkinson, ed., *Alternative Approaches to Second Language Acquisition* (London/New York: Routledge, 2011), 73–94, 87.

13 Bonny Norton, *Identity and Language Learning: Gender, Ethnicity and Educational Change* (Harlow: Pearson Education, 2000), 5.

14 Norton and McKinney, 'An Identity Approach to Second Language Acquisition', 74.

15 Bonny Norton, *Identity and Language Learning: Extending the Conversation* (Bristol/Buffalo/Toronto: Multilingual Matters, 2013), 4.

position may be able to reframe their relationship with others and claim alternative, more powerful identities from which to speak, read or write, thereby enhancing language acquisition.'[16] Besides, learning a foreign language constitutes an investment on the part of the migrant learner, to gain access to the target society's material and symbolic resources, which so far have been out of reach for them. In this way, they can increase the value of their cultural capital – as defined by Bourdieu – and actually satisfy their desires and goals for the future:

> If learners 'invest' in a second language, they do so with the understanding that they will acquire a wider range of symbolic and material resources, which will in turn increase the value of their cultural capital. As the value of their cultural capital increases, so learners' sense of themselves and their desires for the future are reassessed. Hence the integral relationship between investment and identity.[17]

For Abbas Khider too, learning the German language constitutes an investment with the purpose of fulfilling his dream to study, freely and safely, in a new linguistic and cultural context. Furthermore, it was a central concern for him to be able to communicate with the members of his new living environment and to become part of that society.[18] This required, at the beginning, great effort because he had to pay for a German course from his own resources and he struggled to acquire the language.[19] His first contact with German was Bavarian, which he found incomprehensible.[20] Phonetics, especially *umlauts*, caused him great difficulties too:

> Und ich dachte, ich würde diese Sprache niemals lernen. Und ich hatte auch Probleme irgendwann mit diesen Umlauten. [...] Jeder Araber hat dieses Problem. Umlaute. Das gibt es nicht in der arabischen Welt, da gibt es nur ein O und das war's. Oder ein

---

16   Ibid., 3.
17   Carolyn McKinney and Bonny Norton, 'Identity in Language and Literacy Education', in Bernard Spolsky and Francis M. Hult, eds., *The Handbook of Educational Linguistics* (Oxford: Blackwell, 2008), 192–205, 195.
18   Interview in ARD-alpha (16:39–17:09/44:54).
19   Ibid. (16:12–16:33/44:54). The so-called integration courses for asylum seeker were first introduced in Germany on the 1st January 2005 under the Residence Act.
20   Ibid. (15:17–15:19/44:54).

Ö, Ü. Das ist immer noch ein Drama. Ich habe später einen Phonetik-Kurs besucht und bestanden mit 4,0, bin ich stolz darauf.[21]

[And I thought, I would never learn this language. And, at some point, I had problems with these umlauts [...] Every Arab has this problem. Umlauts. This doesn't exist in the Arabic world, there is only one O and that's it. Or an Ö, Ü. That's still a drama. I attended a course in Phonetics later and passed it with a 4.0, I'm proud of that.]

However, for Khider, the acquisition of the German language is far from being just an investment in his personal and future social life. On the contrary, this becomes for him a fundamental instrument to raise his voice and increase its expressiveness. Therefore, the extension of his linguistic identity, which Khider experiences in an utterly physical way, contributes to the development of a *new tongue* and, as a consequence, to a more complex, hybrid identity.[22]

---

21   Ibid. (15:40–16:04/44:54).

22   'Manchmal durchlebt man eine Phase, in der man schreien möchte, aber keinen Ton herausbekommt. Eine Phase der Müdigkeit, der Erschöpfung, in der man merkt, dass man eine andere Sprache braucht. [...] Die Lage in meinem Heimatland hat mich beschäftigt, ich wollte mich dazu äußern, aber auf Arabisch konnte ich das irgendwie nicht. Die deutsche Sprache hat mir diese Möglichkeit gegeben, und seitdem ist sie *meine neue Zunge*. [...] Sowohl mit dem Arabischen als auch mit dem Deutschen bin ich verbunden. In dieser Mischung sehe ich inhaltlich und sprachlich einen Vorteil' [Sometimes you go through a period during which you would like to scream, but no sound comes out. A period of tiredness, of exhaustion in which you notice, you need another language. [...] I was concerned about the situation in my homeland and I wanted to speak out about it, but in Arabic I somehow couldn't. The German language gave me this chance, and since then it is *my new tongue* [...] I am bound to both Arabic and German. In this mixture I see an advantage both for the content and the language]. – Abderrahmane Ammar, 'Deutsch ist meine neue Zunge – Ein Interview mit Abbas Khider', Goethe Institute (2014), <http://www.goethe.de/ins/it/lp/prj/lit/bue/bmt/hin/de14101779.htm>, accessed 25 July 2018. In the recent past, foreign language research has increasingly dealt with the relationship between language, foreign language learning and (hybrid) identity constructions, cf. Eva Burwitz-Melzer, Frank G. Königs and Claudia Riemer, eds. *Identität und Fremdsprachenlernen: Anmerkungen zu einer komplexen Beziehung. Arbeitspapiere der 33. Frühjahrskonferenz zur Erforschung des Fremdsprachenunterrichts* (Tübingen: Narr, 2013).

'What I Can't Live With Is That I Don't Know Who I Really Am'

As in all of Khider's works, including his first novel *Der falsche Inder* (2008) [*The Village Indian*, 2013], the use of the German language as a means of literary expression plays a crucial role for identity. In fact, it is exactly the distance from the foreign language that gives the author the freedom to play with its linguistic forms and structures in an extremely creative way, by means of images, unusual metaphors, phrasemes, sayings literally translated from Arabic and, not least, by means of the sensory and corporeal plane. It is exactly the foreign language, employed in this way, that reveals the author's linguistic and cultural context of origin and creates an estrangement effect. This way of using the German language already emerges in this first novel, an autobiographic work 'als Roman getarnt[-]'²³ [camouflaged as novel], in which the identity issue constitutes a central topic, as is already made clear in the German title. The title refers to a false classification by the outside world, which, due to merely external, physical characteristics, assigns to the main character, Rasul Hamid, a specific ethnic identity and causes him to reflect on it. To find an explanation for his dark skin, Rasul puts forward many possible reasons, which are intended to disprove any stereotypical attributions by means of historical-cultural, climatic and family aspects.²⁴

23   Carola Hilmes, 'Jedes Kapitel ein Anfang und zugleich ein Ende: Abbas Khiders fiktionalisierte Lebensbeschreibung', in Monika Wolting, ed., *Identitätskonstruktionen in der deutschen Gegenwartsliteratur* (Göttingen: V & R unipress, 2017), 135–46, 136.

24   The natural element of fire with its positive and negative effects represents the main component that connects three spheres: the fire lit by Kalif Al-Mansur, in the place where the city of Baghdad was built as City of Freedom in 762; the 'Gespenster des Feuers' [the ghosts of the fire] (FI, 12) that constantly haunted the city with wars; die 'unbarmherzige Sonne' [merciless sun] (FI, 13) that rolls like 'eine Kutsche aus Eisen und Feuer' [a carriage of iron and fire] (FI, 13) through Baghdad. All this – says Rasul – could explain why he goes 'mit brauner Haut, tiefschwarzen Haaren und dunklen Augen durchs Leben' [through life with brown skin, the darkest black hair and dark eyes] (FI, 13).

However, Rasul not only experiences the uncertainty of his origin as an identity problem, but also his time in prison and the long years on the run are destined to make the feeling of uncertainty over his own self be a constant factor in his life. To protect his own existence, he is temporarily forced to take on several names and identities, as he does, for example, in the time between his release from prison and his escape from Iraq:

Er [Mahdis friend Abba] versorgte mich innerhalb einiger Monate mit mehr als fünfzehn gefälschten Ausweisen, mit ebenso vielen unterschiedlichen Namen und Berufen. Jedes Mal musste ich meinen neuen Namen mitsamt den zugehörigen Informationen auswendig lernen. Ich frage mich bis heute, wer von ihnen ich eigentlich war, und vor allem, wer sie waren (FI, 103).

[For the next few months, he [Mahdi's friend Abba] supplied me with more than fifteen fake IDs, with just as many names and professions. Each time, I had to learn by heart my new name and all the details that went with it. Even today, I wonder which one of them I really was. And who they all were.]

That his name has for him an identity-shaping meaning is testified by his joy over the passport with his real name: 'Endlich kam der Tag, an dem ich alle meine Namen hinter mir lassen konnte, um mit meinem richtigen Namen durch die Weltmeere zu segeln' [The day finally came when I could leave all those names behind and sail the seas, using my real name] (FI, 103). Additionally, he learns during his years on the run to use his names or rather his identities even in a humorous and playful way, for example, when dealing with violence and power (FI, 88–9). He experiences his escape from Iraq as 'eine Art Krankheit' [a kind of illness], as 'Keinen-Zustand' [no-one state] and 'große Leere' [great emptiness] (FI 67; 70). This has a strong impact on his existential sense of self, since he sees from now on in his life 'nur noch zwei Möglichkeiten: die Leere zu bekämpfen oder meinem Leben ein Ende zu setzen' [Only two choices lay before me – to fight this emptiness or to put an end to my life] (FI, 71). He chooses the first option and with it the life of a refugee, marked by restlessness, distrust and anxiety. The plague of emptiness, the wandering and the insecurity over present and future do not just cause instability in his inner state, but the *symptoms* of his illness are also visible in his behaviour and his appearance:

Ein Flüchtling geht nicht wie ein normaler Mensch auf die Straße. Er hält alle um sich herum für Polizisten. Alle sind ihm verdächtig. Ihn interessieren weder Schaufenster noch Plakate noch Frauen. Er beobachtet nur die Gesichter der Menschen, und seine Augen wandern unruhig hin und her. Wie eine verrückt gewordene Uhr. Er dreht sich ständig um, und die Angst steht ihm im Gesicht geschrieben. Bei mir waren diese Symptome wohl sehr deutlich ausgeprägt und leicht zu erkennen (FI, 109).

[A refugee doesn't behave like a normal person when he's out and about. He thinks everyone is a policeman. He's suspicious of everyone. He's not interested in shop windows or posters or women. He watches only people's faces, his eyes wander restlessly. Like a clock that has gone mad. He keeps looking over his shoulder, fear written on his face. In my case, the symptoms were probably very evident.]

Initially he considers the vicissitudes of this difficult period from an extremely negative perspective, which casts a cloud over his own existence. He sees himself as 'Unheilbringer für die Menschheit' [a bringer of bad luck], as a 'Pechvogel' [jinx] and 'Unglücksrabe' [unlucky raven], even when he is already in Germany, where he encounters '[k]eine wirklichen Probleme, nur kleinere, wenn auch lästigere' [[n]o big problems. Only small ones] (FI, 123–32). So, for example, Rasul blames himself for the university tuition fee increase:

'Es tut mir leid!'
'Was?'
'Das mit der Studiengebühr.'
'Wieso Studiengebühr? Was ist damit?'
'Das ist alles wegen meines Vogels.'
'Vogel? Du hast wohl einen? Bist du jetzt ganz durchgedreht, oder was?'
'Nein, ich meine doch einen anderen Vogel!'
'Welchen denn?'
[…]
'Na ja, ein Unglücksvogel eben, der vor Kurzem Deutschland erreicht hat.'
'Ist das wieder eines deiner arabischen Märchen?
'Ja, es ist ein echtes arabisches Märchen. Die tausendundzweite Nacht.' (FI, 130–1)

['I'm sorry!'
'What?'
'The whole fee thing.'
'What about the fees?'
'It's all because of my raven!'

Raven? Have you gone completely mad or what?'
'No, I mean a different kind of raven!'
'Which then?'
[...]
'Well, you know, the unlucky raven that reached Germany not so long ago.'
'Is this one of your Arabian fairy tales again?'
'Yes, it's a real Arabian tale. Arabian Night Number 1002.']

This dialogue clearly reflects the role of the German language for Khider's writing. In fact, the author does not just play with typical German sayings but also shows his linguistic creativity by introducing the neologism 'tausendundzweite Nacht'. In this way, he transforms the title of the famous *Tales from the Thousand and One Nights*, to which Rasul adds his own personal story. Having learned the German language is a relatively recent achievement for him, but Khider, just like the protagonist Rasul, *genetically* possesses the best prerequisites to come into contact with the language, having his family background near Babel and 'babylonisches Blut' [Babylonian blood] (FI, 57), a humorous pun that alludes to the alleged connection between his natural origins, multilingualism and his ability to communicate. But if on the one hand he wonders 'welches Schicksal die Sprachen haben, dass sie als Fluch auf die Welt kamen' [about the fate of languages, given that they entered the world as a curse] (FI, 57), on the other hand, he is convinced that

[d]as einzig Wichtige ist, dass der Turm der Grund für die Menschen war, neben den Sprachen auch das Aufzeichnen und Schreiben beherrschen zu wollen. Warum? Ganz einfach: Wenn die Leute viele Sprachen haben, dann schreiben sie, um ihre Sprachen zu schützen und auch, um miteinander zu kommunizieren (FI, 58).

[[t]he one important thing was that the tower was the reason for human beings to want to be able to record and write things as well as to speak languages. Why? Quite simple: if people have many languages, they write in order to protect their own as well as to communicate with others.]

Furthermore, writing takes on an identity-shaping function in the quest for the self, a quest which, also in his new living context in Germany, seems far from being over: 'Es ist sicherlich erträglich, Zigeuner, Iraker, Inder oder gar ein Außerirdischer zu sein, wieso auch nicht! Aber es mir unerträglich, dass ich bis heute nicht genau weiß, wer ich wirklich bin' [I can live, of course, with being a gypsy, an Iraqi, an Indian, an extraterrestial, even – why not? What I can't live with is that I don't know who I really am] (FI, 22). In that regard, for Khider/Rasul, (the German) language and writing not only contribute to new and hopeful trust in life and in the future, but writing is above all a precious opportunity for introspection and, by so doing, to reflect on himself and to discover his new self.[25]

'The Gentle Sway of Your Single Unbroken Wing'

In his second autofictional novel, *Die Orangen des Präsidenten* (2011) [The President's Oranges], language and writing also play a significant role. This applies particularly to the main character, Madhi Muhsin (or rather: Madhi Hamama), for whom reading and writing become a survival strategy during his two years in prison to endure the inflicted physical and mental atrocities:

> Und ich? Ich jagte Wanzen, und meine zweite Beschäftigung wurde bald das Lesen, und zwar alles, was die anderen Gefangenen an die Wände geschrieben hatten. Ich hätte gern Bücher gehabt, aber so etwas existierte in diesem Leben nicht. Später

25   'Wenn ich schreibe, sehe ich alles wie beim ersten Mal und versuche es nachzufühlen und neu zu begreifen. Ich bin nun Schüler und Lehrer zugleich. Ich unterrichte mich und lerne von mir. Und so kam ich auf die verrückte Idee, meine eigene Geschichte aufzuschreiben. Ich verriegelte fast täglich die Tür meines Zimmers, blendete die Außenwelt aus und tauchte in mich hinein, um jedes Mal ein weiteres verborgenes Stück meiner selbst an der Oberfläche zu ziehen. Ich entdeckte mich und die Welt neu und brachte diese Erkenntnis zu Papier. Ob das, was ich schreibe, das wahre Leben ist? Ich kann es nicht sagen' [When I write, I see everything as if for the first time, I try to empathise, to understand anew. I am both the student and the teacher. I teach myself and learn from myself. One day I came up with the mad idea of writing my story. I locked myself in my room, blocked out the external world and plunged deep within each time to bring another concealed part of myself to the surface. I discovered myself and the world anew and committed this insight to paper. Is what I write real life? I can't say] (FI, 24).

begann ich selbst, die Wände zu beschreiben, Wörter und Sätze, die ich für Gedichte hielt (OdP, 61–2).

[And I? I hunted bugs and my second occupation soon became reading, pretty much everything other prisoners had written on the walls. I would have liked to have books, but such things did not exist in that life. Later, I myself started writing on the walls, words or sentences that I considered as poems.]

Khider himself consciously decided to narrate these terrible experiences in a laconic way, so to speak, with a certain 'offhandedness, which is in large part due to the protective distance created by the use of the foreign language'[26] that means for him, at the same time, choosing life:

Wenn ich über all das schreibe, wenn ich alle Türen öffne und das alles, das Ganze, wortwörtlich wiedergebe, ich überlebe das nicht. Das weiß ich. Und deswegen, glaube ich, ist es eben eine Entscheidung für das Leben. Deswegen versuche ich immer, über ernsthafte Themen zu schreiben, über bittere Wirklichkeiten, über Folter, aber ich versuche die Leser nie zu foltern.[27]

[If I wrote about all of this, if I opened doors and related it all, word-for-word, I would not survive it. I know it. And that's why I believe that this exactly means choosing life. That's why I always try to write about serious subjects, about harsh reality and torture, but I never try to torture the readers.]

It is precisely the experience of physical and psychological violence that changes Mahdi's identity deeply. And in this case too, it is exactly the use of the foreign language which allows Khider to narrate the 'bitteren Wirklichkeiten' [harsh reality] of his protagonist. He does not always do it in an emotionally detached way, but occasionally gives his emotions free rein, as happens in the following example, in which some German words

---

26 'Beiläufigkeit, die sich nicht zuletzt der schützenden Distanz der verwendeten Fremdsprache verdankt'. – Andreas Pflitsch, 'Abbas Khider: *Die Orangen des Präsidenten*', *Der Tagesspiegel* (16 March 2011), <https://www.tagesspiegel.de/kultur/abbas-khider-die-orangen-des-praesidenten/3953848.html>, accessed 8 August 2018.

27 Interview in ARD-alpha (24:48–25:15/44:54).

most assuredly reflect Arabic cultures and expressions, also through the use of literal translation:[28]

> Ich taumelte und sackte in mich zusammen wie ein nasses Wäschebündel. So sehr ich auch durch meinen reglosen Körper gezwungen war, reglos zu liegen, so wild tobte mein Geist: Ich wollte Saddam, dieses Mistschwein, diesen Sohn einer trächtigen Flussratte, foltern, seine Haut langsam aufschneiden und Zentimeter für Zentimeter vom Körper ziehen, um sein verdorbenes Inneres und das Fehlen seines Herzens mit eigenen Augen zu sehen (OdP, 71).

> [I staggered and slumped into a heap, like a bundle of wet clothes. As much as I was forced to lay still from my still body, my spirit went wild: I wanted to torture Saddam, that bloody swine, that son of a gravid river rat, to rip off his skin, pull it from off his body, centimetre after centimetre, see with my own eyes his corrupt interior and the lack of his heart.]

On the other hand, Khider narrates such extreme, degrading conditions and violent situations that are able to destroy the body and the self almost always in a laconic way and with a certain situational humour, like Mahdi's fully unexpected, incomprehensible and uncontrolled reaction to physical and psychological violence. He laughs and laughs uncontrollably at the torture:

> Ich prustete laut los und schrie in allen Tonlagen, krümmte und gebärdete mich, als hätte ich Lachgas geatmet. Den Wärtern fielen vor Überraschung fast die Knüppel aus der Hand […]. Einer brach schließlich das Schweigen und forderte, ich solle aufhören. Ich konnte aber nicht. Ich versuchte es, musste aber doppelt so laut und heftig wie zuvor loslachen. […] Irgendwann hörte ich ebenso plötzlich mit dem Lachen auf, wie es begonnen hatte. Und ich stellte zu meiner eigenen Verwunderung fest, dass ich bei äußerst klarem Verstand und anscheinend doch nicht verrückt geworden war (OdP, 6–7).

> [I burst out laughing and shrieking in all possible pitches, I bent over and behaved as if I had inhaled laughing-gas. Caught by surprise, the guards almost let their

---

28   The use of literal translation as linguistic strategy plays an important role in the affective negation of traumatic events not only in Khider's texts, but also in other authors like Emine Sevgi Özdamar. – Cf. Yasemin Yildiz, 'Political Trauma and Literal Translation: Emine Sevgi Özdamar's *Mutterzunge*', *Gegenwartsliteratur* 7 (2008), 248–70.

clubs fall out of their hands. [...] One of them eventually broke the silence and commanded me to stop it. But I couldn't. I tried, but I had to laugh twice as loud and hard as before. [...] At some point I stopped laughing just as suddenly as I had started. And I realised to my own surprise that I was perfectly lucid and that I apparently had not gone crazy.]

In this way, not only does he save his life but also his own self, which the inhuman violence was not able to destroy. The secret of his laughter is disclosed in an emotionally contradictory expression, in his 'Trauerlachen' [grief-laughing] (OdP, 5). The creation of this original compound noun, for which Khider maximises the morphological productivity of the German language, is a demonstration of the author's linguistic creativity. However, the German language not only helps him to escape to a very safe world, but also to discover German literature, specifically a poem by Hilde Domin, which prefaces his novel.[29] The *Trauerlachen* of his protagonist is indeed like 'the gentle sway of the single unbroken dove wing' on which he flies to the world of imagination. A world where language, thanks to Mahdi's narration and to Khider's writing, has a special power, as happens with the tales of *One Thousand and One Nights* that also kept Scheherazade alive.[30]

'I Felt Like a Ball Thrown Back and Forth'

As demonstrated earlier, Khider's novels usually present a main character who in some ways becomes the author's autofictional double. In his third

29   See Hilde Domin's poem 'Versprechen an eine Taube': '[...] wenn ich alles verliere / dich nehme ich mit, / Taube aus wurmstichigem Holz, / wegen des sanften Schwungs deines einzigen ungebrochenen Flügels' [when I lose everything / I'll take you with me, / dove of worm-eaten wood, / because of the gentle sway of your single unbroken wing] (OdP, 11).

30   Wolfgang Günter Lerch, 'Die Frucht der Freiheit', *Frankfurter Allgemeine Zeitung* (8 April 2011), <http://www.faz.net/aktuell/feuilleton/buecher/rezensionen/belletristik/abbas-khider-die-orangen-des-praesidenten-die-frucht-der-freiheit-1628121.html>, accessed 8 August 2018.

novel, *Brief in die Auberginenrepublik* (2013) [Letter to the Aubergine Republic], each chapter has instead a different protagonist, who in turn takes on the role of narrator and tells one part of the story from their point of view. This novel focuses once again on the characters' personalities and the way they construct their identity, whether by writing, thinking or speaking. Identity is thus obviously linked to a specific language which is here once again, not by chance, German. Yet, as seen before, Khider's use of the German language is a peculiar one, one in which Arabic, the author's mother tongue, makes frequent re-appearances – whether in a direct or in an indirect way. Therefore, his fictional characters can be conceived in an in-between space where they are able to use typical German sayings and Arabic expressions at one and the same time. For instance, Salim Al-Kateb, the protagonist of the first chapter, uses the German expression 'ohne Punkt und Komma' [endlessly, without stopping] but also many Arabic denominations (followed by their German translation) like 'Midan Al-Schajare – […] Baum-Platz […]' [Midan Al-Schajare – Tree Square] or 'ein Reisebüro, das Al-Amel – Hoffnung – heißt' [a travel agency named Al-Amel – hope] (BiA, 14–6).

Each protagonist is introduced in the chapter title, where a brief identikit of the character is provided. This clearly constitutes the character's public image as it includes their name, age and profession, the date when and the place where they are at the time of the narration. However, within the chapter, the reader follows the protagonists through their interior monologue as they develop their own sense of self. This provides a sudden change of perspective in the text because the reader moves quickly from an external to an internal perception of the character. This literary device seems to prove that one's sense of self is very much influenced from others' opinions of themselves and that social and individual identity are not detachable. There is strong evidence for this in the novel, for instance, when Salim-Al-Kateb feels like 'ein Ball, der hin und her geworfen wird' [a ball thrown back and forth] (BiA, 14) because he has been sent away from several countries before arriving in Libya, where he does not feel welcome either. Furthermore, identity is not fixed and stable, and sometimes characters have a different perception of themselves depending on the situation they are in. For example, the 54-year-old taxi-driver Haytham Mursi feels like a 'Knecht' [a servant] when his boss treats him like one, but he feels like a 'König auf seinem Thron' [a king on his throne] in his modern Kombitaxi (BiA, 25–6). Sometimes the characters' external perception does not correspond to how they feel and what they think about themselves. This is what happens to Miriam (Ahmed Kader's wife), who is seen as a 'Glückspilz' [lucky one] by her friends but personally does not feel this way (BiA, 134).

The characters' identity is also constructed through their interactions with each other, which can show their social status as well as their social consideration. Thus, Ahmed Kader is addressed, according to his military rank, as 'Oberst Ahmed Kader' [Colonel Ahmed Kader] but also with his nickname, 'Ahmed der Wolf' [Ahmed the wolf], which reflects the brutality he uses with political suspects (BiA, 108; 119). Social hierarchies and social divides also emerge from the characters' interactions. So, for instance, Haytham Mursi uses the title 'Herr' [Mister] to address his boss, but the latter sends him off with a 'Verschwinde jetzt' [Get lost now] (BiA, 23). The words people use can also become a sign of their high or low level of education as happens to a young man in Haytham's taxi who mistakenly understands 'Perialia' instead of 'Imperialistisches Spiel' [imperialistic game] (BiA, 35).

All in all, as the text's polyphonic structure anticipates, the novel not only shows how identity is socially constructed, but also to what extent language can influence this construction process. This applies to every language but obviously has different implications when the identity construction process involves a foreign language, as with German in this case. In fact, in the novel, Khider is not only writing the stories of his characters but also re-writing his own personal story. He does so by re-living the journey from Bengasi to Bagdad, a journey he also undertook – albeit in the opposite direction: 'Der Brief reist von Libyen, Bengasi, bis Bagdad und meine Reise war umgekehrt von Bagdad bis Bengasi' [The letter travels from Libya, Bengasi, to Bagdad and my journey was in the opposite direction, from Bagdad to Bengasi].[31] Hence, in the text, there is another perspective shift, a constant and almost undetectable one, from the authorial instance to the characters' point of view. Although there is no real protagonist

---

31   'Abbas Khider und "Brief in die Auberginenrepublik"' (22:53–23:03).

in the novel, there are various hints at Khider's special connection with Salim Al-Kateb's character, the protagonist of the first chapter. Salim is a 27-year-old man who escaped from Iraq after a short time in prison and currently lives in Libya. Additionally, the young man becomes, in a certain way, the protagonist of the entire novel because the letter he is trying to send to his girlfriend Samia serves as *fil rouge* and establishes a link between the different characters in the text. From the very beginning of the novel, Khider openly seals his profound connection with Salim's character, since he mentions in the initial epigraph some letters he personally sent to and received from a mysterious *You* (BiA, 5). The simple act of writing establishes a parallelism between the two because by writing, they are attempting to affirm their own existence and yet, this also constitutes the point at which Khider and Salim part ways. If identity is indeed socially and relationally constructed, Salim is being denied this opportunity because Samia will never receive his letter and he is only writing to himself and 'Nichts' [nothingness] (BiA, 18). This also implies that he cannot affirm his identity because having no addressee, he also has no voice. In this regard, Khider is different from his fictional counterpart because the German language constitutes the author's *new tongue*, one which gives him the chance to finally deal with his personal struggle.[32] In conclusion, if Salim still feels 'like a ball thrown back and forth', Khider has eventually succeeded in finding a new home or, more precisely, he has created in the German language a new homeland for himself.

---

32   'Mein Alltag ist ein deutscher Alltag geworden [...] Ich bin ein Teil der Gesellschaft geworden und meine Probleme sind auch Probleme der Gesellschaft' [My everyday life has become a German everyday life [...] I've become part of society and my problems are problems of society as well]. – Interview in ARD-alpha (38:17–38:19, 39:05–39:11/44:54).

'What Does It Mean For Me, If I Can Neither Live In My Homeland Nor Away From Home?'[33]

The confrontation with the foreign language as a means of shaping identity emerges in an even more immediate way in Khider's 2016 novel, *Ohrfeige* [*A Slap in the Face*, 2019], in which the protagonist is an Iraqi asylum seeker named Karim Mensy, who struggles with the bureaucracy of his host country, which is not coincidentally Germany. The protagonist's identity construction is revealed in his interactions (both real and imagined) with other characters but also in his interior monologues. Although German apparently is the main language in the novel, this is just a textual artifice which is unmasked in the passages where German is mixed with other languages: English, which functions as a sort of *lingua franca* and appears when migrants who have just arrived in Germany need it to interact with the police or other civil servants, and Arabic, Karim's mother tongue, which emerges in a rather spontaneous way when referring to concepts which have a strong connection with his country of origin. Arabic also appears in many other passages in which it is disguised as German. In the text, there are at least two ways of using German: as a language, when Karim is actually speaking it, and as a textual instance, when, despite the text being written in German, the protagonist is actually speaking in his mother tongue. In fact, the real German conversations only take place when Karim is talking (or rather imagines talking) to Frau Schulz [Mrs Schulz], an immigration authority official. In these interactions, the confrontation with the German language constitutes a real 'site of struggle' because the protagonist is not able to communicate well and produces grammatically incorrect sentences, such as: 'Sie ruhig sind und bleiben still' [You quiet are and remain silent], 'Nix ich will hören!' [Nothing I want to hear] (OF, 9). What emerges quite evidently is the role of language as an instrument of power, one that can create hierarchies by putting some people

---

33   'Was bedeutet es für mich, wenn ich weder in der Heimat noch in der Fremde leben darf?' (OF, 19).

in a privileged position (native speakers) and undermine others' (non-native speakers')[34] capacity to express themselves. But language is not the only problem. These social dynamics are indeed even more manifest when the native speaker has an influential social position, as is the case with Frau Schulz. Hence, Karim will never be able to speak with Frau Schulz 'von Mensch zu Mensch' [from human to human] and compares the distance between himself and her to that between a human and a 'Gott' or 'Göttinnen' [god/goddesses] or an 'Erdling' [Earthling] and a 'Marsianer' [Martian] (OF, 10–2).

However, Frau Schulz is just a symbol for German bureaucracy, and Karim's marginalisation is just the reflection of a wider process. This can be seen, to some extent, as a result of German post-unification national policies which highlighted the role of linguistic unity and paved the way to a sort of 'linguistic nationalism'.[35] In a wider European context, it can be related to the tendency to affirm Europeanness by contrast to what is considered as non-European, mainly the construct of the 'Muslim Other'.[36] The latter became indeed a receptacle for difference and alterity,[37] especially since September 2001 when, as Karim Mensy also points out, there emerged a tendency to eliminate all those traits, which were considered as typical of Muslims – from the side of Muslims as well: 'Früher [...] hatte ich ein unrasiertes Kinn. Wie Sie sehen, trage ich jetzt keinen Bart mehr. Seit dem 11. September [...] laufen alle arabischen Männer mit glatt rasierten Gesichtern herum, sie sehen aus wie Babypopos' [In the past, [...] I had an unshaven chin. Now you see, I have no beard. Since September 11 [...] all Arabic men go around with clean-shaven faces, they look like babies' tushies] (OF, 12). This is the natural consequence of the fact that to be accepted/naturalised in a European State, a 'performance of citizenship' was required, '[including] appearance and dress code but also [...] the acquisition of language proficiency'.[38] The latter officially

34   These terms are used here in a neutral way and do not imply any racialisation of language.
35   Linke, 'Language as Battleground', 50.
36   Ibid., 48.
37   Ibid.
38   Ibid.

came to constitute a prerequisite to enrol for German citizenship, which was previously guaranteed only by *ius sanguinis*, and if on the one hand, it gave way to the naturalisation of new citizens, it was also followed on the other hand by a process of 'racialisation of language': namely the call for language purity and the consequent marginalisation of different accents and improper ways of speaking.[39] Thus, people who were not able to speak the national language became isolated, as happens in the novel to Karim and his friends who, as a result, constantly feel unwelcome in the host community.

It is highly likely that, at a certain point, the protagonist starts interiorising his external perception and changes his own self-concept. There is a sort of dehumanisation of the character, as it prominently emerges in the metaphors and comparisons he uses to describe himself or other migrants, which usually involve the semantic field of trade goods:

> Wir sind alle wie die geschmacklosen und billigen Produkte aus dem Ausland, die man bei Aldi und Lidl finden kann. Wir werden mit dem Lastwagen hierhergeschleppt wie Bananen oder Rinder, werden aufgestellt, sortiert, aufgeteilt und billig verkauft. Was übrig bleibt, kommt in den Müll (OF, 216).

> [We are all like the tasteless and cheap products from abroad, those that one can find in Aldi and Lidl. We are dragged all the way here on a lorry like bananas or beef, we are arranged, sorted out, divided and sold cheap. What's left goes in the bin.]

All this makes the identity issue even deeper, as it digs into the reason why Karim left his homeland: during his adolescence he had developed woman's breasts, and since then, he had always dreamt of getting rid of them with surgery. Hence, Karim came to Germany to 'become a normal man', but instead, he does not even feel like a human being anymore (OF, 93). The ending of Karim's story is thus not a happy one. When he left his homeland, Karim knew that he could no longer live in Iraq, and now, he knows as well that he can no longer live in Germany: his right to exist has been denied, once again.

39 Ibid., 56–8.

The New German as a Well-Tempered Home

His past experiences, which have, to a considerable extent, shaped his identity, also play a very important role in Abbas Khider's latest autofictional novel *Deutsch für alle: Das endgültige Lehrbuch* (2019) [German for Everyone: The Ultimate Textbook], which opens with his first contact with the German language: 'Als ich in der Bundesrepublik ankam, kannte ich lediglich drei Wörter: HITLER, SCHEISSE und LUFTHANSA' [When I arrived in the Federal Republic, I only knew three words: HITLER, SCHEISSE and LUFTHANSA] (DfA, 11). He learnt the word 'Hitler' during his adolescence in Bagdad, when the book *Mein Kampf*, 'das Lieblingsbuch des älteren Sohnes des irakischen Diktators' [the favourite book of the Iraqi dictator's eldest son], was available in the bookshops in Arabic translation (DfA, 11). He first heard the word 'Lufthansa' while he was fleeing to Jordan, although the German airline was 'so unerreichbar wie Europa, so märchenhaft wie ein fliegender Teppich' [as unattainable as Europe, as fabled as a flying carpet], and could not bring him by air to a safe country of refuge; in fact, only 'die Reichen und Mächtigen unter den Flüchtlingen' [the rich and powerful refugees] could afford it (DfA, 12). He learnt the word 'Scheisse' at Bolzano central station, as an answer to the question of how life in Germany was. On this occasion, he infers the signified of the unknown word from its signifier, that is, from its phonetic realisation: 'Allein der zischende, spitze Klang dieses Wortes machte uns die Bedeutung schon klar' [Merely the sizzling, acute sound of the word already made its meaning clear to us] (DfA, 12).

The narrator/author arrives in Germany with only these language skills and understands very soon that the German language is not only the main factor for integration, but also the greatest obstacle to the achievement of this objective. It is especially its complex grammatical structures that have '[in seinem] Gehirn [...] vieles durcheinandergebracht' [messed up his mind], so that now he feels like a 'gespaltene Persönlichkeit' [split personality] (DfA, 14). This is what leads him to revolutionise the German grammar and to do so from the perspective of a German learner. With this revolution of the German grammar, which the author himself considers as 'ernsthafter sprachwissenschaftlicher Schwachsinn' [serious linguistic nonsense], the German reader, who 'sich höchstwahrscheinlich nicht vorstellen [kann], was diese grammatischen Phänomene im Kopf eines Menschen veranstalten, der all das neu lernen muss' [mostly likely cannot imagine what such grammatical phenomena can generate in the mind of people who must learn it all from the start], is forced to change his/her perspective (DfA, 9; 14). The greatest obstacles for German learners are, above all, the pronunciation of the vowels and the *umlauts*, the three grammatical genders and the cases (especially the genitive and the dative), the sentence structure and the position of the verb, the declination of the pronouns, the endings of the adjectives, the prepositions and the verbs. Hence, the rules conceived by the author for his 'New German' are mainly based on the principle of simplification and standardisation. This happens, as in all his other novels, in a very ironic way, whereby, on the one hand, he expresses his immersion in the German culture – for example, through his suggestion to eliminate the definite and the indefinite articles as well as the three grammatical genders and to substitute them with a general article:

> Man sollte dringend etwas gegen die Autorität des Artikels unternehmen. Wenn man daran festhalten will, dass die Zeit der autoritären Regime seit dem Mauerfall vorbei ist, dann sollte auch in der deutschen Sprache die Zeit reif dafür sein, der zwischen dem Rest der Menschheit und den Deutschen steht, zu beseitigen. […] Aber wie? Ich habe einen einfachen und praktischen Vorschlag: Man führt einen Universal-Artikel für die ganze Sprache ein. Die Lernenden müssen dann den Artikel nicht mehr auswendig lernen. […]
>
> *Bestimmter Artikel:* DE
>
> *Unbestimmter Artikel:* E
>
> *Plural:* DIE
>
> Wenn die Ausländer in Deutschland von meinem Vorschlag erfahren, vermute ich, werden alle auf die Straße gehen, tagelang tanzen, feiern und jubeln. Bestimmt lassen einige ihrem Hass auf die Artikel freien Lauf und brüllen: 'Wir sind de Volk' (DfA, 33).
>
> [One should urgently do something against the authority of the articles. When one really wants to hold on to the fact that the era of the authoritarian regime after the fall of the Berlin wall is over, then the time should also be right in the German language to remove what's standing between the rest of humankind and the German

people. […] But how? I have a simple and practical proposal: one should introduce a general article for the whole language. Then learners won't have to learn the article by heart anymore […]

Definite article: DE

Indefinite article: E

Plural: DIE

When foreigners in Germany learn of my proposal, then, I imagine, they will all go out on the street and dance, celebrate and rejoice for days. Some people will certainly let their hatred for the articles run wild and yell: 'Wir sind de Volk'.]

On the other hand, the new rules are often formulated in association with a contrastive approach, that is, against the background of the Arabic language and culture, as happens, for example, with the introduction of the 'Arabic accusative', which is based on the pronunciation rules of the Arabic language: 'Mündlich kann man im Akkusativ einfach den letzten Buchstaben stark betonen und in einem dominierenden höheren Ton in die Länge ziehen, wie es die Araber tun, wenn sie etwas Wichtiges hervorheben wollen: Männer.rrr' [Orally one can simply emphasise the final letter and prolong it in a dominant higher-pitched tone, as the Arabs do when they want to highlight something important: Männer rrr] (DfA, 34).

The creation of a new German language, which arises also from the creative interaction between the German linguistic structures and the elements of the author's original language system, is the result of a language hybridisation, which is, not least, also a sign of the hybridisation of the author's/narrator's identity. Thus, it is not exactly Germany that has become his home in the meantime but rather the German language, even though the author had to 'renovate' and 'refurbish' it in some parts so that he can really be able to open up his new world:

Wenn man eine Sprache wie ein Zuhause wahrnimmt, geht man tatsächlich anders damit um. Man reinigt sie zum Beispiel wöchentlich wie die eigene Wohnung. […] Ich persönlich bin schon vor langer Zeit ins Deutsche umgezogen und fühle mich hier längst zu Hause. Nun habe ich ein bisschen renoviert und einiges saniert, ich habe endlich mein Ziel erreicht: Das Neudeutsche ist für mich eine wohltemperierte Wohnung aus klaren Buchstaben und feinen grammatischen Fällen (DfA, 119).

[When one perceives a language as a home, one really deals with it differently. One cleans it weekly, for example, as one's own home. […] I personally moved into German a long time ago and there, by now, I have started feeling at home. Meanwhile I have renovated a little bit and refurbished a few things, I have finally reached my goal: The New German is for me like a well-tempered home made out of clear letters and fine grammatical cases.]

In doing so, the narrator, and Khider as well, has not carried out a 'Sprachrevolution' [language revolution] but rather simply scratched the surface of the German language, even though this work has constituted 'eine Art Traumabewältigung' [a way to overcome traumas] (DfA, 120). Yet the result is precisely the creation of a linguistic home, which corresponds to his essence, that is, his plural, hybrid identity, a 'well-tempered home' in which he was able to overcome not just the 'Traumata der Nomina' [traumas of the nouns] (DfA, 29).

Final Considerations

Dealing with traumas is surely the starting point and at the same time the main goal of Khider's writing, a goal which is closely bound up with German as a foreign language, the author's own identity construction and his agency, based on an intentional choice, to claim a more powerful identity from which to communicate and write. In this way, learning the German language becomes not only an investment to integrate into German society, but also a fundamental instrument to realise his autofictional narration with *a new tongue*, in a *well-tempered home* where he can deal with his identity and shape it consciously: 'Schreiben ist für mich keine Therapie, es ist viel mehr als das. Das Schreiben ist ein Projekt, mit dem ich mein Leben neu gestaltet, neu aufgebaut habe – in einer ästhetischen Form' [Writing is not therapy for me, it is much more than that. Writing is a project through which I reshaped my life, I rebuilt it – in an aesthetic form].[40] To be able to tell his Arabic tale of

---

40   Ammar, '*Deutsch ist meine neue Zunge* – Ein Interview mit Abbas Khider'.

'tausendundzweite Nacht' [One thousand second [Arabian] Night] (FI, 131), Khider himself had to undergo a language change and he not only changed himself in the process – as many other authors of transcultural literature did – but he also 'trans-formed the German language' too.[41]

41   'die deutsche Sprache ver-wandelt'. – Harald Weinrich, 'Sprachwandler im Namen Chamissos', *Chamisso: Viele Kulturen – eine Sprache* 10 (2014), 18–21, 21.

KAROLIN MACHTANS

Multilingual Aesthetics in Abbas Khider's *Deutsch für alle: Das endgültige Lehrbuch*

In interviews, Abbas Khider has described German (not Arabic) as the language that allows him to approach his traumatic experiences as a refugee from Iraq.[1] Having started to learn German only in his late twenties when he first arrived in Germany, he – as he admits himself – still struggles with the complex grammatical structures and especially the pronunciation of the German language.[2] Unlike authors such as Yoko Tawada and Samuel Beckett, who voluntarily immersed themselves in unfamiliar language environments, Khider's confrontation with the German language was not a free choice, but a consequence of flight and expulsion. Consequently, his engagement with the German language goes beyond a playful exploration of linguistic phenomena. Rather, he examines the relationship between multilingual realities and monolingual power structures in Germany and the sociopolitical consequences of Germany's institutionalised monolingualism. His protagonists with their multilingual, literalising gaze uncover unexpected patterns of sound and meaning, thus deconstructing the alleged unity of signifier and signified, and destabilising presumably fixed meanings.

---

1   'I was very preoccupied with the situation in my country and wanted to say something about it, but somehow I could not do that in Arabic. But German gave me the possibility, and since then it has been my new language.' – Abderrahmane Ammar, ' "German is My New Language": Interview with Abbas Khider', trans. Pauline Cumbers, Goethe Institute (2014), <https://www.goethe.de/en/kul/lit/20437059.html>, accessed 10 March 2020.

2   Christian Erber, ' "Besonders übel sind die Umlaute": Interview mit Abbas Khider', Radio Bremen (2019), <https://www.radiobremen.de/bremenzwei/sendungen/gespraechszeit/abbas-khider112-popup.html>, accessed 10 March 2020.

From code-switching to code-mixing, from seemingly accidental phonetic slippages to the use of homographs and homophones from other languages, and from literal translations to the creation of entirely new linguistic forms, Khider's texts challenge the notion of languages as clearly distinct, separate entities, and point to new linguistic and cultural affiliations instead. Furthermore, they question the concept of *one* 'mother tongue' through which one is – as Yasemin Yildiz put it – 'organically linked to an exclusive, clearly demarcated ethnicity, culture, and nation'.[3]

With its grammatical explanations, its declension and conjugation tables and its sample sentences, Khider's 2019 ethnographic 'grammar book' *Deutsch für alle: Das endgültige Lehrbuch* [German for Everyone: The Ultimate Textbook] is structured like a German grammar – yet obviously not one that is meant to be taken seriously. Or is it? 'Dieses Büchlein ist ernsthafter, sprachwissenschaftlicher Schwachsinn' [this little book is serious, linguistic nonsense'] is what we read in the preliminary remarks. And obviously Khider's 'simplifications' of the German grammar that follow are an ironic nod to the many pitfalls of the German language – suggestions that many learners of German as a second language would certainly support as well, especially the replacement of the three German articles *der, die, das* by only one: *de* (*de Mann* instead of *der Mann, de Frau* instead of *die Frau* and *de Buch* instead of *das Buch*). Linguistic nonsense? Not necessarily. What deserves further attention are the introductory paragraphs of the individual chapters as well as the sample sentences that Khider inserts throughout the text to illustrate his new grammar rules. Here, Khider deals *en passant* with topics such as European refugee policies and procedures, physical violence against refugees and migrants in Germany as well as linguistic stereotyping and accent discrimination. He also questions the German language level needed to gain access to the German university system, thus highlighting the privileges of certain groups of refugees and migrants over others. Furthermore, he contrasts the prescriptive, normative

---

3   Yasemin Yildiz, *Beyond the Mother Tongue: The Postmonolingual Condition* (New York: Fordham University Press, 2012), 2.

role of Germany's institutional monolingualism with the multilingual realities of a growing number of non-native speakers living in Germany.

Hence, Khider's humorous suggestions hint at larger and much more serious issues than just 'linguistic nonsense'. First, *Deutsch für alle*, written as a language autobiography, highlights the role that language plays for questions of cultural and national belonging, specifically in the context of Germany's and Europe's language politics and citizenship laws. Second, Khider's confrontation with Germany's educational system emphasises the inequalities refugees are faced with, caused by its inherent structural monolingualism. And third, by focusing on the use of dialects, words of foreign derivation [*Fremdwörter*] and highly specialised philosophical terminology, Khider deconstructs the assumed 'purity' of the German language and highlights its hybrid, integrative nature instead. Creating a new hybrid language [*Neudeutsch*] himself, Khider challenges the assumption that languages 'belong' to a national collective that excludes its minoritarian subjects, and reclaims linguistic agency in German. Hence, Khider's humorous 'ethnographic grammar' *Deutsch für alle*, which suggests nothing less than a complete renewal of the German language, can be read as a plea for heightened critical language awareness and appreciation for multilingual realities in Germany.

German as Cultural Capital: Khider's Language Biography

Deutsch für alle begins with Khider's German language biography: his development from his first words to a fluent, yet not always confident speaker of German. Khider has invested a lot of time and energy into acquiring the German language: 'Ich kämpfte so sehr. Ich fing so oft an. Ich gab so oft auf. Aber ich wollte es unbedingt. Ich wollte Deutsch lernen' ['I struggled so much. I began so many times. I gave up so many times. But I really wanted it. I wanted to learn German'] (DfA, 28). It is only through the acquisition of the German language that he is able to finally develop a new, 'German' identity and a sense of cultural belonging: 'So ist ein zweiter Abbas in mir gewachsen, gewissermaßen ein

Herr Abbas Müller-Schmidt' ['As such a second Abbas grew inside me, a certain Mr Abbas Müller-Schmidt'] (DfA, 18). Yet as much as he tries to assimilate linguistically into the German culture, there are aspects of the German language that are beyond his control – elements that will forever mark him as an outsider in the German language and, consequently, German society and culture. As Etienne Balibar has argued with reference to Pierre Bourdieu, ' "foreign" or "regional" accent, [...] language "errors" or, conversely, ostentatious "correctness" immediately designat[e] a speaker's belonging to a particular population and [are] spontaneously interpreted as reflecting a specific family origin and a hereditary disposition.'[4] Not unlike national migration policies, grammars and dictionaries determine what is right and wrong, what belongs and what does not belong to a language – and, ultimately, *who* belongs to the collective of 'native' speakers – in Khider's words, a 'grammatikalisch-diktatorische[r] Albtraum, der zwischen dem Rest der Menschheit und den Deutschen steht' ['a grammatical-dictatorial nightmare that stands between the rest of humanity and the Germans'] (DfA, 26). Hence, his only goal in life is to renew the German language by simplifying the German grammar in order to overcome his linguistic traumas (DfA, 26). In order to reach this goal, Khider suggests changing the word order of the German subordinate clauses by moving the verb to the second place, changing the personal and possessive pronouns, getting rid of all separable-prefix verbs, abolishing the genitive and the dative cases and so on. By completely renewing the German language, Khider questions the authority of institutions such as the German *Duden*, the normative dictionary of the German language that used to be the prescriptive source for the correct use of German, defining the norms for its grammar and spelling between 1955 and 1996, and the Standing Conference of the Ministers of Education and Cultural Affairs [*Kultusministerkonferenz*] which, since 1996, has been responsible for official changes to German grammar and spelling rules, including the infamous German spelling reform [*Rechtschreibreform*] in 1996, a reform that was supposed to make the German language more

---

4   Etienne Balibar, 'The Nation Form', in Etienne Balibar and Immanuel Wallerstein, eds., *Race, Nation, Class* (London: Verso, 1995), 86–106, 104.

logical and intuitive.[5] His humouristic interventions also respond to the growing number of purist language associations in Germany such as the Dortmund-based *Verein deutsche Sprache* (VDS, founded in 1997) that attempt to keep the German language free from the influence of other languages.[6]

Yet even the most accessible new grammar rules do not protect Khider from being othered based on his foreign accent and his pronunciation of German words. As early as the biblical story of the murder of the Ephraimites, who mistakenly pronounced the word 'shibboleth' as 'sibboleth', accents and dialects have been markers of linguistic and cultural otherness.[7] For Khider, it is specifically the German *umlauts* that exclude him from the collective of native speakers:

> Natürlich hört man auch ansonsten einen arabischen Akzent, wenn ich spreche, vor allem, wenn ich nervös und müde bin. Aber die Umlaute führen dazu, dass ich wirklich sofort als Fremder identifiziert werden kann. Sie isolieren mich von den Muttersprachlern und wirken so, als hätte man mir eine leuchtend rote Clownsnase aufgesetzt. [...] Manchmal frage ich mich sogar, [...] ob einige spezielle Geschöpfe unter den Urdeutschen diese verfluchten Umlaute Ä, Ö, Ü absichtlich erfunden haben, um schneller herauszufinden, wer ein Inländer und wer ein Ausländer, wer ein Urbewohner und wer ein Neubewohner ist (DfA, 19–21).

> [Naturally one otherwise hears an Arabic accent when I speak, especially when I'm nervous or tired. But the umlauts really cause me to be identified as a foreigner. They isolate me from the native speakers and make it look as if I have had put on a

5   Georges Lüdi, 'German and Its Norms', trans. Chris Cave, Goethe Institute (2014), <https://www.goethe.de/en/spr/mag/sta/20456023.html>, accessed 10 March 2020.

6   Karoline Wirth, *Der Verein Deutsche Sprache: Hintergrund, Entstehung, Arbeit und Organisation eines deutschen Sprachvereins* (Bamberg: Bamberg University Press, 2008).

7   'And the Gileadites took the passages of Jordan before the Ephraimites: and it was so, that when those Ephraimites which were escaped said, Let me go over; that the men of Gilead said unto him, Art thou an Ephraimite? If he said, Nay; Then said they unto him, Say now Shibboleth: and he said Sibboleth: for he could not frame to pronounce it right. Then they took him, and slew him at the passages of Jordan: and there fell at that time of the Ephraimites forty and two thousand.' – *Judges* 12:5–6 KJV.

shiny red clown's nose. [...] Sometimes I ask myself if some special creatures among the *Ur*-Germans purposefully invented these damned umlauts, Ä, Ö, Ü, in order to find out more quickly who is a local and who is a foreigner, who is native and who is an immigrant.]

To veil his linguistic otherness, Khider tries to use sentences without *umlauts* whenever possible ('Umlaut-Umgehungssätze'). Hence, Khider does not say what he wants to say, but rather, what he *can* say, determined by the pronounceability of specific German words. Whereas his accent is not noticeable in his books, it becomes noticeable in public readings, making him more 'authentic' and 'exotic' in the ears of his audience (DfA, 24).[8]

Just how seriously Khider's humorous reflections must be taken becomes obvious in the context of Europe's and Germany's current language politics. While language competency has always been a sign of cultural belonging in European history, in recent years, national identity politics have become language politics: 'The presence of diverse populations in the European Union, whether immigrants, refugees or citizens, has complicated matters of national belonging by the signs of colour: the racialializing codes of "whiteness" or "blackness" are no longer reliable visual tools for ascertaining national membership. In turn, language practices have become new signposts of belonging.'[9] At Europe's outer borders as well as within the European member states, asylum seekers are linguistically screened by Frontex officials to determine their country of origin. Based on Eurocentric assumptions of nationality, this procedure neglects local language variations and individual histories of displacement.[10]

---

8   It is interesting to note that Khider – unlike Saša Stanišić and others – is not the speaker of the audiobook of *Deutsch für alle*. The relationship between text and audio versions of multilingual literature is an under-researched topic that certainly deserves much more attention.

9   Uli Linke, 'Language as Battleground: "Speaking" the Nation, Lingual Citizenship and Diversity Management in Post-unification Germany', in Jan-Jonathan Bock and Sharon Macdonald, eds., *Refugees Welcome? Difference and Diversity in a Changing Germany* (New York/Oxford: Berghahn, 2019), 41–66, 60.

10   'It is facile to assume that Arabic is the mother tongue and universally spoken language in a region as diverse as the Middle East. Even when migrants speak the right language, the interpreter sometimes makes the wrong assessment. In

This is all the more problematic as interpreters are often not sufficiently trained.[11]

In post-unification Germany, as a consequence of the changes in Germany's citizenship law from being solely based on *ius sanguinis* to the introduction of *ius soli*, and especially in light of the 'refugee crisis' since 2015, Germany's population has become increasingly diverse.[12] Consequently, the call for unity of the German nation state as a language-body, based on an assumed community of native-language speakers that has a long tradition in Germany's national history, has re-emerged.[13] Foreigners are increasingly 'ethnicized through language'.[14] This becomes especially obvious in right-wing, anti-immigration circles. In their manifesto, the *Alternative für Deutschland* (AfD) for instance reminds us that the German language is the 'focal point of our identity':

> Our culture is inextricably linked to the German language, which has developed over centuries and which in itself is a reflection of its intellectual history, national identity

---

particular, in the case of persons who had lived as refugees for a long period of time in a third country, such as Afghans in refugee camps in Iran or Iraqis in Syria, wrong assessments have been made due to accent or lack of country knowledge. The situation is more tricky for Palestinians, many of whom are born and brought up in other countries, such as Syria or Iraq, and are thus displaced once more by the wars there, and are either deemed stateless and sent back, or assigned Syrian or Iraqi nationality, and thus cannot benefit from the status accorded to Palestinian nationals.' – Aisha Maniar, '(Language) Policing at Europe's Borders', Institute of Race Relations (2016), <http://www.irr.org.uk/news/language-policing-at-europes-borders/>, accessed 10 March 2020. – See also the findings of the Language & Asylum Research Group at the University of Essex, <https://www1.essex.ac.uk/larg/>, accessed 10 March 2020.

11   This process is further complicated by the introduction of voice recognition software to determine refugees' countries of origin – see the BBC, 'Germany to Use Voice Recognition to Identify Migrant Origins' (2017), <https://www.bbc.com/news/world-europe-39307155>, accessed 10 March 2020.

12   Jan-Jonathan Bock and Sharon Macdonald, 'Introduction: Making, Experiencing and Managing Difference in a Changing Germany', in Bock and Macdonald, eds., *Refugees Welcome?*, 1–38, 1–2.

13   Linke, 'Language as Battleground', 52.

14   Ibid., 54.

within central Europe, and German set of basic values, which have all changed over time but have retained a unique core inventory. The bond which language creates amongst people should be maintained and protected.[15]

Following the logic of the AfD manifesto, the German language should be 'declared as the official language of the country and enacted as such in the German Constitution'.[16]

While this is undoubtedly an extreme position, sufficient command of the German language is in fact one of the requirements for becoming a naturalised German citizen. The German Ministry of the Interior lists the ability to speak German as an 'absolute necessity' and a prerequisite for successful integration into German society: 'Being able to communicate in German is essential for social and economic integration.'[17]

Thus, linguistic homogeneity continues to be the norm and a sign of successful integration in Germany. Based on Pierre Bourdieu's concept of

15   Alternative für Deutschland, 'Manifesto for Germany: The Political Programme of the Alternative für Deutschland' (2016), <https://www.afd.de/wp-content/uploads/sites/111/2017/04/2017-04-12_afd-grundsatzprogramm-englisch_web.pdf>, accessed 10 March 2020, 46.

16   Ibid.

17   'Sufficient command' is defined as oral and written German-language skills equivalent to level B 1 of the Common European Framework of Reference for languages. – Federal Ministry of the Interior, Building and Community, 'What Are the Requirements for Becoming a Naturalized German Citizen?' <https://www.bmi.bund.de/SharedDocs/faqs/EN/themen/migration/staatsang/Erwerb_der_deutschen_Staatsbuergerschaft_durch_Eingbuergerung_en.html>, accessed 10 March 2020. – As part of the National Action Plan on Integration, on October 21, 2019, the Federal Ministry of the Interior, Building and Community invited about seventy experts to discuss the question of how language teaching for immigrants and immigrants' German-language skills can be improved. Coming from a wide variety of different professional backgrounds, the participants – academics, practitioners and representatives of immigrant organisations – discussed the use of digital technologies in language teaching, the practical use of the language, obstacles to learning and the testing of German-language skills. The results will be presented at the Integration Summit in the third quarter of 2020 and published as a conference report. – Federal Ministry of the Interior, Building and Community, 'The Key to Integration is Language' (2019),

language proficiency as cultural capital and the relationship between language and symbolic power in societies, Ingrid Gogolin and others have argued that migrants in Germany are often unable to make use of their own cultural capital, as their first languages have a low status in German society and are considered 'undesirable'.[18] This is all the more problematic as for non-native speakers, it is often multilingualism – and the innovative, integrative appropriation of the target language through one's first language – that serves as a medium of identification with the target culture.[19] A creative appropriation of the German language such as Khider's, however, runs counter to Germany's official language politics, where linguistic otherness is still perceived as problematic and different ways of speaking the national language are censored. Whereas curricula framework specifications in Germany do acknowledge increased linguistic diversity in the classroom, linguistic competencies other than the idealised, monolingual standard German continue to meet with negative stereotyping and devaluations in the classroom. This holds true for different languages in different ways: while English, Spanish and French are regularly taught as a second language in German schools and international schools such as the American and French schools in Germany are welcome, low-status languages such as Turkish and Arabic are rarely offered in German schools – a development that Yildiz, borrowing from Ruth Mandel's term 'selective cosmopolitanism', aptly terms 'selective multilingualism'.[20] Such a 'selective multilingualism' has become apparent in the most recent debates about the establishment of Turkish schools as well as bilingual Turkish-German kindergartens and elementary schools in Germany.[21]

<https://www.bmi.bund.de/SharedDocs/kurzmeldungen/EN/2019/10/key-to-integration-is-language.html>, accessed 10 March 2020.

18 Pierre Bourdieu, *Distinctions* (London: Routledge & Kegan Paul, 1984). – Ingrid Gogolin, Sarah McMonagle and Tanja Salem, 'Germany: Systemic, Sociocultural and Linguistic Perspectives on Educational Inequality', in Peter A. J. Stevens and A. Gary Dworkin, eds., *The Palgrave Handbook of Race and Ethnic Inequalities in Education* (London: Palgrave Macmillan, 2014), 557–602.

19 Jörg Roche, 'Sprache als Medium von (Des-)Integration', in Till Dembeck and Rolf Parr, eds., *Literatur und Mehrsprachigkeit: Ein Handbuch* (Tübingen: Narr Francke Attempto, 2017), 45–52, 49–50.

20 Yildiz, *Beyond the Mother Tongue*, 209.

21 See, for example, Austin Davis, 'Would Turkish Schools in Germany Influence Erdogan's Influence Abroad?', Deutsche Welle (2020), <https://www.dw.com/en/turkish-schools-germany-erdogan-influence/a-51948242>, accessed 10 March

Institutionalised Monolingualism: Refugees' Access to Higher Education

The exclusionary nature of Germany's official language politics, based on its structural monolingualism, is not only prevalent in primary and secondary schools, but also in higher education. In *Deutsch für alle*, Khider is denied access to the German university system due to his lack of the required proficiency level of German: 'Um überhaupt studieren zu können, musste ich zuvor natürlich ein gewisses Maß an Sprachfertigkeit erlangt haben, das mich, das ist kein Witz, fünf Jahre und tausende Unterrichtsstunden gekostet hat' ['In order to study at all, I had to first acquire a certain language proficiency level, that cost me, and this is no joke, five years and thousands of hours of instruction'] (DfA, 15). It is not only the required German-language proficiency level that stands in his way, but also the lack of a university entrance certificate from Iraq that would allow him to directly enrol at a German university. In Iraq, Khider was eligible to study at the university level, but only to major in accounting, not in literature, as he had wanted to. After two semesters, he was exmatriculated on political grounds. In Germany, the Bavarian *Zeugnisanerkennungsstelle* (the office that decides whether a foreign school qualification is sufficient) decided that his Iraqi high-school diploma does not allow him to enrol directly in a German university.[22] He is not even

---

2020, or Sabine Kinkartz, 'Aufregung um türkische Schulen in Deutschland', Deutsche Welle (2020), <https://www.dw.com/de/aufregung-um-türkische-schulen-in-deutschland/a-51947633>, accessed 10 March 2020.

22   While in theory, access to German institutes of higher education is granted with a foreign secondary school-leaving qualification, in practice, it is up to the International Students' Office (*Akademisches Auslandsamt*) or the Registrar's Office of the German institution of higher education to decide whether the foreign school qualifications are sufficient or whether the applicant has to complete a preparatory course at a *Studienkolleg* beforehand. International applicants who possess a university entrance certificate from their country of origin that does not authorise them to directly enrol at a German university are required to undergo an assessment – the so-called *Feststellungsprüfung* or university qualification exam – by the German university before starting a degree programme. This assessment

eligible for a preparatory course, the *Studienkolleg*, that prepares international students for an assessment demonstrating that the applicant has the necessary German-language skills and fulfils the subject requirements to study at a German university. When the *Zeugnisanerkennungsstelle* finally revises their decision, Khider is informed that he must attend a preparatory course first. However, despite his goal to major in the humanities later on, he is assigned to a so-called 'T-Kurs', focusing on engineering, maths and sciences, as his Iraqi high-school diploma does not list enough humanities subjects – a decision that clearly disregards the special challenges refugee students face in their countries of origin. After the fall of Saddam Hussein, Khider is able to obtain a second high-school diploma from Iraq via distance learning, this time with a focus on the humanities. Yet even both Iraqi high-school diplomas combined still do not provide him with access to the German university system – not even to the *Studienkolleg*, as he still does not possess the necessary language skills that are the prerequisite to study at a German university. When he finally passes the *Zentrale Mittelstufenprüfung* of the Goethe Institute, he still must sit an entrance examination, which consists of a German-language test and further criteria for admission, set by the individual university and *Studienkolleg*. These requirements vary by subject and by state, creating unequal preconditions reinforced by the distribution of refugees among the twelve German *Länder* based on the 'Königstein Key'.[23] Khider is ultimately accepted into the *Studienkolleg* in Potsdam and Halle – yet not in any other German state, hinting once more at the educational inequalities refugees face, based on their distribution among the German

---

test is officially called the 'Examination to Assess Aptitude of Foreign Applicants for Acceptance to an Institution of Higher Education in the Federal Republic of Germany'. See the website of the University of Hamburg, 'Studienkolleg Hamburg: Preparing for the Assessment Exam', <https://www.uni-hamburg.de/en/campuscenter/studienangebot/international/studienkolleg-hamburg.html>, accessed 10 March 2020.

23 For an explanation of the distribution of refugees in Germany based on the Königstein Key, see the Federal Office for Migration and Refugees (BAMF), 'Initial Distribution of Asylum-Seekers (EASY)', <https://www.bamf.de/EN/Themen/AsylFluechtlingsschutz/AblaufAsylverfahrens/Erstverteilung/erstverteilung-node.html>, accessed 10 March 2020.

Länder. Furthermore, not every state offers each focus course, creating additional inequalities for refugees who are allocated to more rural areas.

After several years, Khider finally passes the so-called *Feststellungsprüfung* or university qualification exam, the equivalent of the German high-school diploma, and is now able to pursue his studies in comparative literature with minors in philosophy and German literature at the University of Munich. What sounds like a truly Kafkaesque scenario is in fact the common procedure for non-European citizens in Germany: unlike EU citizens who are granted access to German universities with no further entrance exams, applicants from outside the European Union face an entirely different situation.

Luckily, since the arrival of over a million refugees in Germany in 2015 and 2016, things have started to change, and many German universities now offer special study programmes for refugees.[24] In addition, progress has been made to facilitate admission for refugees without official documentation.[25] Furthermore, the so-called *Integrationskurse* [integration courses], consisting of a German-language course and an orientation course, provide refugees with access to subsidised language learning.[26] At the end of the language course, participants have to pass the 'German language test for immigrants' before being able to enrol in the orientation course that prepares them for the mandatory 'Life in Germany' test.[27] Access to the subsidised

24   See the following study published by the German Academic Exchange Service: 'The Integration of Refugees at German Higher Education Institutions: Findings from Higher Education Programmes for Refugees' (2017), <https://www2. daad.de/medien/downloads/studie_hochschulzugang_fluechtlinge_engl.pdf>, accessed 10 March 2020.

25   Council of Europe, 'Education Department News: New Recommendation on Recognition of Qualifications held by Refugees' (2017), <https://www.coe.int/en/web/education/-/new-recommendation-on-recognition-of-qualifications-held-by-refugees>, accessed 10 March 2020.

26   For a description of the Integration Courses, see the following website of the Federal Office for Migration and Refugees (BAMF), 'Integration Courses', <https://www.bamf.de/EN/Themen/Integration/ZugewanderteTeilnehmende/Integrationskurse/integrationskurse-node.html>, accessed 10 March 2020.

27   Federal Office for Migration and Refugees (BAMF), 'The Content and Stages of the Procedure', <https://www.bamf.de/EN/Themen/Integration/ZugewanderteTeilnehmende/Integrationskurse/InhaltAblauf/inhaltablauf-node.html>, accessed 10 March 2020.

integration courses as well as their duration, intensity and costs are regulated by the German state and depend on the date of the applicant's residence title as well as the applicant's nationality and immigration status.[28] Thus, the state's intervention in refugees' access to German-language courses still creates a de-facto linguistic segregation, making it much more difficult for certain groups to integrate, linguistically and culturally.

Reclaiming Agency: German as a Hybrid Language

Against a standardised German language whose access for non-German citizens is regulated by the German state, Khider sets his own, hybrid version of German. In so doing, Khider not only reminds us that languages are dynamic and in constant flux, but also reclaims the German language for himself, a language that has always also been the language of Germany's many minorities.[29]

By using the Bavarian dialect as an example of how best to simplify the German language, he affirms his familiarity with the German language and thus his level of integration. More importantly, he turns the hierarchy between standard German and its many dialects upside down.

---

28   While foreign nationals with residence titles issued after 2005 must currently pay EUR 1.95 for every lesson of the integration course (amounting to EUR 1,365 for the entire course), ethnic German resettlers are legally entitled to a free integration course. – Federal Office for Migration and Refugees (BAMF), 'Foreign Nationals with Residence Titles Issued From 2005 Onwards', <https://www.bamf. de/EN/Themen/Integration/ZugewanderteTeilnehmende/Integrationskurse/ TeilnahmeKosten/Titelab2005/titelab2005.html>, accessed 10 March 2020. – Federal Office for Migration and Refugees (BAMF), 'Ethnic German Resettlers', <https://www.bamf.de/EN/Themen/Integration/ZugewanderteTeilnehmende/ Integrationskurse/TeilnahmeKosten/Spaetaussiedler/spaetaussiedler.html>, accessed 10 March 2020.

29   Till Dembeck and Rolf Parr provide the most recent overview of multilingual aesthetics in German literature. – Dembeck and Parr, eds., *Literatur und Mehrsprachigkeit*.

And he goes even further: he replaces the many German directional prepositions with the Arabic prepositions *min* and *ila* which, as he assures us,
have been invented by no one less than Allah himself, thus 'Arabising' the
German language and deconstructing the conflation of language, nation
and religion. Not only are these Arabic prepositions themselves borrowed
from other languages and thus linguistic hybrids, as Khider explains, but
he also mixes them with the Bavarian dialect, resulting in the creation of a
'bayerisch-arabische Min-Form' ['Bavarian-Arabic Min form'] (DfA, 92–
6). Fusing standard German with words and grammatical structures from
Arabic and the Bavarian dialect, Khider challenges the normative role of
standard German and questions the supposed homogeneity of the German
language, thus deconstructing the notion of any language as a 'clearly demarcated entity that has a name, is countable, and is the property of the group
that speaks it'.[30] Borrowing from Stephan Braese's concept of German as a
Jewish language, one could thus argue that in *Deutsch für alle*, German becomes an 'Arabic' language, or rather: a German-Arabic-Bavarian hybrid.[31]
Additionally, Khider points to the Anglicisation of the German language
by emphasising the mass media influence on everyday German in an age
of rapid language change, thus further engaging with 'the tension between
monolingual paradigm and multilingual practice'.[32] As Yildiz has convincingly argued, this 'monolingual paradigm', emerging in the course of the
eighteenth century and promoted by German thinkers Johann Gottfried
Herder, Wilhelm von Humboldt and Friedrich Schleiermacher, was closely
tied to the birth of the modern nation state and is still prominent today,
despite the multilingual realities in Germany.[33]

   In *Deutsch für alle*, the hybrid, multilingual nature of the German language is further emphasised through the use of words of foreign derivation
[*Fremdwörter*] and highly specialised philosophical language [*Fachsprache*].
As Khider observes, German academics are obsessed with the use of words
of foreign derivation. Jokingly pointing at the elitist use of *Fremdwörter*

30   Yildiz, *Beyond the Mother Tongue*, 7.
31   Stephan Braese, *Eine europäische Sprache: Deutsche Sprachkultur von Juden 1760–
     1930* (Göttingen: Wallstein, 2010).
32   Yildiz, *Beyond the Mother Tongue*, 20.
33   Ibid., 6–8.

in the German academy, Khider deconstructs the exclusionary nature of what Adorno in his essay 'Words from Abroad' has termed a 'language of initiates'.[34] As Adorno argues in 'On the Use of Foreign Words', the German language has always been inherently multilingual, as it incorporates words of foreign derivation that remain unassimilated, non-naturalised words. Other, supposedly 'organic' German words have been assimilated into the language throughout history and are not experienced as 'foreign' any longer – such as *Bank* or *Acker*.[35]

Like words of foreign derivation, the artificial language of philosophy 'moves away from the organic nature of the language when the latter is no longer adequate to grasp ideas'.[36] Yet unlike words of foreign derivation that stand out and do not pretend to assimilate, highly specialised scholarly language like philosophical terminology is unsettling precisely *because* of its supposed familiarity. As a philosophy major at the University of Munich, Khider is introduced to the inaccessible philosophical language of Kant and Heidegger. While on the surface, the expressions used by Kant and Heidegger seem familiar, their meaning is unexpected, foreign. Neither Arabic dictionaries nor *Fremdwörterbücher* help him decipher the meaning behind the supposedly familiar German words. Interestingly, this defamiliarising effect is something that both ethnic Germans and Khider, as a minoritarian subject, share vis-à-vis the Kantian German language: 'Selbst die deutschen Studenten mussten sich die Texte wortweise erschließen, als seien sie in einer Fremdsprache geschrieben' ['Even the German students had to decipher the texts word by word, as if they were written in a foreign language'] (DfA, 15–6). Losing their literal, dictionary sense when used by these philosophers, they blur the boundaries between *Muttersprache* and *Fremdsprache*, highlighting the inherent multilingual character of the German language instead. Even for the average German speaker, there is 'so

34 Theodor W. Adorno, 'Words from Abroad', in Rolf Tiedemann, ed., *Notes to Literature*, trans. Shierry Weber Nicholson, Vol. 1 (New York: Columbia University Press, 1991), 185–99, 190.

35 Theodor W. Adorno, 'On the Use of Foreign Words', in Rolf Tiedemann, ed., *Notes to Literature*, trans. Shierry Weber Nicholson, Vol. 2 (New York: Columbia University Press, 1992), 286–91, 287.

36 Ibid., 290.

much compressed' into these expressions that the philosophical concept behind them is incomprehensible.[37] Being at the same time familiar and *fremd*, these expressions simultaneously belong and do not belong to the everyday lexicon of the average German speaker, thus questioning an alleged familiarity with one's own language. Even for ethnic Germans, their language can become uncanny at times. Interestingly, it is this ultimate strangeness that, for Khider, paves the way for him to an advanced level of proficiency of German. In other words: it is the *Fremdheit* of the highly stylised, philosophical terminology that brings Khider closer to his new language, German.

Towards a Multilingual Aesthetics

Khider's oeuvre as a whole does not fit into the German monolingual paradigm at all. Not only does he utilise different strategies of multilingual literature in his texts, but he also chooses to write in German despite his first language being Arabic, thus highlighting his multilingual attachments and questioning his identification with one language only.[38] Furthermore, he challenges the assumption that one can only express oneself properly in one's 'mother tongue'. As Yildiz has convincingly argued, individuals and social formations are 'imagined to possess one "true" language only, their "mother tongue," and through this possession to be organically linked to an exclusive, clearly demarcated ethnicity, culture, and nation.'[39] Having one – and only one – mother tongue was (and is) considered to be the natural norm. Literary creation in a language other than one's mother tongue or even several languages was considered impossible, as Schleiermacher famously argued: 'Every writer can produce original work only in his mother tongue.'[40] Khider's oeuvre, in contrast,

37   Adorno, 'Words from Abroad', 197.
38   See Beate Baumann's and Corinne Puglisi's contribution in this volume.
39   Yildiz, *Beyond the Mother Tongue*, 2.
40   Friedrich Daniel Ernst Schleiermacher, '*From* On the Different Methods of Translating', trans. Waltraud Bartscht, in Rainer Schulte and John Biguenet,

highlights multiple linguistic attachments instead and can be read as a plea for recognising non-ethnic Germans as legitimate speakers of their own versions – not deficient, but simply different versions – of German as a lingua franca that is not reduced to ethnic or national belonging.[41]

Hence, Khider's humorous grammar book *Deutsch für alle* is much more than just 'linguistic nonsense'. Rather, it offers a serious critique of and engagement with a number of pressing issues regarding Germany's treatment of its many non-native speakers and its official language politics. By changing the German grammar rules to his liking, Khider appropriates the German language and subverts it from within, thus constructing his own, unique voice in German that is distinct from the dominant 'standard German'. The playful, ironic appropriation of multiple language sources from the standpoint of a critical, distant insider can be liberating and empowering. Alienation is turned into linguistic agency – or, as Salman Rushdie put it with regard to the English language:

> And I hope all of us share the opinion that we can't simply use the language the way the British did; that it needs remaking for our own purposes. Those of us who do use English do so in spite of our ambiguity towards it, or perhaps because of that, perhaps because we can find in that linguistic struggle a reflection of other struggles taking place in the real world, struggles between the cultures within ourselves and the influences at work upon our societies. To conquer English may be to complete the process of making ourselves free.[42]

It comes as no surprise that the appropriation of German, more than that: the transformation of the German language by a non-ethnic speaker of German whose first language is Arabic has triggered responses from the far-right and other 'concerned citizens'. How seriously Khider's humorous interventions have been taken can be illustrated by the racist attacks that he is confronted with on a regular basis on Facebook and Twitter by self-proclaimed 'rightful owners' of the German language and

---

Theories of Translation: An Anthology of Essays from Dryden to Derrida (Chicago: University of Chicago Press, 1992), 36–54, 50.

41   Cf. Yildiz, *Beyond the Mother Tongue*, 210.

42   Salman Rushdie, *Imaginary Homelands: Essays and Criticism 1981–1991* (London: Penguin Books, 1992), 17.

German nationality who feel threatened by his creative use of 'their' language, reminding him of the fact that neither is Germany his *Heimat*, nor does the German language 'belong' to him. However, as Khider stated in our interview, it is precisely these attacks that make him feel even more at home in Germany, as they make his interventions more needed than ever: 'I think that the right-wing extremists gave me the possibility to really arrive psychologically. There is finally this feeling that this country needs me.'[43]

43   See my interview with Khider in this volume, p. 31; 33.

Bibliography

1. Works by Khider (in Chronological Order)

Khider, Abbas, *Der falsche Inder* (Hamburg: Edition Nautilus, 2008).
——, *Der falsche Inder* (Munich: btb, 2013).
——, *The Village Indian*, trans. Donal McLaughlin (Calcutta/London/ New York: Seagull Books, 2013).
——, *Die Orangen des Präsidenten* (Hamburg: Edition Nautilus, 2011).
——, *Die Orangen des Präsidenten* (Munich: btb, 2013).
——, *Brief in die Auberginenrepublik* (Hamburg: Edition Nautilus, 2013).
——, *Brief in die Auberginenrepublik* (Munich: btb, 2015).
——, *Ohrfeige* (Munich: Hanser, 2016).
——, *A Slap in the Face*, trans. Simon Pare (Calcutta/London/New York: Seagull Books, 2019).
——, *Deutsch für alle: Das endgültige Lehrbuch* (Munich: Hanser, 2019).

2. Interviews with Khider

Ammar, Abderrahmane, 'Deutsch ist meine neue Zunge – Ein Interview mit Abbas Khider', Goethe Institute (2014), <http://www.goethe.de/ins/it/lp/prj/lit/ bue/bmt/hin/de14101779.htm>, accessed 25 July 2018.
——, '"German is My New Language": Interview with Abbas Khider', trans. Pauline Cumbers, Goethe Institute (2014), <https://www.goethe.de/en/kul/lit/ 20437059.html>, accessed 10 March 2020.
Düker, Ronald, 'Literat Abbas Khider: "Ich stelle der Folter eine sprachliche Form entgegen"', *Cicero: Magazin für politische Kultur* (15 March 2013), <https:// www.cicero.de/kultur/abbas-khider-auberginenrepublik-ich-stelle-der-folter-eine-sprachliche-form-entgegen/53874>, accessed 3 November 2018.

Erber, Christian, ' "Besonders übel sind die Umlaute": Interview mit Abbas Khider', Radio Bremen (2019), <https://www.radiobremen.de/bremenzwei/sendungen/gespraechszeit/abbas-khider112-popup.html>, accessed 10 March 2020.

Heinrich, Kaspar, 'Wir sollten nicht plötzlich alles infrage stellen', *Planet Interview* (11 May 2016), <http://www.planet-interview.de/interviews/abbas-khider/48826/>, accessed 2 July 2018.

Kohlstadt, Michael, 'Abbas Khider und die Liebe zur Sprache der Deutschen', *Westdeutsche Allgemein Zeitung* (11 December 2013), <http://www.derwesten.de/kultur/abbas-khider-und-die-liebe-zur-sprache-der-deutschenid8762981.html>, accessed 1 October 2019.

Rahden, Wolfert von, 'Die fremde Sprache bedeutet Freiheit: Ein Dialog mit Wolfert von Rahden über Grenzgänge zwischen Sprachen, Staaten und Kulturen', *Eurozine* (31 July 2012), <https://www.eurozine.com/die-fremde-sprache-bedeutet-freiheit/>, accessed 22 June 2018.

'Wenn man das Gefängnis hinter sich lässt, oder wenn man entlassen wird, man trägt das Gefängnis in sich mit: Psychisch ist man nicht mehr der alte', ARD-alpha (14 March 2017), <https://www.youtube.com/watch?v=8KyI1d8UB-0>, accessed 25 July 2018.

3. Works about Khider

Anderson, Katherine, *Foreign Writing Agency: Abbas Khider & María Cecilia Barbetta Writing Towards Catharsis in German as a Foreign Language After Trauma* (Philadelphia: The Pennsylvania State University, 2017).

——, 'Von der Wanderung zum Wandel: Die Migration des Abbas Khider in die deutsche Sprache als Traumabewältigung durch Erzählen', in Elke Sturm-Trigonakis, Olga Laskaridou, Evi Petropoulou and Katerina Karakassi, eds., *Turns und kein Ende?: Aktuelle Tendenzen in Germanistik und Komparatistik* (Frankfurt am Main: Peter Lang, 2017), 95–104.

Aydemir, Fatma, 'Eine Sachbearbeiterin wird gefesselt: Sein Roman *Ohrfeige* dreht sich um den Wahnsinn im Alltag eines Asylbewerbers in Deutschland. Eine Begegnung mit Abbas Khider', *taz* (29 January 2016), <http://www.taz.de/Roman-Ohrfeige-von-Abbas-Khider/%215270464/>, accessed 5 November 2018.

Calero Valera, Ana R., 'Diálogo entre memorias: Perpetradores y víctimas en *Brief in die Auberginenrepublik* de Abbas Khider', *Revista de Filología Alemana* 27 (2019), 117–30.

Delius, Friedrich Christian, 'Die deutsche Verlogenheit', *Süddeutsche Zeitung* (9 March 2017), <https://www.sueddeutsche.de/kultur/preisrede-die-deutsche-verlogenheit-1.3412260>, accessed 4 November 2018.

Düker, Ronald, 'Literat Abbas Khider – "Ich stelle der Folter eine sprachliche Form entgegen"', *Cicero* (2013), <https://www.cicero.de/kultur/abbas-khider-auberginenrepublik-ich-stelle-der-folter-eine-sprachliche-form-entgegen/53874>, accessed 25 March 2018.

El-Kaddouri, Warda, '"Gott, rette mich aus der Leere!" Verlust, Religiosität und Radikalisierung in den Fluchtnarrativen von Abbas Khider und Sherko Fatah', in Hardtke, Kleine and Payne, eds., *Niemandsbuchten und Schutzbefohlene* (Göttingen: V&R Unipress, 2017), 39–53.

Encke, Julia, 'Flüchtlingsroman: Vom Warten wird man immer blöder', *Frankfurter Allgemeine Zeitung* (30 January 2016).

Fessmann, Meike, 'Die Freiheit, sein Leben noch einmal zu erzählen: Laudatio auf Abbas Khider', *Sinn und Form*, 66/4 (2014), 705–11.

——, 'Die Blutegel des Unglücks', *Süddeutsche Zeitung* (10 February 2016).

——, 'Lachen unter der Folter', *Süddeutsche Zeitung* (19 April 2011).

Granzin, Katharina, 'Der Mensch im Durchgangsland: Die Katastrophe des Nie-irgendwo-ankommen-Dürfens. Abbas Khider erzählt in seinem neuen Roman *Ohrfeige* die Geschichte eines ewigen Flüchtlings', *Frankfurter Rundschau* (5 February 2016), <http://www.fr.de/kultur/literatur/abbas-khider-ohrfeige-der-mensch-im-durchgangsland-a-372313>, accessed 5 November 2018.

Gropp, Lewis, 'Schöner schreiben als Gott', *Neue Bücher Zeitung* (24 May 2011).

——, 'Writing More Beautifully than God', *Qantara* (30 September 2011), <https://en.qantara.de/content/the-german-iraqi-writer-abbas-khider-writing-more-beautifully-than-god>, accessed 15 June 2020.

Haueis, Eduard, '"Charab Al …" – Fluch(t)punkt Sprache im Roman *Ohrfeige* von Abbas Khider', *OBST: Flucht_Punkt_Sprache* 89 (2016), 53–6.

Hilmes, Carola, '"Jedes Kapitel ein Anfang und zugleich ein Ende." – Abbas Khiders fiktionalisierte Lebensbeschreibung', in Monika Wolting, ed., *Identitätskonstruktionen in der deutschen Gegenwartsliteratur* (Göttingen: V&R Unipress, 2017), 135–46.

——, 'Zum DORT verflucht: Grußwort', *Hamburger Abendblatt*, four-paged special *Tage des Exils* (12 October 2018).

——, 'Zum Dort verflucht', opening event of *Tage des Exils* 2018, <https://www.koerber-stiftung.de/mediathek/zum-dort-verflucht-1642>, accessed 9 November 2018.

Hofmann, Hanna Maria, 'Erzählungen der Flucht aus raumtheoretischer Sicht: Abbas Khiders *Der falsche Inder* und Anna Seghers' *Transit*', in Hardtke, Kleine and Payne, eds., *Niemandsbuchten und Schutzbefohlene*, 97–124.

Jessen, Jens, 'Was den Erniedrigten schützt', *Zeit Online* (5 May 2011), <https://www.zeit.de/2011/19/L-B-Khider>, accessed 9 January 2020.

Lerch, Wolfgang Günter, 'Die Frucht der Freiheit', *Frankfurter Allgemeine Zeitung* (8 April 2011), <http://www.faz.net/aktuell/feuilleton/buecher/rezensionen/belletristik/abbas-khider-die-orangen-des-praesidenten-die-frucht-der-freiheit-1628121.html>, accessed 8 August 2018.

Mangold, Ijoma, 'Ein guter Burger', *Zeit Online* (18 February 2016), <http://www.zeit.de/2016/06/ohrfeige-abbas-khider>, accessed 17 September 2018.

März, Ursula, 'Abbas Khider: *Ohrfeige*. Die Wutrede eines abgelehnten Asylbewerbers', *Deutschlandfunk Kultur* (30 January 2016), <https://www.deutschlandfunkkultur.de/abbas-khider-ohrfeige-die-wutrede-eines-abgelehnten.950.de.html?dram:article_id=343983>, accessed 3 November 2018.

Pflitsch, Andreas, 'Abbas Khider: Die Orangen des Präsidenten', *Der Tagesspiegel* (16 March 2011), <https://www.tagesspiegel.de/kultur/abbas-khider-die-orangen-des-praesidenten/3953848.html>, accessed 8 August 2018.

Schneider, Ulrike, 'Darstellungsweisen von Fluchtprozessen in der Gegenwartsliteratur am Beispiel von Merle Kröger und Abbas Khider sowie den Reportagen von Wolfgang Bauer und Navid Kermani', *Argonautenschiff: Jahrbuch der Anna-Seghers-Gesellschaft Berlin und Mainz e.V.* 25 (2017), 82–92.

Schramm, Moritz, 'Experimentelle Erkundungen: Überlegungen zum Verhältnis von Anerkennungstheorie und Literaturwissenschaft am Beispiel von Abbas Khiders Roman *Die Orangen des Präsidenten*', in Martin Baisch, ed., *Anerkennung und die Möglichkeiten der Gabe* (Frankfurt am Main: Peter Lang, 2017), 177–95.

——, 'Ironischer Realismus: Selbstdifferenz und Wirklichkeitsnähe bei Abbas Khider', in Søren R. Fauth and Rolf Parr, eds., *Neue Realismen in der Gegenwartsliteratur* (Munich: Fink, 2016), 71–84.

Spiegel, Hubert, 'Ein Schutzwall aus Worten gegen Gewalt, Not und Elend: Abbas Khiders "Rache des Poeten"', *Chamisso: Viele Kulturen – eine Sprache* 16 (2017), 4–9.

——, ' "Wenn ich auf Arabisch schreibe, handelt alles von Leid. Das Deutsche hält mich auf Distanz": Abbas Khider wird für seinen Debütroman ausgezeichnet', *Chamisso: Viele Kulturen – eine Sprache* 4 (2010), 10–3.

Stan, Corina, 'Novels in the Translation Zone: Abbas Khider, *Weltliteratur*, and the Ethics of the Passerby', *Comparative Literature Studies*, 55/2 (2018), 285–302.

Steidl, Sarah, 'Der Flüchtling als Grenzgestalter? Zur Dialektik des Grenzverletzers in Abbas Khiders Debütroman *Der falsche Inder*', in Hardtke, Kleine and Payne, eds., *Niemandsbuchten und Schutzbefohlene*, 305–20.

Tafazoli, Hamid, 'Flüchtlingsfiguren im kulturellen Gedächtnis Europas: Konstruktionen einer Grenzfigur in den Romanen *Schlafgänger*, *Ohrfeige* und *Gehen, ging, gegangen*', *Weimarer Beiträge: Zeitschrift für Literaturwissenschaft, Ästhetik und Kulturwissenschaften* 64/2 (2018), 222–43.

Trojanow, Ilija, 'Wie lange reißt ein Mensch sich am Riemen? Die Erfahrungen des Exils sind voller Widersprüchlichkeiten: Die Romane von Abbas Khider erzählen davon', *Süddeutsche Zeitung* (18 March 2018).

Welebil, Simon, 'Monolog für mehr Verständnis: In seinem neuen Roman *Ohrfeige* feuert Abbas Khider eine Breitseite auf das europäische Asylsystem ab', *FM4* (27 March 2016), <https://fm4v3.orf.at/stories/1768692/index.html>, accessed 5 November 2018.

4. Works Cited

Adelson, Leslie A., 'Against Between: A Manifesto', in Tom Cheesman and Karin E. Yeşilada, eds., *Zafer Şenocak* (Cardiff: University of Wales Press, 2003), 130–43.

——, *The Turkish Turn in Contemporary German Literature: Toward a New Critical Grammar of Migration* (New York: Palgrave Macmillan, 2005).

Adorno, Theodor W., 'On the Use of Foreign Words', in Rolf Tiedemann, ed., *Notes to Literature*, trans. Shierry Weber Nicholson, Vol. 2 (New York: Columbia University Press, 1992), 286–91.

——, 'Words from Abroad', in Rolf Tiedemann, ed., *Notes to Literature*, trans. Shierry Weber Nicholson, Vol. 1 (New York: Columbia University Press, 1991), 185–99.

Agamben, Giorgio, *Homo Sacer: Sovereign Power and Bare Life*, trans. Daniel Heller-Roazen (Stanford: Stanford University Press, 1998).

——, *State of Exception*, trans. Kevin Attell (Chicago: University of Chicago Press, 2005).

——, 'We Refugees', *Symposium* 49/2 (1995), 114–9.

Agier, Michel, *Managing the Undesirables: Refugee Camps and Humanitarian Government* (Cambridge/Malden: Polity Press, 2011).

Allen, Barry, 'The Ethical Artefact: On Junk', in John Knechtel, ed., *TRASH* (Cambridge/MA: MIT Press, 2007), 196–213.

Alternative für Deutschland, 'Manifesto for Germany: The Political Programme of the Alternative für Deutschland' (2016), <https://www.afd.de/wp-content/uploads/sites/111/2017/04/2017-04-12_afd-grundsatzprogramm-englisch_web.pdf>, accessed 10 March 2020.

Amati-Mehler, Jacqueline, Simona Argentieri and Jorge Canestri, *The Babel of the Unconscious: Mother Tongue and Foreign Tongues in the Psychoanalytic Dimension* (Madison/CT: International Universities Press, 1993).

Amery, Jean, *At the Mind's Limits: Contemplations by a Survivor on Auschwitz and Its Realities*, trans. Sidney Rosenfeld and Stella P. Rosenfeld (Bloomington: Indiana University Press, 2009).

Anderson, Benedict R., *Imagined Communities: Reflections on the Origin and Spread of Nationalism* (London/New York: Verso, 2006).

Arendt, Hannah, *The Human Condition*, 2nd edn (Chicago: University of Chicago Press, 1998).

——, *The Origins of Totalitarianism* (Cleveland/NY: Meridian Books, 1958).

——, 'We Refugees', in Marc Robinson, ed., *Altogether Elsewhere: Writers on Exile* (Boston: Faber and Faber, 1994), 111–9.

Assmann, Aleida, *Auf dem Weg zu einer europäischen Gedächtniskultur?* (Wien: Picus, 2012).

Bachtin, Michail M., *Literatur und Karneval: Zur Romantheorie und Lachkultur* (Frankfurt am Main: Fischer, 1990 [1969]).

——, *Rabelais und seine Welt: Volkskultur als Gegenkultur* (Frankfurt am Main: Suhrkamp, 2015 [1987]).

Bahoora, Haytham, 'Writing the Dismembered Nation: The Aesthetics of Horror in Iraqi Narratives of War', *The Arab Studies Journal*, 23/1 (2015), 184–208, <https://www.jstor.org/stable/44744904>, accessed 8 January 2020.

Balibar, Etienne, 'The Nation Form', in Etienne Balibar and Immanuel Wallerstein, eds., *Race, Nation, Class* (London: Verso, 1995), 86–106.

Bauman, Zygmunt, *Strangers at Our Door* (Cambridge/Malden: Polity Press, 2016).

——, *Wasted Lives: Modernity and Its Outcasts* (Cambridge/Malden: Polity Press, 2004).

Baumann, Gerd, and Thijl Sunier, 'Introduction: De-Essentializing Ethnicity', in Gerd Baumann and Thijl Sunier, eds., *Post-Migration Ethnicity: De-Essentializing Cohesion, Commitments and Comparison* (Amsterdam: Het Spinhuis, 1995), 1–8.

Bay, Hansjörg, 'Migrationsliteratur (Gegenwartsliteratur III)', in Dirk Göttsche, Axel Dunker and Gabriele Dürbeck, eds., *Handbuch Postkolonialismus und Literatur* (Stuttgart: Springer, 2017), 323–32, <https://doi.org/10.1007/978-3-476-05386-2_60>, accessed 9 May 2018.

Beck, Ulrich, 'Multiculturalism or Cosmopolitanism: How Can We Describe and Understand the Diversity of the World?', *Social Sciences in China* 32/4 (2011), 52–8, <http://dx.doi.org/10.1080/02529203.2011.625169>, accessed 19 January 2018.

Behre, Maria, 'Hölderlin in der Lyrik des 20. Jahrhunderts', *Lyrik des 20. Jahrhunderts* (Munich: text + kritik 1999), 107–24.

Benhabib, Seyla, *The Rights of Others: Aliens, Residents, and Citizens* (Cambridge: Cambridge University Press, 2004).

Benn, Gottfried, 'Only two things', in David Paisey, ed. and trans., *Selected Poems and Prose* (Manchester: Fyfield Books, 2013).

——, *Sämtliche Werke. Band I: Gedichte 1*. Stuttgarter Ausgabe, ed. Gerhard Schuster (Stuttgart: Klett-Cotta, 2006).

Betts, Alexander, and Paul Collier, *Refuge: Rethinking Refugee Policy in a Changing World* (Oxford: Oxford University Press, 2017).

Bhabha, Homi, *The Location of Culture* (London/New York: Routledge, 1994).

——, *Our Neighbours, Ourselves: Contemporary Reflections on Survival* (Berlin: De Gruyter, 2011).

Bieritz, Karl-Heinrich, 'Anthropologische Grundlegung', in Hans-Christoph Schmidt-Lauber, ed., *Handbuch der Liturgik: Liturgiewissenschaft in Theologie und Praxis der Kirche* (Göttingen: Vandenhoeck & Ruprecht, 2003), 95–128.

Blumer, Herbert, *Symbolic Interactionism: Perspective and Method* (Englewood Cliffs, NJ: Prentice-Hall, 1969).

Bock, Jan Jonathan, and Sharon Macdonald, 'Introduction: Making, Experiencing and Managing Difference in a Changing Germany', in Bock and Macdonald, eds., *Refugees Welcome?*, 1–38.

——, eds., *Refugees Welcome? Difference and Diversity in a Changing Germany* (New York: Berghahn Books, 2019).

Borso, Vittoria, 'Transitorische Räume', in Jörg Dünne and Andreas Mahler, eds., *Handbuch Literatur & Raum* (Berlin/Boston: de Gruyter, 2015), 947–96, <http://dx.doi.org/10.1515/9783110301403>, accessed 20 August 2018.

Boscagli, Maurizia, *Stuff Theory: Everyday Objects, Radical Materialism* (London: Bloomsbury, 2014).

Bottici, Chiara, and Benoît Challand, *Imagining Europe: Myth, Memory, and Identity* (New York: Cambridge University Press, 2013).

Boulé, Jean-Pierre, 'Writing Selves as Mourning and *Vita Nova*: Abdellah Taïa's *Un Pays Pour Mourir*', *Contemporary French Civilization*, 41/1 (2016), 25–47.

Bourdieu, Pierre, *Distinctions* (London: Routledge & Kegan Paul, 1984).

Braese, Stephan, *Eine europäische Sprache: Deutsche Sprachkultur von Juden 1760–1930* (Göttingen: Wallstein, 2010).

Braidotti, Rosi, *Nomadic Subjects: Embodiment and Sexual Difference in Contemporary Feminist Theory* (New York: Columbia University Press, 1994).

Brylla, Ute, 'Die Maske des Unmaskierten: Eine Zusammenschau von Bruno Schulz und Michail Bachtin', in Elfi Bettinger and Julika Funk, eds., *Maskeraden: Geschlechterdifferenz in der literarischen Inszenierung* (Berlin: Erich Schmidt Verlag, 1995), 307–22.

Burwitz-Melzer, Eva, Frank G. Königs and Claudia Riemer, eds, *Identität und Fremdsprachenlernen: Anmerkungen zu einer komplexen Beziehung. Arbeitspapiere der 33. Frühjahrskonferenz zur Erforschung des Fremdsprachenunterrichts* (Tübingen: Narr, 2013).

Busch, Brigitta, *Mehrsprachigkeit* (Wien: Facultas, 2013).

Butler, Judith, *Frames of War: When Is Life Grievable?* (London/ New York: Verso, 2009).

——, *Giving an Account of Oneself* (New York: Fordham University Press, 2005).

——, *Precarious Life: The Powers of Mourning and Violence* (London/ New York: Verso, 2004).

——, *Undoing Gender* (New York: Routledge, 2004).

Caplan, Eric Michael, 'Trains, Brains, and Sprains: Railway Spine and the Origins of Psychoneuroses', *Bulletin of the History of Medicine*, 69/3 (1995), 387–419.

Caplan, Jane, and John Torpey, *Documenting Individual Identity: State Practices in the Modern World* (Princeton: Princeton University Press, 2001).

Caruth, Cathy, *Unclaimed Experience: Trauma, Narrative, and History* (Baltimore: Johns Hopkins University Press, 1996).

Casella, Eleanor Conlin, 'Enmeshed Inscriptions: Reading the Graffiti of Australia's Convict Past', *Australian Archaeology*, 78/1 (2014), 108–12, <https://doi.org/10.1080/03122417.2014.11682006>, accessed 7 January 2020.

Charim, Isolde, *Ich und die Anderen: Wie die neue Pluralisierung uns alle verändert* (Wien: Zsolnay, 2018).

Chemmachery, Jaine, 'Spatial, Temporal and Linguistic Displacement in Kipling's and Maugham's Colonial Short Stories: The Disrupting Power of the "Colonial" in Modern Short Fiction', *Journal of the Short Story in English*, 64 (2015), 47–65.

Cresswell, Tim, *On the Move: Mobility in the Modern Western World* (New York: Routledge, 2006).

Crewe, Ben, et al., 'The Emotional Geography of Prison Life', *Theoretical Criminology*, 18/1 (2014), 56–74, <https://doi.org/10.1177/1362480613497778>, accessed 6 January 2020.

de Certeau, Michel, *The Practice of Everyday Life*, trans. Steven Rendall (Berkeley/ Los Angeles/London: University of California Press, 1984).

Damai, Puspa, 'The Killing Machine of Exception: Sovereignty, Law, and Play in Agamben's State of Exception', *The New Centennial Review*, 5/3 (2005), 255–76.

Deleuze, Gilles, and Félix Guattari, 'What Is a Minor Literature?', trans. Robert Brinkley, *Mississippi Review* 11/3 (1983), 13–33, <http://www.jstor.org/stable/20133921>, accessed 21 August 2017.

Dembeck, Till, 'Sprachliche und kulturelle Identität', in Dembeck and Parr, eds., *Literatur und Mehrsprachigkeit*, 27–34.

——, and Rolf Parr, eds., *Literatur und Mehrsprachigkeit: Ein Handbuch* (Tübingen: Narr Francke Attempto, 2017).

Derrida, Jacques, *Archive Fever: A Freudian Impression*, trans. Eric Prenowitz (Chicago: The University of Chicago Press, 1995).

Doubrovsky, Serge, 'Nah am Text', *Kultur & Gespenster: Autofiktion* 7 (2008), 123–33.

Douglas, Mary, *Purity and Danger: An Analysis of the Concepts of Pollution and Taboo* (New York: Routledge, 2002).

Eaglestone, Robert, 'Knowledge, "Afterwardness" and the Future of Trauma Theory', in Gert Buelens, Sam Durrant and Robert Eaglestone, eds., *The Future of Trauma Theory* (London: Routledge, 2013), 11–21.

El-Tayeb, Fatima, *Undeutsch: Die Konstruktion des Anderen in der postmigrantischen Gesellschaft* (Bielefeld: transcript, 2016).

Ellermann, Antje, 'The Rule of Law and the Right to Stay: The Moral Claims of Undocumented Migrants', *Politics & Society*, 42/3 (2014), 293–308.

——, 'Undocumented Migrants and Resistance in the Liberal State', *Politics & Society* 38/3 (2010), 408–29.

Erickson, Gregory, *The Absence of God in Modernist Literature* (New York: Palgrave Macmillan, 2007).

Erpenbeck, Jenny, *Gehen, ging, gegangen* (Munich: Albrecht Knaus, 2015).

Fiddian-Qasmiyeh, Elena, ed., *The Oxford Handbook of Refugee and Forced Migration Studies* (Oxford: Oxford University, Press 2014).

FitzGerald, William, *Spiritual Modalities: Prayer as a Rhetoric and as a Performance* (Philadelphia: Penn State University Press, 2012).

Foroutan, Naika, 'Postmigrantische Gesellschaften', in Heinz Ulrich Brinkmann and Martina Sauer, eds., *Einwanderungsgesellschaft Deutschland: Entwicklung und Stand der Integration* (Wiesbaden: Springer Fachmedien, 2016), 227–54, <https://doi.org/10.1007/978-3-658-05746-6_9>, accessed 20 August 2018.

——, 'The Post-Migrant Paradigm', in Bock and Macdonald, eds., *Refugees Welcome?*, 142–67.

——, and Dorte Huneke, '"Wir brauchen neue Narrationen von einem pluralen Deutschland": Interview', in Dorte Huneke, ed., *Ziemlich deutsch: Betrachtungen aus dem Einwanderungsland Deutschland* (Bonn: Bundeszentrale für politische

Bildung, 2013), 43–55, <http://www.bpb.de/system/files/dokument_pdf/ Dorte Huneke_Ziemlich_deutsch.pdf>, accessed 20 August 2018.

'Forum: Migration Studies (with contributions by Gizem Arslan, Brooke Kreitinger, Deniz Göktürk, David Gramling, B. Venkat Mani, Olivia Landry, Barbara Mennel, Scott Denham, Robin Ellis, and Roman Utkin)', *The German Quarterly* 90/2 (2017), 212–34, <https://onlinelibrary.wiley.com/doi/full/ 10.1111/gequ.12033>, accessed 24 September 2017.

Foucault, Michel, *Die Heterotopien: Der utopische Körper. Zwei Radiovorträge* (Frankfurt am Main: Suhrkamp, 2005 [1966]).

——, *Discipline and Punish: The Birth of the Prison*, trans. Alan Sheridan (New York: Random House, 1977).

——, *Dispositive der Macht: Michel Foucault über Sexualität, Wissen und Wahrheit* (Berlin: Merve, 1978).

Freud, Sigmund, *Jenseits des Lustprinzips*, 2nd edn (Leipzig: Internationaler Psychoanalytischer Verlag, 1921).

Friedländer, Saul, *Nazi Germany and the Jews*, Vol. I: *The Years of Persecution, 1933– 1939* (New York: Harper Collins, 2007).

Fuchs, Thomas, *Ecology of the Brain* (Oxford: Oxford University Press, 2018).

Geißler, Christoph, 'Eine Begegnung mit Abbas Khider: Die deutsche Sprache ist wie eine schöne Frau', *Berliner Zeitung* (27 January 2016).

Gellner, Christoph, and Georg Langenhorst, *Blickwinckel öffnen: Interreligiöses Lernen mit literarischen Texten* (Ostfildern: Patmos, 2013).

Goffman, Erving, *Asylums: Essays on the Social Situation of Mental Patients and Other Inmates* (Garden City/NY: Anchor Books, 1961).

Gogolin, Ingrid, Sarah McMonagle and Tanja Salem, 'Germany: Systemic, Sociocultural and Linguistic Perspectives on Educational Inequality', in Peter A. J. Stevens and A. Gary Dworkin, eds., *The Palgrave Handbook of Race and Ethnic Inequalities in Education* (London: Palgrave Macmillan, 2014), 557–602.

Gramling, David, 'The New Cosmopolitan Monolingualism: On Linguistic Citizenship in Twenty-First Century Germany', *Die Unterrichtspraxis / Teaching German* 42/2 (2009), 130–40, <http://www.jstor.org/stable/ 40608632>, accessed 25 July 2017.

Gregory, Derek, 'The Black Flag: Guantánamo Bay and the Space of Exception', *Geografiska Annaler: Series B, Human Geography*, 88/4 (2006), <https:// www.jstor.org/stable/4621537>, accessed 8 January 2020.

Green, Todd H., *The Fear of Islam: An Introduction to Islamophobia in the West*, 2nd edn (Minneapolis: Fortress Press 2019).

Gueydan-Turek, Alexandra, '"Homeland Beyond Homelands": Reinventing Algeria Through A Transnational Literary Community: Assia Djebar's "Le Blanc De L'Algérie"', *Cincinnati Romance Review* 31 (2011), 85–102.

Habermas, Jürgen, 'The Concept of Human Dignity and the Realistic Utopia of Human Rights' in Claudio Corradetti, ed., *Philosophical Dimensions of Human Rights: Some Contemporary Views* (2012), 63–79.

Hallensleben, Markus, 'Introduction: Performative Body Spaces', in Markus Hallensleben, ed., *Performative Body Spaces: Corporeal Topographies in Literature, Theatre, Dance, and the Visual Arts* (Amsterdam: Rodopi, 2010), 9–27.

Hardtke, Thomas, Johannes Kleine and Charlton Payne, eds., *Niemandsbuchten und Schutzbefohlene: Flucht-Räume und Flüchtlingsfiguren in der deutschsprachigen Gegenwartsliteratur* (Göttingen: V&R unipress, 2016).

Harrison, Brian A., *The Tower of London Prisoner Book: A Complete Chronology of the Persons Known to Have Been Detained at Their Majesties' Pleasure, 1100–1941* (London: Trustees of the Royal Armouries, 2004).

Hawkins, Gay, *The Ethics of Waste: How We Relate to Rubbish* (Lanham: Rowman & Littlefield, 2006).

Heine, Heinrich, *Sämtliche Werke in vier Bänden*, eds Jost Perfahl and Werner Vortriede (Munich: Winkler, 1969).

Hempelmann, Heinzpeter, *Gott, ein Schriftsteller: Johann Georg Hamann über die End-Äusserung Gottes ins Wort der Heiligen Schrift und ihre hermeneutischen Konsequenzen* (Wuppertal: Brockhaus, 1988).

Herman, Judith Lewis, *Trauma and Recovery* (New York: Basic Books, 1992).

Heselhaus, Herrad, 'Transnationale Elemente im Flüchtlingsroman', *Studies in Language and Literature [文藝言語研究]* 72 (2017), 47–65, <https://tsukuba.repo.nii.ac.jp/?action=repository_uri&item_id=43525&file_id=17&file_no=1>, accessed 22 March 2018.

Hofmann, Michael, and Julia-Karin Patrut, *Einführung in die interkulturelle Literatur* (Darmstadt: WBG, 2015).

Hoven, Bettina van, and David Sibley, '"Just Duck": The Role of Vision in the Production of Prison Spaces' (2015), <https://journals.sagepub.com/doi/10.1068/d5107>, accessed 8 January 2020.

Huntington, Samuel P., *The Clash of Civilizations and the Remaking of World Order* (New York: Simon & Schuster, 1996).

Hutchings, John, 'Folklore and Symbolism of Green', *Folklore*, 108 (1997), 55–63.

Ismail, Khairul Azril, 'Pudu Jail's Graffiti: Aesthetics Beyond the Walls of the Prison Cells', in *Proceedings of ISEA2008: The 14th International Symposium on Electronic Art*, Isea Archives (2008), 248–50, <http://www.isea-archives. org/docs/2008/proceedings/ISEA2008_proceedings.pdf>, accessed 8 January 2020.

Janet, Pierre, *Psychological Healing* (New York: Macmillan Company, 1925).

Jones, Richard, and Thomas Schmid, *Doing Time: Prison Experience and Identity among First-Time Inmates* (Stamford/CT: Jai, 2000).

Kabir, Ananya Jahanara, 'Diasporas, Literature and Literary Studies' in Kim Knott and Sean McLoughlin, eds., *Diasporas: Concepts, Intersections, Identities* (London: Zed Books, 2010), 145–50.

Kansteiner, Wulf, 'Genealogy of a Category Mistake: A Critical Intellectual History of the Cultural Trauma Metaphor', *Rethinking History*, 8/2 (2004), 193–221.

Kaplan, Caren, *Questions of Travel: Postmodern Discourses of Displacement* (Durham: Duke University Press, 1996), <http://read.dukeupress.edu/content/questions-of-travel>, accessed 15 February 2018.

Kennedy, Greg, *The Ontology of Trash: The Disposable and Its Problematic Nature* (New York: SUNY Press, 2007).

Kermani, Navid, *Der Schrecken Gottes: Attar, Hiob und die metaphysische Revolte* (Munich: C.H. Beck, 2011).

——, *Gott ist schön: Das ästhetische Erleben des Korans* (Munich: C.H. Beck, 2011).

——, *Upheaval: The Refugee Trek through Europe* (Cambridge/Malden: Polity, 2017).

Keupp, Heiner, Thomas Ahbe and Wolfgang Gmür, *Identitätskonstruktionen: Das Patchwork der Identitäten in der Spätmoderne* (Reinbek: Rowohlt, 2006).

Kleine, Johannes, 'Navid Kermani's Poetic Hermeneutics of Religious Experiences', in Thomas Hardtke, ed., *Religious Experience Revisited: Expressing the Inexpressible?* (Leiden: Brill 2016), 123–36.

Knechtel, John, ed., *TRASH* (Cambridge, MA: MIT Press, 2007).

Kolk, Bessel van der, *The Body Keeps the Score* (London: Penguin Books, 2014).

Koudelka, Josef, 'The Refugee Regime and Its Weaknesses: Prospects for Human Rights and Kant's Ethic', *Human Affairs*, 26 (2016), 356–70.

Lacan, Jacques, *The Four Fundamental Concepts of Psycho-Analysis*, in Jacques-Alain Miller, ed., trans. Alan Sheridan (New York: W. W. Norton & Company, 1978).

Lachmann, Renate, 'Vorwort', in Michail M. Bachtin, *Rabelais und seine Welt: Volkskultur als Gegenkultur* (Frankfurt am Main: Suhrkamp, 2015 [1987]), 7–46.

Lefebvre, Henri, *The Production of Space*, trans. Donald Nicholson-Smith (Oxford/ Cambridge: Blackwell, 1991).

Legros, Waltraud, *Was die Wörter erzählen* (Munich: dtv, 2003).

Linke, Uli, 'Language as Battleground: "Speaking" the Nation, Lingual Citizenship and Diversity Management in Post-unification Germany', in Bock and Macdonald, eds., *Refugees Welcome?*, 41–66.

Lüdi, Georges, 'German and Its Norms', trans. Chris Cave, Goethe Institute (2014), <https://www.goethe.de/en/spr/mag/sta/20456023.html>, accessed 10 March 2020.

Lyndsey Stonebridge, *Placeless People: Writings, Rights and Refugees* (Oxford: Oxford University Press, 2018).

Machtans, Karolin, 'Navid Kermani: Advocate for an Antipatriotic Patriotism and a Multireligious, Multicultural Europe', in Axel Hildebrandt and Jill Twark, eds., *Envisioning Social Justice in Contemporary German Culture* (Rochester/NY: Camden House, 2015), 290–311.

Malak, Amin, *Muslim Narratives and the Discourse of English* (New York: State University of New York Press, 2005).

Malkki, Liisa, 'National Geographic: The Rooting of Peoples and the Territorialization of National Identity among Scholars and Refugees', *Cultural Anthropology* 7/1 (1992), 24–44, <http://www.jstor.org/stable/656519>, accessed 18 October 2017.

——, 'Speechless Emissaries: Refugees, Humanitarianism, and Dehistoricization', *Cultural Anthropology* 11/3 (1996), 377–404.

Malone, David, *The International Struggle Over Iraq: Politics in the UN Security Council 1980–2005* (Oxford: Oxford University Press, 2006).

Mani, B. Venkat, *Cosmopolitical Claims: Turkish-German Literatures from Nadolny to Pamuk* (Iowa City: University of Iowa Press, 2007).

Maniar, Aisha, '(Language) Policing at Europe's Borders', Institute of Race Relations (2016), <http://www.irr.org.uk/news/language-policing-at-europes-borders/>, accessed 10 March 2020.

Massey, Doreen, 'Politics and Space/Time', *New Left Review* (1992), 65–84.

Matthes, Frauke, *Writing and Muslim Identity: Representations of Islam in German and English Transcultural Literature, 1990–2006* (London: IGRS, 2011).

McKinney, Carolyn, and Bonny Norton, 'Identity in Language and Literacy Education', in Bernard Spolsky and Francis M. Hult, eds., *The Handbook of Educational Linguistics* (Oxford: Blackwell, 2008), 192–205.

McLeod, Hugh, *Religion and the People of Western Europe 1789–1989* (Oxford: Oxford University Press, 1997).

Mead, George Herbert, *Mind, Self, and Society: From the Standpoint of a Social Behaviorist* (Chicago: University of Chicago Press, 1934).

Mirón, Louis F., and Jonathan Xavier Inda, 'Race as a Kind of Speech Act', in Norman K. Denzin, ed., *Cultural Studies: A Research Volume* (Greenwich: JAI Press, 2000), 85–107.

Moslund, Sten Pultz, Anne Ring Petersen and Moritz Schramm, eds., *The Culture of Migration: Politics, Aesthetics and Histories, International Library of Migration Studies,* Vol. 6 (London: I. B. Tauris, 2015).

Moslund, Sten Pultz, Anne Ring Petersen, Hans Christian Post, Moritz Schramm, Mirjam Gebauer, Sabrina Vitting-Seerup and Frauke Wiegand, *Reframing Migration, Diversity and the Arts: The Postmigrant Condition* (New York: Routledge, 2019), <https://www.routledge.com/Migration-Diversity-and-the-Arts-The-Postmigrant-Condition/Schramm-Moslund-Petersen/p/book/9781138584099>, accessed 26 April 2019.

Nail, Thomas, *The Figure of the Migrant* (Stanford: Stanford University Press, 2015).

Nashif, Esmail, *Palestinian Political Prisoners: Identity and Community* (New York: Routledge, 2008).

Nassehi, Armin, 'Überraschte Identitäten', in Jürgen Straub and Joachim Renn, eds., *Transitorische Identität: Der Prozesscharakter des modernen Selbst* (Frankfurt am Main/New York: Campus, 2002), 211–37.

Neuner, Frank, et al., 'Narrative Exposition', in Andreas Maercker, ed., *Posttraumatische Belastungsstörungen*, 4th edn (Berlin: Springer Medizin, 2013), 327–47.

Norton, Bonny, *Identity and Language Learning: Gender, Ethnicity and Educational Change* (Harlow: Pearson Education, 2000).

——, *Identity and Language Learning: Extending the Conversation* (Bristol: Multilingual Matters, 2013).

——, and Carolyn McKinney, 'An Identity Approach to Second Language Acquisition', in Dwight Atkinson, ed., *Alternative Approaches to Second Language Acquisition* (London: Routledge, 2011), 73–94.

Oberndörfer, Dieter, 'Einwanderung wider Willen: Deutschland zwischen historischer Abwehrhaltung und unausweichlicher Öffnung gegenüber (muslimischen) Fremden', in Thorsten G. Schneiders, ed., *Islamfeindlichkeit* (Wiesbaden: Springer, 2009), 127–42.

Omar, Irfan A., 'Khiżr-i Rāh: The Pre-Eminent Guide to Action in Muhammad Iqbal's Thought', *Islamic Studies*, 43/1 (2004), 39–50.

Peter, Frank, 'Welcoming Muslims Into the Nation: Tolerance, Politics and Integration in Germany', in Jocelyne Cesari, ed., *Muslims in the West after 9/11* (New York: Routledge, 2010), 119–44.

Petersen, Anne Ring, and Moritz Schramm, '(Post-)Migration in the Age of Globalisation: New Challenges to Imagination and Representation', *Journal of Aesthetics & Culture* 9/2 (2017), 1–12, <https://doi.org/10.1080/20004214.2017.1356178>, accessed 12 May 2018.

Pries, Ludger, *Migration und Ankommen: Die Chancen der Flüchtlingsbewegung* (Frankfurt am Main/New York: Campus, 2016).

Rancière, Jacques, *The Politics of Literature* (Cambridge/Malden, MA: Polity, 2011), trans. Julie Rose.

Reno, Joshua, 'Waste and Waste Management', *Annual Review of Anthropology* 44 (2015), 557–72.

Roche, Jörg, 'Sprache als Medium von (Des-)Integration', in Dembeck and Parr, eds., *Literatur und Mehrsprachigkeit*, 45–52.

Rorty, Richard, 'Human Rights, Rationality, and Sentimentality', in Christopher Voparil and Richard Bernstein, eds., *The Rorty Reader* (Hoboken, NJ: Wiley-Blackwell, 2010), 351–65.

Rosello, Mireille, *The Reparative in Narratives: Works of Mourning in Progress* (Liverpool: Liverpool University Press, 2010).

Rushdie, Salman, *Imaginary Homelands: Essays and Criticism 1981–1991* (London: Penguin Books, 1992).

Said, Edward W., 'Reflections on Exile', in Marc Robinson, ed., *Altogether Elsewhere: Writers on Exile* (Boston: Faber and Faber, 1994), 137–49.

Schiffauer, Werner, 'Enemies Within the Gates: The Debate About the Citizenship of Muslims in Germany', in Tariq Modood, ed., *Multiculturalism, Muslims and Citizenship* (London: Routledge, 2006), 94–116.

Schleiermacher, Friedrich Daniel Ernst, 'From On the Different Methods of Translating', trans. Waltraud Bartscht, in Rainer Schulte and John Biguenet, eds., *Theories of Translation: An Anthology of Essays from Dryden to Derrida* (Chicago: University of Chicago Press, 1992), 36–54.

Schmidt, Jara, *Literarische Narreteien: Karnevaleske Strategien in deutsch- und englischsprachigen Migrationsromanen der Gegenwart* (Würzburg: Königshausen & Neumann, 2019).

Schulze Wessel, Julia, *Grenzfiguren: Zur politischen Theorie des Flüchtlings* (Bielefeld: transcript, 2017).

Senoçak, Zafer, *Deutschsein: Eine Aufklärungsschrift* (Hamburg: Körber Stiftung, 2011).

Spickard, Paul R., ed., *Multiple Identities: Migrants, Ethnicity, and Membership* (Bloomington: Indiana University Press, 2013).

Spolsky, Bernard, and Francis M. Hult, eds., *The Handbook of Educational Linguistics* (Oxford: Blackwell, 2008), 192–205.

Stevens, Peter A. J., and A. Gary Dworkin, eds., *The Palgrave Handbook of Race and Ethnic Inequalities in Education* (London: Palgrave Macmillan, 2014).

Straub, Jürgen, 'Identitätstheorie, empirische Identitätsforschung und die "postmoderne" armchair psychology', *Zeitschrift für qualitative Bildungs-, Beratungs- und Sozialforschung* 1 (2002), 167–94.

Sykes, Gresham M., *The Society of Captives: A Study of Maximum Security Prison*, Rev. edn (Princeton: Princeton University Press, 2007).

Taberner, Stuart, *Transnationalism and German-Language Literature in the Twenty-First Century* (Cham: Palgrave Macmillan, 2017).

Terkessidis, Mark, *Nach der Flucht: Neue Ideen für die Einwanderungsgesellschaft* (Ditzingen: Reclam, 2017).

Travers, Martin, *The Poetry of Gottfried Benn: Text and Selfhood* (Bern: Peter Lang, 2007).

Trojanow, Ilija, and Ranjit Hoskote, *Confluences: Forgotten Histories from East and West* (New Delhi: Yoda Press, 2012).

——, *Kampfabsage: Kulturen bekämpfen sich nicht, sie fließen zusammen* (Frankfurt am Main: Fischer, 2016).

Urry, John, 'Moving on the Mobility Turn', in Weert Canzler, Vincent Kaufmann and Sven Kesselring, eds., *Tracing Mobilities: Towards a Cosmopolitan Perspective* (Aldershot/Burlington: Ashgate, 2008), 13–23.

——, *Sociology beyond Societies: Mobilities for the Twenty-First Century* (London: Routledge, 2000), <http://www.myilibrary.com?id=35426>, accessed 25 November 2017.

Vertovec, Steven, ' "Diversity" and the Social Imaginary', *European Journal of Sociology/Archives Européennes de Sociologie* 53/3 (2012), 287–312, <http://dx.doi.org/10.1017/S000397561200015X>, accessed 16 September 2017.

——, 'Super-Diversity and its Implications', *Ethnic and Racial Studies* 30/6 (2007), 1024–54, <http://dx.doi.org/10.1080/01419870701599465>, accessed 16 September 2017.

——, 'Super-Diversity in Frankfurt' (2009), <http://www.mmg.mpg.de/fileadmin/user_upload/powerpoint/Super-diversity_in_Frankfurt/Super-diversity_in_Frankfurt.pdf>, accessed 16 September 2017.

Wagner-Egelhaaf, Martina, 'Einleitung: Was ist Auto(r)fiktion?', in Wagner-Egelhaaf, ed., *Auto(r)fiktion: Literarische Verfahren der Selbstkonstruktion* (Bielefeld: Aisthesis, 2013), 7–21.

Wagner, Peter, 'Hat Europa eine kulturelle Identität?', in Hans Joas and Klaus Wiegandt, eds., *Die kulturellen Werte Europas* (Frankfurt am Main: Fischer, 2010), 494–511.

Waldenfels, Bernhard, 'Flüchtlinge als Gäste in Not', *Deutsche Zeitschrift für Philosophie*, 64/1 (2017), 89–105.

Weinrich, Harald, 'Sprachwandler im Namen Chamissos', *Chamisso: Viele Kulturen – eine Sprache* 10 (2014), 18–21.

——, 'Um eine deutsche Literatur von außen bittend', *Merkur*, 37/422 (1983), 911–20.

Welsch, Wolfgang, 'Was ist eigentlich Transkulturalität?', in Lucyna Darowska, Thomas Lüttenberg and Claudia Machold, eds., *Hochschule als transkultureller Raum? Beiträge zu Kultur, Bildung und Differenz* (Bielefeld: transcript, 2003), 39–66.

Williams, Philip F., and Yenna Wu, *The Great Wall of Confinement: The Chinese Prison Camp through Contemporary Fiction and Reportage* (Berkeley/Los Angeles/London: University of California Press, 2004).

Wirth, Karoline, *Der Verein Deutsche Sprache: Hintergrund, Entstehung, Arbeit und Organisation eines deutschen Sprachvereins* (Bamberg: Bamberg University Press, 2008).

Yeşilada, Karin E., 'Gottes Krieger und Jungfrauen: Islam im Werk Feridun Zaimoğlus', in Michael Hofmann and Klaus von Stosch, eds., *Islam in der deutschen und türkischen Literatur* (Paderborn: Ferdinand Schöningh, 2012), 175–92.

Yildiz, Erol, 'Postmigrantische Perspektiven: Aufbruch in eine neue Geschichtlichkeit', in Erol Yildiz and Marc Hill, eds., *Nach der Migration: Postmigrantische Perspektiven jenseits der Parallelgesellschaft* (Bielefeld: transcript, 2015), 19–36.

Yildiz, Yasemin, *Beyond the Mother Tongue: The Postmonolingual Condition* (New York: Fordham University Press, 2012).

——, 'Political Trauma and Literal Translation: Emine Sevgi Özdamar's *Mutterzunge*', *Gegenwartsliteratur* 7 (2008), 248–70.

——, 'Turkish Girls, Allah's Daughters, and the Contemporary German Subject: Itinerary of a Figure', in *German Life and Letters* 62/3 (2009), 465–81.

Zeller, Claudia, 'Antrag abgelehnt: Eine literarische Case-Study über Bürokratie, Illegalität und Asyl', *Trajectoires: Travaux des jeunes chercheurs du CIERA* 11 (2018), <https://journals.openedition.org/trajectoires/2571>, accessed 9 May 2018.

Notes on Contributors

KATHERINE ANDERSON successfully defended her dissertation 'Foreign Writing Agency: Abbas Khider & Maria Cecilia Barbetta Writing Towards Catharsis in German as a Foreign Language After Trauma' 15 March 2017 at The Pennsylvania State University. She worked as a Visiting Assistant Professor of German at the College of the Holy Cross in Worcester, Massachusetts. Her research interests include Chamisso Literature and non-native writers of German, the intersections of trauma and foreign language writing, the German Romantic and Optimism in the GDR.

BEATE BAUMANN is an Associate Professor in German Linguistics and Translation at the Department of Humanities, University of Catania (Italy). Her main research interests are intercultural studies, didactics of GFL, plurilinguism and language creativity in transcultural literature, applied linguistics and empirical research methodologies in the area of language acquisition. She is vice director of the inter-university research centre Polyphonie (University of Genoa and University of Catania) and co-editor of the research project and web portal 'Polyphonie. Plurilinguismus_Kreativität_Schreiben'.

DAVID N. COURY is Frankenthal Professor of the Humanities, German, and Global Studies at the University of Wisconsin-Green Bay. He is the author of *The Return of Storytelling in Contemporary German Literature and Film* (Mellen, 2004) and co-editor of *The Works of Peter Handke: International Perspectives* (Ariadne, 2007). He co-edited with Sabine von Dirke a special issue of *Seminar* on 'Globalization, German Literature, and the New Economy' (2011) and has published widely on contemporary German literature and film as well as the transnational works of the writers Navid Kermani, Orhan Pamuk and Sarah Khan.

WARDA EL-KADDOURI holds a PhD in German literature. She defended her dissertation on religion and identity in the works of Abbas Khider, Sherko Fatah and Navid Kermani in 2019. She studied English and German language and literature at Ghent University and Westphälische Wilhelmsuniversität Münster, and European Studies at the Catholic University in Leuven. Currently she is working as an investigative journalist at *De Groene Amsterdammer*.

MARKUS HALLENSLEBEN is Associate Professor in the Department of Central, Eastern and Northern European Studies, Affiliated Faculty Member of the Institute for European Studies and Steering Committee Member of the Center for Migration Studies at the University of British Columbia, Vancouver, Canada. He was an adjunct lecturer at the Free University Berlin, a visiting scholar at Nagoya City University, and a DAAD Lecturer at the University of Tokyo. His publications range from nineteenth-century to contemporary German and Austrian literature, and from early twentieth-century art movements to theories of performativity (*Performative Body Spaces: Corporeal Topographies in Literature, Theatre, Dance, and the Visual Arts; Critical Studies* Vol. 33, Amsterdam, 2010). He has covered authors and artists such as Heinrich Heine, Else Lasker-Schüler (*Avantgardismus und Kunstinszenierung;* Tübingen, 2000), Hannah Höch, Wolfgang Paalen, Yōko Tawada, Ilija Troanow, Jenny Erpenbeck, Marlene Streeruwitz, Robert Schindel, Bodo Hell, VALIE EXPORT, ORLAN and Stelarc. His current research projects deal with literature and aesthetics in the postmigrant condition, and with narratives and politics of *Belonging in Unceded Territories* (<https://migration.ubc.ca/research/narratives>).

KAROLIN MACHTANS is Associate Professor of German Studies at Connecticut College. She is the author of *Zwischen Wissenschaft und autobiographischem Projekt: Saul Friedländer und Ruth Klüger* (Niemeyer: Conditio Judaica, 2009); co-editor, with Martin Ruehl, of *Hitler – Films from Germany: History, Cinema, and Politics since 1945* (Palgrave Macmillan, 2012) as well as co-editor, with Helga Druxes and Alexandar Mihailovic, of the first volume of criticism in English dedicated to Iranian-German author and scholar of Islam Navid Kermani (Peter Lang, 2016). She has published numerous articles in the fields of Holocaust, refugee and migration studies and is currently working on her new research project about multilingualism in contemporary literature of refuge.

CAROLIN MÜLLER (is a research associate at the Media Center at the Technical University Dresden.) She holds a PhD and a MA in German Studies from The Ohio State University and an MEd in English and Art Studies from the Technical University Dresden. Her research is informed by critical theory in citizenship and race and migration studies and looks at creative acts of citizenship through music, film and the arts. She also works on recent activist movements, the politics of migrancy as well as representations of oppression and flight in Germany. Her work has been published by *on_culture, textpraxis, Crossings: Journal of Migration & Culture* and the *Activist History Review*.

CORINNE PUGLISI is a Master's graduate in Comparative Literature and Languages (November 2018) at the University of Catania (Italy). Her main academic interests are Transcultural Literature, Translation and Linguistics. She previously graduated in Euro-American and Oriental Languages and Civilization (BA) at the University of Catania (March 2015). She was Erasmus exchange-student at the Johannes Gutenberg-Universität Mainz (Germany) during the winter semester 2013–2014. Her publications include two articles on Abbas Khider, '*Devo parlare arabo con lei*. Peculiarità linguistiche e aspetti traduttologici del romanzo *Ohrfeige* di Abbas Khider', and 'Das Übersetzen transkultureller Literatur. Übersetzungsproblematiken in Abbas Khiders Roman *Ohrfeige*' as well as on work on Uwe Timm.

JARA SCHMIDT is a research assistant at the German Department of Universität Hamburg. After studying English and German Literature as well as Modern History, she earned her doctorate in Intercultural Literature with a thesis entitled *Literarische Narreteien. Karnevaleske Strategien in deutsch- und englischsprachigen Migrationsromanen der*

Gegenwart (*Literary Follies. Carnivalesque Strategies in Contemporary German and English Novels of Migration*, 2019). Teaching and research stays took her to the University of Mumbai and Istanbul University. Her main areas of research are: Intercultural Literature; Postmigrant Studies; Postcolonial Studies; Gender Studies; Queer Studies.

SABINE ZIMMERMANN is currently earning her doctoral degree in Germanic Studies at the University of British Columbia, Canada. Her fields of research are post-migration literature, refugee resettlement in Germany and Canada, and ethics of migration. She volunteers with private refugee sponsorship organisations active in Vancouver's Lower Mainland.

Index

CONTEMPORARY GERMAN WRITERS AND FILMMAKERS

Edited by

Julian Preece (Swansea University)
Frank Finlay (University of Leeds)

Editorial Board

Professor Stephen Brockmann (Carnegie Mellon University)
Professor Friederike Eigler (Georgetown University)
Dr Michael Minden (University of Cambridge)
Professor Moritz Baßler (Westfälische Wilhelms-Universität Münster)
Professor Sabine Hake (University of Texas at Austin)

Contemporary German Writers and Filmmakers aims to reflect the continuing and dynamic developments in German culture since the reunification of Germany in 1990. The fall of communism, the forging of the new Berlin Republic and increasing ethnic diversity have coincided with growing international acclaim for writers of German (such as Nobel Laureates Günter Grass, Elfriede Jelinek and Herta Müller) and renewed interest in German cinema (such as award-winning film *Das Leben der Anderen / The Lives of Others*).

Each volume is devoted to the work of a contemporary German-speaking novelist, poet, playwright or filmmaker, containing an interview with its subject and, in the case of writers, an original piece of previously unpublished writing presented in parallel English translation. The other chapters on key aspects of the emerging oeuvre and its international significance are by scholars in the field. As the volumes are intended for readers with little or no knowledge of German, all quotations are translated into English. The volumes are designed as a resource for specialists and students alike and to stimulate debate within and beyond the academy.

Proposals for new volumes on significant contemporary practitioners in the literary and cinematic fields are welcomed. The language of the series is English.